STANDARDS

for educational and psychological testing

American Educational Research Association
American Psychological Association
National Council on Measurement in Education

Published by
American Educational Research Association
1230 17th St., NW
Washington, DC 20036

Library of Congress Card number: 99-066845
ISBN: 0-935302-25-5

Printed in the United States of America

First Impression 2002

Second Impression 2004

The *Standards for Educational and Psychological Testing* will be under continuing review by the three sponsoring organizations. Comments and suggestions will be welcome and should be sent to The Committee to Develop Standards for Educational and Psychological Testing in care of the Executive Office, American Psychological Association, 750 First Street, NE, Washington, DC 20002-4242.

Prepared by the
Joint Committee on Standards for Educational and Psychological Testing of the American Educational Research Association, the American Psychological Association, and the National Council on Measurement in Education.

TABLE OF CONTENTS

PREFACE

There have been five earlier documents from three sponsoring organizations guiding the development and use of tests. The first of these was *Technical Recommendations for Psychological Tests and Diagnostic Techniques,* prepared by a committee of the American Psychological Association (APA) and published by that organization in 1954. The second was *Technical Recommendations for Achievement Tests,* prepared by a committee representing the American Educational Research Association (AERA) and the National Council on Measurement Used in Education (NCMUE) and published by the National Education Association in 1955. The third, which replaced the earlier two, was published by APA in 1966 and prepared by a committee representing APA, AERA, and the National Council on Measurement in Education (NCME) and called the *Standards for Educational and Psychological Tests and Manuals.* The fourth, *Standards for Educational and Psychological Tests,* was again a collaboration of AERA, APA and NCME, and was published in 1974. The fifth, *Standards for Educational and Psychological Testing,* also a joint collaboration, was published in 1985.

In 1991 APA's Committee on Psychological Tests and Assessment suggested the need to revise the 1985 *Standards.* Representatives of AERA, APA and NCME met and discussed the revision, principles that should guide that revision, and potential Joint Committee members. By 1993, the presidents of the three organizations appointed members and the Committee had its first meeting November, 1993.

The *Standards* has been developed by a joint committee appointed by AERA, APA and NCME. Members of the Committee were:

Eva Baker, *co-chair*
Paul Sackett, *co-chair*
Lloyd Bond
Leonard Feldt

David Goh
Bert Green
Edward Haertel
Jo-Ida Hansen
Sharon Johnson-Lewis
Suzanne Lane
Joseph Matarazzo
Manfred Meier
Pamela Moss
Esteban Olmedo
Diana Pullin

From 1993 to 1996 Charles Spielberger served on the Committee as co-chair. Each sponsoring organization was permitted to assign up to two liaisons to the Joint Committee's project. Liaisons served as the conduits between the sponsoring organizations and the Joint Committee. APA's liaison from its Committee on Psychological Tests and Assessments changed several times as the membership of the Committee changed.

Liaisons to the Joint Committee:
AERA -William Mehrens
APA - Bruce Bracken, Andrew Czopek, Rodney Lowman, Thomas Oakland
NCME - Daniel Eignor

APA and NCME also had committees who served to monitor the process and keep relevant parties informed.

APA Ad Hoc Committee of the Council of Representatives:
Melba Vasquez
Donald Bersoff
Stephen DeMers
James Farr
Bertram Karon
Nadine Lambert
Charles Spielberger

NCME Standards and Test Use Committee:
Gregory Cizek
Allen Doolittle
Le Ann Gamache

Donald Ross Green
Ellen Julian
Tracy Muenz
Nambury Raju

A management committee was formed at the beginning of this effort. They monitored the financial and administrative arrangements of the project, and advised the sponsoring organizations on such matters.

Management Committee:
Frank Farley, APA
George Madaus, AERA
Wendy Yen, NCME

Staffing for the revision included Dianne Brown Maranto as project director, and Dianne L. Schneider as staff liaison. Wayne J. Camara served as project director from 1993 to 1994. APA's legal counsel conducted the legal review of the *Standards*. William C. Howell and William Mehrens reviewed the standards for consistency across chapters. Linda Murphy developed the indexing for the book.

The Joint Committee solicited preliminary reviews of some draft chapters, from recognized experts. These reviews were primarily solicited for the technical and fairness chapters. Reviewers are listed below:

Marvin Alkin
Philip Bashook
Bruce Bloxom
Jeffery P. Braden
Robert L. Brennan
John Callender
Ronald Cannella
Lee J. Cronbach
James Cummins
John Fremer
Kurt F. Geisinger
Robert M. Guion
Walter Haney
Patti L. Harrison
Gerald P. Koocher
Richard Jeanneret

Frank Landy
Ellen Lent
Robert Linn
Theresa C. Liu
Stanford von Mayrhauser
Milbrey W. McLaughlin
Samuel Messick
Craig N. Mills
Robert J. Mislevy
Kevin R. Murphy
Mary Anne Nester
Maria Pennock-Roman
Carole Perlman
Michael Rosenfeld
Jonathan Sandoval
Cynthia B. Schmeiser
Kara Schmitt
Neal Schmitt
Richard J. Shavelson
Lorrie A. Shepard
Mark E. Swerdlik
Janet Wall
Anthony R. Zara

Draft versions of the *Standards* were widely distributed for public review and comment three times during this revision effort, providing the Committee with a total of nearly 8,000 pages of comments. Organizations who submitted comments on drafts are listed below. Many individuals contributed to the input from each organization, and although we wish we could acknowledge every individual who had input, we cannot do so due to incomplete information as to who contributed to each organization's response. The Joint Committee could not have completed its task without the thoughtful reviews of so many professionals.

Sponsoring Associations
American Educational Research
Association (AERA)
American Psychological Association (APA)
National Council on Measurement in
Education (NCME)

Membership Organizations (Scientific, Professional, Trade & Advocacy)

American Association for Higher Education (AAHE)

American Board of Medical Specialties (ABMS)

American Counseling Association (ACA)

American Evaluation Association (AEA)

American Occupational Therapy Association

American Psychological Society (APS)

APA Division of Counseling Psychology (Division 17)

APA Division of Developmental Psychology (Division 7)

APA Division of Evaluation, Measurement, and Statistics (Division 5)

APA Division of Mental Retardation & Developmental Disabilities (Division 33)

APA Division of Pharmacology & Substance Abuse (Division 28)

APA Division of Rehabilitation Psychology (Division 22)

APA Division of School Psychology (Division 16)

Asian American Psychological Association (AAPA)

Association for Assessment in Counseling (AAC)

Association of Test Publishers (ATP)

Australian Council for Educational Research Limited (ACER)

Chicago Industrial/Organizational Psychologists (CIOP)

Council on Licensure, Enforcement, and Regulation (CLEAR), Examination Resources & Advisory Committee (ERAC)

Equal Employment Advisory Council (EEAC)

Foundation for Rehabilitation Certification, Education and Research

Human Sciences Research Council, South Africa

International Association for Cross-Cultural Psychology (IACCP)

International Brotherhood of Electrical Workers

International Language Testing Association

International Personnel Management Association Assessment Council (IPMAAC)

Joint Committee on Testing Practices (JCTP)

National Association for the Advancement of Colored People (NAACP), Legal Defense and Educational Fund, Inc.

National Center for Fair and Open Testing (Fairtest)

National Organization for Competency Assurance (NOCA)

Personnel Testing Council of Metropolitan Washington (PTC/MW)

Personnel Testing Council of Southern California (PTC/SC)

Society for Human Resource Management (SHRM)

Society of Indian Psychologists (SIP)

Society for Industrial and Organizational Psychology (APA Division 14)

Society for the Psychological Study of Ethnic Minority Issues (APA Division 45)

State Collaborative on Assessment & Student Standards Technical Guidelines for Performance Assessment Consortium (TGPA)

Telecommunications Staffing Forum

Western Region Intergovernmental Personnel Assessment Council (WRIPAC)

Credentialing Boards

American Board of Physical and Medical Rehabilitation

American Medical Technologists

Commission on Rehabilitation Counselor Certification

National Board for Certified Counselors (NBCC)

National Board of Examiners in Optometry

National Board of Medical Examiners

National Council of State Boards of Nursing

Government and Federal Agencies

Army Research Institute (ARI)

California Highway Patrol, Personnel and Training Division, Selection Research Program

City of Dallas, Civil Service Department

Commonwealth of Virginia, Department of Education

Defense Manpower Data Center (DMDC), Personnel Testing Division

Department of Defense (DOD), Office of the Assistant Secretary of Defense

Department of Education, Office of Educational Improvement, National Center for Education Statistics

Department of Justice, Immigration and Naturalization Service (INS)

Department of Labor, Employment and Training Administration (DOL/ETA)

U.S. Equal Employment Opportunity Commission (EEOC)

U.S. Office of Personnel Management (OPM), Personnel Resources & Development Center

Test Publishers/Developers

American College Testing (ACT)

CTB/McGraw-Hill

The College Board

Educational Testing Service (ETS)

Highland Publishing Company

Institute for Personality & Ability Testing (IPAT)

Professional Examination Service (PES)

Academic Institutions

Center for Creative Leadership

Gallaudet University, National Task Force on Equity in Testing Deaf Professionals

University of Haifa, Israeli Group

Kansas State University

National Center on Educational Outcomes (NCEO)

Pennsylvania State University

University of North Carolina – Charlotte

University of Southern Mississippi, Department of Psychology

When the Joint Committee completed its task of revising the *Standards*, it then submitted its work to the three sponsoring organizations for approval. Each organization had its own governing body and mechanism for approval, as well as definitions for what their approval means.

AERA: This endorsement carries with it the understanding that, in general, we believe the *Standards* to represent the current consensus among recognized professionals regarding expected measurement practice. Developers, sponsors, publishers, and users of tests should observe these *Standards*.

APA: The APA's approval of the *Standards* means the Council adopts the document as APA policy.

NCME: NCME endorses the *Standards for Educational and Psychological Testing* and recognizes that the intent of these *Standards* is to promote sound and responsible measurement practice. This endorsement carries with it a professional imperative for NCME members to attend to the *Standards*.

Although the *Standards* are prescriptive, the *Standards* itself does not contain enforcement mechanisms. These standards were formulated with the intent of being consistent with other standards, guidelines and codes of conduct published by the three sponsoring organizations, and listed below. The reader is encouraged to obtain these documents, some of which have references to testing and assessment in specific applications or settings.

The Joint Committee on the
Standards for Educational and Psychological Testing

References

American Educational Research Association. (June, 1992). *Ethical Standards of the American Educational Research Association.* Washington, DC: Author.

American Federation of Teachers, National Council on Measurement in Education, & National Education Association. *Standards for Teacher Competence in Educational Assessment of Students.* (1990). Washington, DC: National Council on Measurement in Education.

American Psychological Association. (December, 1992). Ethical Principles of Psychologists and Code of Conduct. *American Psychologist, 47* (12), 1597-1611.

Joint Committee on Testing Practices. (1988). *Code of Fair Testing Practices in Education.* Washington, DC: American Psychological Association.

National Council on Measurement in Education. (1995). *Code of Professional Responsibilities in Educational Measurement.* Washington, DC: Author.

INTRODUCTION

Educational and psychological testing and assessment are among the most important contributions of behavioral science to our society, providing fundamental and significant improvements over previous practices. Although not all tests are well-developed nor are all testing practices wise and beneficial, there is extensive evidence documenting the effectiveness of well-constructed tests for uses supported by validity evidence. The proper use of tests can result in wiser decisions about individuals and programs than would be the case without their use and also can provide a route to broader and more equitable access to education and employment. The improper use of tests, however, can cause considerable harm to test takers and other parties affected by test-based decisions. The intent of the *Standards* is to promote the sound and ethical use of tests and to provide a basis for evaluating the quality of testing practices.

Participants in the Testing Process

Educational and psychological testing and assessment involve and significantly affect individuals, institutions, and society as a whole. The individuals affected include students, parents, teachers, educational administrators, job applicants, employees, clients, patients, supervisors, executives, and evaluators, among others. The institutions affected include schools, colleges, businesses, industry, clinics, and government agencies. Individuals and institutions benefit when testing helps them achieve their goals. Society, in turn, benefits when testing contributes to the achievement of individual and institutional goals.

The interests of the various parties involved in the testing process are usually, but not always, congruent. For example, when a test is given for counseling purposes or for job placement, the interests of the individual and the institution often coincide. In contrast, when a test is used to select from among many individuals for a highly competitive job or for entry into an educational or training program, the preferences of an applicant may be inconsistent with those of an employer or admissions officer. Similarly, when testing is mandated by a court, the interests of the test taker may be different from those of the party requesting the court order.

There are many participants in the testing process, including, among others: (a) those who prepare and develop the test; (b) those who publish and market the test; (c) those who administer and score the test; (d) those who use the test results for some decision-making purpose; (e) those who interpret test results for clients; (f) those who take the test by choice, direction, or necessity; (g) those who sponsor tests, which may be boards that represent institutions or governmental agencies that contract with a test developer for a specific instrument or service; and (h) those who select or review tests, evaluating their comparative merits or suitability for the uses proposed.

These roles are sometimes combined and sometimes further divided. For example, in clinics the test taker is typically the intended beneficiary of the test results. In some situations the test administrator is an agent of the test developer, and sometimes the test administrator is also the test user. When an industrial organization prepares its own employment tests, it is both the developer and the user. Sometimes a test is developed by a test author but published, advertised, and distributed by an independent publisher, though the publisher may play an active role in the test development. Given this intermingling of roles, it is difficult to assign precise responsibility for addressing various standards to specific participants in the testing process.

This document begins with a series of chapters on the test development process, which focus primarily on the responsibilities of test developers, and then turns to chapters on specific uses and applications, which focus primarily on responsibilities of test users. One chapter is devoted specifically to the rights and responsibilities of test takers.

The *Standards* is based on the premise that effective testing and assessment require that all participants in the testing process possess the knowledge, skills, and abilities relevant to their role in the testing process, as well as awareness of personal and contextual factors that may influence the testing process. They also should obtain any appropriate supervised experience and legislatively mandated practice credentials necessary to perform competently those aspects of the testing process in which they engage. For example, test developers and those selecting and interpreting tests need adequate knowledge of psychometric principles such as validity and reliability.

The Purpose of the Standards

The purpose of publishing the *Standards* is to provide criteria for the evaluation of tests, testing practices, and the effects of test use. Although the evaluation of the appropriateness of a test or testing application should depend heavily on professional judgment, the *Standards* provides a frame of reference to assure that relevant issues are addressed. It is hoped that all professional test developers, sponsors, publishers, and users will adopt the *Standards* and encourage others to do so.

The *Standards* makes no attempt to provide psychometric answers to questions of public policy regarding the use of tests. In general, the *Standards* advocates that, within feasible limits, the relevant technical information be made available so that those involved in policy debate may be fully informed.

Categories of Standards

The 1985 *Standards* designated each standard as "primary" (to be met by all tests before operational use), "secondary" (desirable, but not feasible in certain situations), or "conditional" (importance varies with application). The present *Standards* continues the tradition of expecting test developers and users to consider all standards before operational use; however, the *Standards* does not continue the practice of designating levels of importance. Instead, the text of each standard, and any accompanying commentary, discusses the conditions under which a standard is relevant. It was not the case that under the 1985 *Standards* test developers and users were obligated to attend only to the primary standards. Rather, the term "conditional" meant that a standard was primary in some settings and secondary in others, thus requiring careful consideration of the applicability of each standard for a given setting.

The absence of designations such as "primary" or "conditional" should not be taken to imply that all standards are equally significant in any given situation. Depending on the context and purpose of test development or use, some standards will be more salient than others. Moreover, some standards are broad in scope, setting forth concerns or requirements relevant to nearly all tests or testing contexts, and other standards are narrower in scope. However, all standards are important in the contexts to which they apply. Any classification that gives the appearance of elevating the general importance of some standards over others could invite neglect of some standards that need to be addressed in particular situations.

Further, the current *Standards* does not include standards considered secondary or "desirable." The continued use of the secondary designation would risk encouraging both the expansion of the *Standards* to encompass large numbers of "desirable" standards and the inappropriate assumption that any guideline not included in the *Standards* as at least "secondary" was inconsequential.

Unless otherwise specified in the standard or commentary, and with the caveats outlined below, standards should be met before operational test use. This means that each standard should be carefully considered to determine its applicability to the testing context under consideration. In a given case there may be a sound professional reason why adherence to the standard is unnecessary. It is also possible that there may be occasions when technical feasibility may influence whether a standard can be met prior to operational test use. For example, some standards may call for analyses of data that may not be available at the point of initial operational test use. If test developers, users, and, when applicable, sponsors have deemed a standard to be inapplicable or unfeasible, they should be able, if called upon, to explain the basis for their decision. However, there is no expectation that documentation be routinely available of the decisions related to each standard.

Tests and Test Uses to Which These Standards Apply

A test is an evaluative device or procedure in which a sample of an examinee's behavior in a specified domain is obtained and subsequently evaluated and scored using a standardized process. While the label *test* is ordinarily reserved for instruments on which responses are evaluated for their correctness or quality and the terms *scale* or *inventory* are used for measures of attitudes, interest, and dispositions, the *Standards* uses the single term *test* to refer to all such evaluative devices.

A distinction is sometimes made between *test* and *assessment*. *Assessment* is a broader term, commonly referring to a process that integrates test information with information from other sources (e.g., information from the individual's social, educational, employment, or psychological history). The applicability of the *Standards* to an evaluation device or method is not altered by the label applied to it (e.g., test, assessment, scale, inventory).

Tests differ on a number of dimensions: the mode in which test materials are presented (paper and pencil, oral, computerized administration, and so on); the degree to which stimulus materials are standardized; the type of response format (selection of a response from a set of alternatives as opposed to the production of a response); and the degree to which test materials are designed to reflect or simulate a particular context. In all cases, however, tests standardize the process by which test-taker responses to test materials are evaluated and scored. As noted in prior versions of the *Standards*, the same general types of information are needed for all varieties of tests.

The precise demarcation between those measurement devices used in the fields of educational and psychological testing that do and do not fall within the purview of the *Standards* is difficult to identify. Although the *Standards* applies most directly to standardized measures generally recognized as "tests," such as measures of ability, aptitude, achievement, attitudes, interests, personality, cognitive functioning, and mental health, it may also be usefully applied in varying degrees to a broad range of less formal assessment techniques. Admittedly, it will generally not be possible to apply the *Standards* rigorously to unstandardized questionnaires or to the broad range of unstructured behavior samples used in some forms of clinic- and school-based psychological assessment (e.g., an intake interview), and to instructor-made tests that are used to evaluate student performance in education and training. It is useful to distinguish between devices that lay claim to the concepts and techniques of the field of educational and psychological testing from those which represent nonstandardized or less standardized aids to day-to-day evaluative decisions. Although the principles and concepts underlying the *Standards* can be fruitfully applied to day-to-day decisions, such as when a business owner interviews a job applicant, a manager evaluates the performance of subordinates, or a coach evaluates a prospective athlete, it would be overreaching to expect that the standards of the educational and psychological testing field be followed by those making such decisions. In contrast, a structured interviewing system developed by a psychologist and accompanied by claims that the system has been found to be predictive of job performance in a variety of other settings falls within the purview of the *Standards*.

Cautions to be Exercised in Using the Standards

Several cautions are important to avoid misinterpreting the *Standards*:

1) Evaluating the acceptability of a test or test application does not rest on the literal satisfaction of every standard in this document, and acceptability cannot be determined by using a checklist. Specific circumstances affect the importance of individual standards, and individual standards should not be considered in isolation. Therefore, evaluating acceptability involves (a) professional judgment that is based on a knowledge of behavioral science, psychometrics, and the community standards in the professional field to which the tests apply; (b) the degree to which the intent of the standard has been satisfied by the test developer and user; (c) the alternatives that are readily available; and (d) research and experiential evidence regarding feasibility of meeting the standard.

2) When tests are at issue in legal proceedings and other venues requiring expert witness testimony it is essential that professional judgment be based on the accepted corpus of knowledge in determining the relevance of particular standards in a given situation. The intent of the *Standards* is to offer guidance for such judgments.

3) Claims by test developers or test users that a test, manual, or procedure satisfies or follows these standards should be made with care. It is appropriate for developers or users to state that efforts were made to adhere to the *Standards*, and to provide documents describing and supporting those efforts. Blanket claims without supporting evidence should not be made.

4) These standards are concerned with a field that is evolving. Consequently, there is a continuing need to monitor changes in the field and to revise this document as knowledge develops.

5) Prescription of the use of specific technical methods is not the intent of the *Standards*. For example, where specific statistical reporting requirements are mentioned, the phrase "or generally accepted equivalent" always should be understood.

The standards do not attempt to repeat or to incorporate the many legal or regulatory requirements that might be relevant to the issues they address. In some areas, such as the collection, analysis, and use of test data and results for different subgroups, the law may both require participants in the testing process to take certain actions and prohibit those participants from taking other actions. Where it is apparent that one or more standards or comments address an issue on which established legal requirements may be particularly relevant, the standard, comment, or introductory material may make note of that fact. Lack of specific reference to legal requirements, however, does not imply that no relevant requirement exists. In all situations, participants in the testing process should separately consider and, where appropriate, obtain legal advice on legal and regulatory requirements.

The Number of Standards

The number of standards has increased from the 1985 *Standards* for a variety of reasons. First, and most importantly, new developments have led to the addition of new standards. Commonly these deal with new types of tests or new uses for existing tests, rather than being broad standards applicable to all tests. Second, on the basis of recognition that some users of the *Standards* may turn only to chapters directly relevant to a given application, certain standards are repeated in different chapters. When such repetition occurs, the essence of the standard is the same. Only the wording, area of application, or elaboration in the comment is changed. Third, standards dealing with important nontechnical issues, such as avoiding conflicts of interest and equitable treatment of all test takers, have been added. Although such topics have not been addressed in prior versions of the *Standards*, they are not likely to be viewed as imposing burdensome new requirements. Thus the increase in the number of standards does not per se signal an increase in the obligations placed on test developers and test users.

Tests as Measures of Constructs

We depart from some historical uses of the term "construct," which reserve the term for characteristics that are not directly observable, but which are inferred from interrelated sets of observations. This historical perspective invites confusion. Some tests are viewed as measures of constructs, while others are not. In addition, considerable debate has ensued as to whether certain characteristics measured by tests are properly viewed as constructs. Furthermore, the types of validity evidence thought to be suitable can differ as a result of whether a given test is viewed as measuring a construct.

We use the term *construct* more broadly as the concept or characteristic that a test is designed to measure. Rarely, if ever, is there a single possible meaning that can be attached to a test score or a pattern of test responses. Thus, it is always incumbent on a testing professional to specify the construct interpretation that will be made on the basis of the score or response pattern. The notion that some tests are not under the purview of the *Standards* because they do not measure constructs is contrary to this use of the term. Also, as detailed in chapter 1, evolving conceptualizations of the concept of validity no longer speak of different types of validity but speak instead of different lines of validity evidence, all in service of providing information relevant to a specific intended interpretation of test scores. Thus, many lines of evidence can contribute to an understanding of the construct meaning of test scores.

Organization of This Volume

Part I of the *Standards*, "Test Construction, Evaluation, and Documentation," contains standards for validity (ch. 1); reliability and errors of measurement (ch. 2); test development and revision (ch. 3); scaling, norming, and score comparability (ch. 4); test administration, scoring, and reporting (ch. 5); and supporting documentation for tests (ch. 6). Part II addresses "Fairness in Testing," and contains standards on fairness and bias (ch. 7); the rights and responsibilities of test takers (ch. 8); testing individuals of diverse linguistic backgrounds (ch. 9); and testing individuals with disabilities (ch. 10). Part III treats specific "Testing Applications," and contains standards involving general responsibilities of test users (ch. 11); psychological testing and assessment (ch. 12); educational testing and assessment (ch. 13); testing in employment and credentialing (ch. 14); and testing in program evaluation and public policy (ch. 15).

Each chapter begins with introductory text that provides background for the standards that follow. This revision of the *Standards* contains more extensive introductory text material than its predecessor. Recognizing the common use of the *Standards* in the education of future test developers and users, the committee opted to provide a context for the standards themselves by presenting more background material than in previous versions. This text is designed to assist in the interpretation of the standards that follow in each chapter. Although the text is at times prescriptive and exhortatory, it should not be interpreted as imposing additional standards.

The *Standards* also contains an index and includes a glossary that provides definitions for terms as they are specifically used in this volume.

PART I

Test Construction, Evaluation, and Documentation

1. VALIDITY

Background

Validity refers to the degree to which evidence and theory support the interpretations of test scores entailed by proposed uses of tests. Validity is, therefore, the most fundamental consideration in developing and evaluating tests. The process of validation involves accumulating evidence to provide a sound scientific basis for the proposed score interpretations. It is the interpretations of test scores required by proposed uses that are evaluated, not the test itself. When test scores are used or interpreted in more than one way, each intended interpretation must be validated.

Validation logically begins with an explicit statement of the proposed interpretation of test scores, along with a rationale for the relevance of the interpretation to the proposed use. The proposed interpretation refers to the construct or concepts the test is intended to measure. Examples of constructs are mathematics achievement, performance as a computer technician, depression, and self-esteem. To support test development, the proposed interpretation is elaborated by describing its scope and extent and by delineating the aspects of the construct that are to be represented. The detailed description provides a conceptual framework for the test, delineating the knowledge, skills, abilities, processes, or characteristics to be assessed. The framework indicates how this representation of the construct is to be distinguished from other constructs and how it should relate to other variables.

The conceptual framework is partially shaped by the ways in which test scores will be used. For instance, a test of mathematics achievement might be used to place a student in an appropriate program of instruction, to endorse a high school diploma, or to inform a college admissions decision. Each of these uses implies a somewhat different interpretation of the mathematics achievement test

scores: that a student will benefit from a particular instructional intervention, that a student has mastered a specified curriculum, or that a student is likely to be successful with college-level work. Similarly, a test of self-esteem might be used for psychological counseling, to inform a decision about employment, or for the basic scientific purpose of elaborating the construct of self-esteem. Each of these potential uses shapes the specified framework and the proposed interpretation of the test's scores and also has implications for test development and evaluation.

Validation can be viewed as developing a scientifically sound validity argument to support the intended interpretation of test scores and their relevance to the proposed use. The conceptual framework points to the kinds of evidence that might be collected to evaluate the proposed interpretation in light of the purposes of testing. As validation proceeds, and new evidence about the meaning of a test's scores becomes available, revisions may be needed in the test, in the conceptual framework that shapes it, and even in the construct underlying the test.

The wide variety of tests and circumstances makes it natural that some types of evidence will be especially critical in a given case, whereas other types will be less useful. The decision about what types of evidence are important for validation in each instance can be clarified by developing a set of propositions that support the proposed interpretation for the particular purpose of testing. For instance, when a mathematics achievement test is used to assess readiness for an advanced course, evidence for the following propositions might be deemed necessary: (a) that certain skills are prerequisite for the advanced course; (b) that the content domain of the test is consistent with these prerequisite skills; (c) that test scores can be generalized across relevant sets of items; (d) that test scores are not unduly influenced by ancillary variables, such as writing ability; (e) that success in the advanced course can be validly assessed; and (f) that examinees with high scores on the test will be more successful in the advanced course than examinees with low scores on the test. Examples of propositions in other testing contexts might include, for instance, the proposition that examinees with high general anxiety scores experience significant anxiety in a range of settings, the proposition that a child's score on an intelligence scale is strongly related to the child's academic performance, or the proposition that a certain pattern of scores on a neuropsychological battery indicates impairment characteristic of brain injury. The validation process evolves as these propositions are articulated and evidence is gathered to evaluate their soundness.

Identifying the propositions implied by a proposed test interpretation can be facilitated by considering rival hypotheses that may challenge the proposed interpretation. It is also useful to consider the perspectives of different interested parties, existing experience with similar tests and contexts, and the expected consequences of the proposed test use. Plausible rival hypotheses can often be generated by considering whether a test measures less or more than its proposed construct. Such concerns are referred to as *construct underrepresentation* and *construct-irrelevant* variance.

Construct underrepresentation refers to the degree to which a test fails to capture important aspects of the construct. It implies a narrowed meaning of test scores because the test does not adequately sample some types of content, engage some psychological processes, or elicit some ways of responding that are encompassed by the intended construct. Take, for example, a test of reading comprehension intended to measure children's ability to read and interpret stories with understanding. A particular test might underrepresent the intended construct because it did not contain a sufficient variety of reading passages or ignored a common type of reading material. As another example, a test of anxiety might measure only physiological reactions and not emotional, cognitive, or situational components.

Construct-irrelevant variance refers to the degree to which test scores are affected by processes that are extraneous to its intended construct. The test scores may be systematically influenced to some extent by components that are not part of the construct. In the case of a reading comprehension test, construct-irrelevant components might include an emotional reaction to the test content, familiarity with the subject matter of the reading passages on the test, or the writing skill needed to compose a response. Depending on the detailed definition of the construct, vocabulary knowledge or reading speed might also be irrelevant components. On a test of anxiety, a response bias to under-report anxiety might be considered a source of construct-irrelevant variance.

Nearly all tests leave out elements that some potential users believe should be measured and include some elements that some potential users consider inappropriate. Validation involves careful attention to possible distortions in meaning arising from inadequate representation of the construct and also to aspects of measurement such as test format, administration conditions, or language level that may materially limit or qualify the interpretation of test scores. That is, the process of validation may lead to revisions in the test, the conceptual framework of the test, or both. The revised test would then need validation.

When propositions have been identified that would support the proposed interpretation of test scores, validation can proceed by developing empirical evidence, examining relevant literature, and/or conducting logical analyses to evaluate each of these propositions. Empirical evidence may include both local evidence, produced within the contexts where the test will be used, and evidence from similar testing applications in other settings. Use of existing evidence from similar tests and contexts can enhance the quality of the validity argument, especially when current data are limited.

Because a validity argument typically depends on more than one proposition, strong evidence in support of one in no way diminishes the need for evidence to support others. For example, a strong predictor-criterion relationship in an employment setting is not sufficient to justify test use for selection without considering the appropriateness and meaningfulness of the criterion measure. Professional judgment guides decisions regarding the specific forms of evidence that can best support the intended interpretation and use. As in all scientific endeavors, the quality of the evidence is primary. A few lines of solid evidence regarding a particular proposition are better than numerous lines of evidence of questionable quality.

Validation is the joint responsibility of the test developer and the test user. The test developer is responsible for furnishing relevant evidence and a rationale in support of the intended test use. The test user is ultimately responsible for evaluating the evidence in the particular setting in which the test is to be used. When the use of a test differs from that supported by the test developer, the test user bears special responsibility for validation. The standards apply to the validation process, for which the appropriate parties share responsibility. It should be noted that important contributions to the validity evidence are made as other researchers report findings of investigations that are related to the meaning of scores on the test.

Sources of Validity Evidence

The following sections outline various sources of evidence that might be used in evaluating a proposed interpretation of test scores for particular purposes. These sources of evidence may illuminate different aspects of validity,

but they do not represent distinct types of validity. Validity is a unitary concept. It is the degree to which all the accumulated evidence supports the intended interpretation of test scores for the proposed purpose. Like the 1985 *Standards*, this edition refers to types of validity evidence, rather than distinct types of validity. To emphasize this distinction, the treatment that follows does not follow traditional nomenclature (i.e., the use of the terms *content validity* or *predictive validity*). The glossary contains definitions of the traditional terms, explicating the difference between traditional and current use.

EVIDENCE BASED ON TEST CONTENT

Important validity evidence can be obtained from an analysis of the relationship between a test's content and the construct it is intended to measure. Test content refers to the themes, wording, and format of the items, tasks, or questions on a test, as well as the guidelines for procedures regarding administration and scoring. Test developers often work from a specification of the content domain. The content specification carefully describes the content in detail, often with a classification of areas of content and types of items. Evidence based on test content can include logical or empirical analyses of the adequacy with which the test content represents the content domain and of the relevance of the content domain to the proposed interpretation of test scores. Evidence based on content can also come from expert judgments of the relationship between parts of the test and the construct. For example, in developing a licensure test, the major facets of the specific occupation can be specified, and experts in that occupation can be asked to assign test items to the categories defined by those facets. They, or other qualified experts, can then judge the representativeness of the chosen set of items. Sometimes rules or algorithms can be constructed to select or generate items that differ systematically on the various facets of content, according to specifications.

Some tests are based on systematic observations of behavior. For example, a listing of the tasks comprising a job domain may be developed from observations of behavior in a job, together with judgments of subject-matter experts. Expert judgments can be used to assess the relative importance, criticality, and/or frequency of the various tasks. A job sample test can then be constructed from a random or stratified sampling of tasks rated highly on these characteristics. The test can then be administered under standardized conditions in an off-the-job setting.

The appropriateness of a given content domain is related to the specific inferences to be made from test scores. Thus, when considering an available test for a purpose other than that for which it was first developed, it is especially important to evaluate the appropriateness of the original content domain for the proposed new use. In educational program evaluations, for example, tests may properly cover material that receives little or no attention in the curriculum, as well as that toward which instruction is directed. Policymakers can then evaluate student achievement with respect to both content neglected and content addressed. On the other hand, when student mastery of a delivered curriculum is tested for purposes of informing decisions about individual students, such as promotion or graduation, the framework elaborating a content domain is appropriately limited to what students have had an opportunity to learn from the curriculum as delivered.

Evidence about content can be used, in part, to address questions about differences in the meaning or interpretation of test scores across relevant subgroups of examinees. Of particular concern is the extent to which construct underrepresentation or construct-irrelevant components may give an unfair advantage or disadvantage to one or more subgroups of examinees. Careful review of the construct and test content domain by a diverse panel of experts may point to potential sources of irrelevant difficulty (or easiness) that require further investigation.

EVIDENCE BASED ON RESPONSE PROCESSES

Theoretical and empirical analyses of the response processes of test takers can provide evidence concerning the fit between the construct and the detailed nature of performance or response actually engaged in by examinees. For instance, if a test is intended to assess mathematical reasoning, it becomes important to determine whether examinees are, in fact, reasoning about the material given instead of following a standard algorithm. For another instance, scores on a scale intended to assess the degree of an individual's extroversion or introversion should not be strongly influenced by social conformity.

Evidence based on response processes generally comes from analyses of individual responses. Questioning test takers about their performance strategies or responses to particular items can yield evidence that enriches the definition of a construct. Maintaining records that monitor the development of a response to a writing task, through successive written drafts or electronically monitored revisions, for instance, also provides evidence of process. Documentation of other aspects of performance, like eye movements or response times, may also be relevant to some constructs. Inferences about processes involved in performance can also be developed by analyzing the relationship among parts of the test and between the test and other variables. Wide individual differences in process can be revealing and may lead to reconsideration of certain test formats.

Evidence of response processes can contribute to questions about differences in meaning or interpretation of test scores across relevant subgroups of examinees. Process studies involving examinees from different subgroups can assist in determining the extent to which capabilities irrelevant or ancillary to the construct may be differentially influencing their performance.

Studies of response processes are not limited to the examinee. Assessments often rely on observers or judges to record and/or evaluate examinees' performances or products. In such cases, relevant validity evidence includes the extent to which the processes of observers or judges are consistent with the intended interpretation of scores. For instance, if judges are expected to apply particular criteria in scoring examinees' performances, it is important to ascertain whether they are, in fact, applying the appropriate criteria and not being influenced by factors that are irrelevant to the intended interpretation. Thus, validation may include empirical studies of how observers or judges record and evaluate data along with analyses of the appropriateness of these processes to the intended interpretation or construct definition.

EVIDENCE BASED ON INTERNAL STRUCTURE

Analyses of the internal structure of a test can indicate the degree to which the relationships among test items and test components conform to the construct on which the proposed test score interpretations are based. The conceptual framework for a test may imply a single dimension of behavior, or it may posit several components that are each expected to be homogeneous, but that are also distinct from each other. For example, a measure of discomfort on a health survey might assess both physical and emotional health. The extent to which item interrelationships bear out the presumptions of the framework would be relevant to validity.

The specific types of analysis and their interpretation depend on how the test will be used. For example, if a particular application posited a series of test components of increasing difficulty, empirical evidence of the extent to which response patterns conformed to this expectation would be provided. A theory that posited unidimensionality would call for evidence of item homogeneity. In this case, the item interrelationships

also provide an estimate of score reliability, but such an index would be inappropriate for tests with a more complex internal structure.

Some studies of the internal structure of tests are designed to show whether particular items may function differently for identifiable subgroups of examinees. Differential item functioning occurs when different groups of examinees with similar overall ability, or similar status on an appropriate criterion, have, on average, systematically different responses to a particular item. This issue is discussed in chapters 3 and 7. However, differential item functioning is not always a flaw or weakness. Subsets of items that have a specific characteristic in common (e.g., specific content, task representation) may function differently for different groups of similarly scoring examinees. This indicates a kind of multidimensionality that may be unexpected or may conform to the test framework.

EVIDENCE BASED ON RELATIONS TO OTHER VARIABLES

Analyses of the relationship of test scores to variables external to the test provide another important source of validity evidence. External variables may include measures of some criteria that the test is expected to predict, as well as relationships to other tests hypothesized to measure the same constructs, and tests measuring related or different constructs. Measures other than test scores, such as performance criteria, are often used in employment settings. Categorical variables, including group membership variables, become relevant when the theory underlying a proposed test use suggests that group differences should be present or absent if a proposed test interpretation is to be supported. Evidence based on relationships with other variables addresses questions about the degree to which these relationships are consistent with the construct underlying the proposed test interpretations.

Convergent and discriminant evidence. Relationships between test scores and other measures intended to assess similar constructs provide convergent evidence, whereas relationships between test scores and measures purportedly of different constructs provide discriminant evidence. For instance, within some theoretical frameworks, scores on a multiple-choice test of reading comprehension might be expected to relate closely (convergent evidence) to other measures of reading comprehension based on other methods, such as essay responses; conversely, test scores might be expected to relate less closely (discriminant evidence) to measures of other skills, such as logical reasoning. Relationships among different methods of measuring the construct can be especially helpful in sharpening and elaborating score meaning and interpretation.

Evidence of relations with other variables can involve experimental as well as correlational evidence. Studies might be designed, for instance, to investigate whether scores on a measure of anxiety improve as a result of some psychological treatment or whether scores on a test of academic achievement differentiate between instructed and noninstructed groups. If performance increases due to short-term coaching are viewed as a threat to validity, it would be useful to investigate whether coached and uncoached groups perform differently.

Test-criterion relationships. Evidence of the relation of test scores to a relevant criterion may be expressed in various ways, but the fundamental question is always: How accurately do test scores predict criterion performance? The degree of accuracy deemed necessary depends on the purpose for which the test is used.

The criterion variable is a measure of some attribute or outcome that is of primary interest, as determined by test users, who may be administrators in a school system, the management of a firm, or clients. The choice of the criterion and the measurement procedures used to obtain criterion scores are of central importance. The value of a test-criterion study depends on the relevance, reliability, and validity of the interpretation based on the criterion measure for a given testing application.

Historically, two designs, often called predictive and concurrent, have been distinguished for evaluating test-criterion relationships. A predictive study indicates how accurately test data can predict criterion scores that are obtained at a later time. A concurrent study obtains predictor and criterion information at about the same time. When prediction is actually contemplated, as in education or employment settings, or in planning rehabilitation regimens, predictive studies can retain the temporal differences and other characteristics of the practical situation. Concurrent evidence, which avoids temporal changes, is particularly useful for psychodiagnostic tests or to investigate alternative measures of some specified construct. In general, the choice of research strategy is guided by prior evidence of the extent to which predictive and concurrent studies yield the same or different results in the domain.

Test scores are sometimes used in allocating individuals to different treatments, such as different jobs within an institution, in a way that is advantageous for the institution and for the individuals. In that context, evidence is needed to judge the suitability of using a test when classifying or assigning a person to one job versus another or to one treatment versus another. Classification decisions are supported by evidence that the relationship of test scores to performance criteria is different for different treatments. It is possible for tests to be highly predictive of performance for different education programs or jobs without providing the information necessary to make a comparative judgment of the efficacy of assignments or treatments. In general, decision rules for selection or placement are also influenced by the number of persons to be accepted or the numbers that can be accommodated in alternative placement categories.

Evidence about relations to other variables is also used to investigate questions of differential prediction for groups. For instance, a finding that the relation of test scores to a relevant criterion variable differs from one group to another may imply that the meaning of the scores is not the same for members of the different groups, perhaps due to construct underrepresentation or construct-irrelevant components. However, the difference may also imply that the criterion has different meaning for different groups. The differences in test-criterion relationships can also arise from measurement error, especially when group means differ, so such differences do not necessarily indicate differences in score meaning. (See chapter 7.)

Validity generalization. An important issue in educational and employment settings is the degree to which evidence of validity based on test-criterion relations can be generalized to a new situation without further study of validity in that new situation. When a test is used to predict the same or similar criteria (e.g., performance of a given job) at different times or in different places, it is typically found that observed test-criterion correlations vary substantially. In the past, this has been taken to imply that local validation studies are always required. More recently, meta-analytic analyses have shown that in some domains, much of this variability may be due to statistical artifacts such as sampling fluctuations and variations across validation studies in the ranges of test scores and in the reliability of criterion measures. When these and other influences are taken into account, it may be found that the remaining variability in validity coefficients is relatively small. Thus, statistical summaries of past validation studies in similar situations may be useful in estimating test-criterion relationships in a new situation. This practice is referred to as the study of validity generalization.

In some circumstances, there is a strong basis for using validity generalization. This would be the case where the meta-analytic database is large, where the meta-analytic data adequately represent the type of situation to which one wishes to generalize, and where correction for statistical artifacts produces a clear and consistent pattern of validity evidence. In such circumstances, the informational value of a local validity study may be relatively limited. In other circumstances, the inferential leap required for generalization may be much larger. The meta-analytic database may be small, the findings may be less consistent, or the new situation may involve features markedly different from those represented in the meta-analytic database. In such circumstances, situation-specific evidence of validity will be relatively more informative. Although research on validity generalization shows that results of a single local validation study may be quite imprecise, there are situations where a single study, carefully done, with adequate sample size, provides sufficient evidence to support test use in a new situation. This highlights the importance of examining carefully the comparative informational value of local versus meta-analytic studies.

In conducting studies of the generalizability of validity evidence, the prior studies that are included may vary according to several situational facets. Some of the major facets are (a) differences in the way the predictor construct is measured, (b) the type of job or curriculum involved, (c) the type of criterion measure used, (d) the type of test takers, and (e) the time period in which the study was conducted. In any particular study of validity generalization, any number of these facets might vary, and a major objective of the study is to determine empirically the extent to which variation in these facets affects the test-criterion correlations obtained.

The extent to which predictive or concurrent evidence of validity generalization can be used in new situations is in large measure a function of accumulated research. Although evidence of generalization can often help to support a claim of validity in a new situation, the extent of available data limits the extent to which the claim can be sustained.

The above discussion focuses on the use of cumulative databases to estimate predictor-criterion relationships. Meta-analytic techniques can also be used to summarize other forms of data relevant to other inferences one may wish to draw from test scores in a particular application, such as effects of coaching and effects of certain alterations in testing conditions to accommodate test takers with certain disabilities.

Evidence Based on Consequences of Testing

An issue receiving attention in recent years is the incorporation of the intended and unintended consequences of test use into the concept of validity. Evidence about consequences can inform validity decisions. Here, however, it is important to distinguish between evidence that is directly relevant to validity and evidence that may inform decisions about social policy but falls outside the realm of validity.

Distinguishing between issues of validity and issues of social policy becomes particularly important in cases where differential consequences of test use are observed for different identifiable groups. For example, concerns have been raised about the effect of group differences in test scores on employment selection and promotion, the placement of children in special education classes, and the narrowing of a school's curriculum to exclude learning of objectives that are not assessed. Although information about the consequences of testing may influence decisions about test use, such consequences do not in and of themselves detract from the validity of intended test interpretations. Rather, judgments of validity or invalidity in the light of testing

consequences depend on a more searching inquiry into the sources of those consequences.

Take, as an example, a finding of different hiring rates for members of different groups as a consequence of using an employment test. If the difference is due solely to an unequal distribution of the skills the test purports to measure, and if those skills are, in fact, important contributors to job performance, then the finding of group differences per se does not imply any lack of validity for the intended inference. If, however, the test measured skill differences unrelated to job performance (e.g., a sophisticated reading test for a job that required only minimal functional literacy), or if the differences were due to the test's sensitivity to some examinee characteristic not intended to be part of the test construct, then validity would be called into question, even if test scores correlated positively with some measure of job performance. Thus, evidence about consequences may be directly relevant to validity when it can be traced to a source of invalidity such as construct underrepresentation or construct-irrelevant components. Evidence about consequences that cannot be so traced—that in fact reflects valid differences in performance—is crucial in informing policy decisions but falls outside the technical purview of validity.

Tests are commonly administered in the expectation that some benefit will be realized from the intended use of the scores. A few of the many possible benefits are selection of efficacious treatments for therapy, placement of workers in suitable jobs, prevention of unqualified individuals from entering a profession, or improvement of classroom instructional practices. A fundamental purpose of validation is to indicate whether these specific benefits are likely to be realized. Thus, in the case of a test used in placement decisions, the validation would be informed by evidence that alternative placements, in fact, are differentially beneficial to the persons and the institution. In the case of employment testing, if a test publisher claims that use of the test will result in reduced employee training costs, improved workforce efficiency, or some other benefit, then the validation would be informed by evidence in support of that claim.

Claims are sometimes made for benefits of testing that go beyond direct uses of the test scores themselves. Educational tests, for example, may be advocated on the grounds that their use will improve student motivation or encourage changes in classroom instructional practices by holding educators accountable for valued learning outcomes. Where such claims are central to the rationale advanced for testing, the direct examination of testing consequences necessarily assumes even greater importance. The validation process in such cases would be informed by evidence that the anticipated benefits of testing are being realized.

Integrating the Validity Evidence

A sound validity argument integrates various strands of evidence into a coherent account of the degree to which existing evidence and theory support the intended interpretation of test scores for specific uses. It encompasses evidence gathered from new studies and evidence available from earlier reported research. The validity argument may indicate the need for refining the definition of the construct, may suggest revisions in the test or other aspects of the testing process, and may indicate areas needing further study.

Ultimately, the validity of an intended interpretation of test scores relies on all the available evidence relevant to the technical quality of a testing system. This includes evidence of careful test construction; adequate score reliability; appropriate test administration and scoring; accurate score scaling, equating, and standard setting; and careful attention to fairness for all examinees, as described in subsequent chapters of the *Standards*.

Standard 1.1

A rationale should be presented for each recommended interpretation and use of test scores, together with a comprehensive summary of the evidence and theory bearing on the intended use or interpretation.

Comment: The rationale should indicate what propositions are necessary to investigate the intended interpretation. The comprehensive summary should combine logical analysis with empirical evidence to provide support for the test rationale. Evidence may come from studies conducted locally, in the setting where the test is to be used; from specific prior studies; or from comprehensive statistical syntheses of available studies meeting clearly specified criteria. No type of evidence is inherently preferable to others; rather, the quality and relevance of the evidence to the intended test use determine the value of a particular kind of evidence. A presentation of empirical evidence on any point should give due weight to all relevant findings in the scientific literature, including those inconsistent with the intended interpretation or use. Test developers have the responsibility to provide support for their own recommendations, but test users are responsible for evaluating the quality of the validity evidence provided and its relevance to the local situation.

Standard 1.2

The test developer should set forth clearly how test scores are intended to be interpreted and used. The population(s) for which a test is appropriate should be clearly delimited, and the construct that the test is intended to assess should be clearly described.

Comment: Statements about validity should refer to particular interpretations and uses. It is incorrect to use the unqualified phrase "the validity of the test." No test is valid for all purposes or in all situations. Each recommended use or interpretation requires validation and should specify in clear language the population for which the test is intended, the construct it is intended to measure, and the manner and contexts in which test scores are to be employed.

Standard 1.3

If validity for some common or likely interpretation has not been investigated, or if the interpretation is inconsistent with available evidence, that fact should be made clear and potential users should be cautioned about making unsupported interpretations.

Comment: If past experience suggests that a test is likely to be used inappropriately for certain kinds of decisions, specific warnings against such uses should be given. On the other hand, no two situations are ever identical, so some generalization by the user is always necessary. Professional judgment is required to evaluate the extent to which existing validity evidence supports a given test use.

Standard 1.4

If a test is used in a way that has not been validated, it is incumbent on the user to justify the new use, collecting new evidence if necessary.

Comment: Professional judgment is required to evaluate the extent to which existing validity evidence applies in the new situation and to determine what new evidence may be needed. The amount and kinds of new evidence required may be influenced by experience with similar prior test uses or interpretations and by the amount, quality, and relevance of existing data.

Standard 1.5

The composition of any sample of examinees from which validity evidence is

obtained should be described in as much detail as is practical, including major relevant sociodemographic and developmental characteristics.

Comment: Statistical findings can be influenced by factors affecting the sample on which the results are based. When the sample is intended to represent a population, that population should be described, and attention should be drawn to any systematic factors that may limit the representativeness of the sample. Factors that might reasonably be expected to affect the results include self-selection, attrition, linguistic prowess, disability status, and exclusion criteria, and others. If the subjects of a validity study are patients, for example, then the diagnoses of the patients are important, as well as other characteristics, such as the severity of the diagnosed condition. For tests used in industry, the employment status (e.g., applicants versus current job holders), the general level of experience and educational background and the gender and ethnic composition of the sample may be relevant information. For tests used in educational settings, relevant information may include educational background, developmental level, community characteristics, or school admissions policies, as well as the gender and ethnic composition of the sample. Sometimes restrictions about privacy preclude obtaining such population information.

Standard 1.6

When the validation rests in part on the appropriateness of test content, the procedures followed in specifying and generating test content should be described and justified in reference to the construct the test is intended to measure or the domain it is intended to represent. If the definition of the content sampled incorporates criteria such as importance, frequency, or criticality, these criteria should also be clearly explained and justified.

Comment: For example, test developers might provide a logical structure that maps the items on the test to the content domain, illustrating the relevance of each item and the adequacy with which the set of items represents the content domain. Areas of the content domain that are not included among the test items could be indicated as well.

Standard 1.7

When a validation rests in part on the opinions or decisions of expert judges, observers, or raters, procedures for selecting such experts and for eliciting judgments or ratings should be fully described. The qualifications, and experience, of the judges should be presented. The description of procedures should include any training and instructions provided, should indicate whether participants reached their decisions independently, and should report the level of agreement reached. If participants interacted with one another or exchanged information, the procedures through which they may have influenced one another should be set forth.

Comment: Systematic collection of judgments or opinions may occur at many points in test construction (e.g., in eliciting expert judgments of content appropriateness or adequate content representation), in formulating rules or standards for score interpretation (e.g., in setting cut scores), or in test scoring (e.g., rating of essay responses). Whenever such procedures are employed, the quality of the resulting judgments is important to the validation. It may be entirely appropriate to have experts work together to reach consensus, but it would not then be appropriate to treat their respective judgments as statistically independent.

Standard 1.8

If the rationale for a test use or score interpretation depends on premises about the psychological processes or cognitive operations used by examinees, then theoretical or empirical evidence in support of those premises should be provided. When statements about the processes employed by observers or scorers are part of the argument for validity, similar information should be provided.

Comment: If the test specification delineates the processes to be assessed, then evidence is needed that the test items do, in fact, tap the intended processes.

Standard 1.9

If a test is claimed to be essentially unaffected by practice and coaching, then the sensitivity of test performance to change with these forms of instruction should be documented.

Comment: Materials to aid in score interpretation should summarize evidence indicating the degree to which improvement with practice or coaching can be expected. Also, materials written for test takers should provide practical guidance about the value of test preparation activities, including coaching.

Standard 1.10

When interpretation of performance on specific items, or small subsets of items, is suggested, the rationale and relevant evidence in support of such interpretation should be provided. When interpretation of individual item responses is likely but is not recommended by the developer, the user should be warned against making such interpretations.

Comment: Users should be given sufficient guidance to enable them to judge the degree of confidence warranted for any use or interpretation recommended by the test developer. Test manuals and score reports should discourage overinterpretation of information that may be subject to considerable error. This is especially important if interpretation of performance on isolated items, small sub-sets of items, or subtest scores is suggested.

Standard 1.11

If the rationale for a test use or interpreta-tion depends on premises about the relation-ships among parts of the test, evidence concerning the internal structure of the test should be provided.

Comment: It might be claimed, for example, that a test is essentially unidimensional. Such a claim could be supported by a mul-tivariate statistical analysis, such as a factor analysis, showing that the score variability attributable to one major dimension was much greater than the score variability attributable to any other identified dimen-sion. When a test provides more than one score, the interrelationships of those scores should be shown to be consistent with the construct(s) being assessed.

Standard 1.12

When interpretation of subscores, score dif-ferences, or profiles is suggested, the ration-ale and relevant evidence in support of such interpretation should be provided. Where composite scores are developed, the basis and rationale for arriving at the composites should be given.

Comment: When a test provides more than one score, the distinctiveness of the separate scores should be demonstrated, and the inter-relationships of those scores should be shown to be consistent with the construct(s) being assessed. Moreover, evidence for the validity of interpretations of two separate scores would not necessarily justify an interpretation of the difference between them. Rather, the rationale and supporting evidence must pertain directly to the specific score or score combination to be interpreted or used.

Standard 1.13

When validity evidence includes statistical analyses of test results, either alone or together with data on other variables, the conditions under which the data were col-lected should be described in enough detail that users can judge the relevance of the statistical findings to local conditions. Attention should be drawn to any features of a validation data collection that are likely to differ from typical operational testing conditions and that could plausibly influ-ence test performance.

Comment: Such conditions might include (but would not be limited to) the following: examinee motivation or prior preparation, the distribution of test scores over examinees, the time allowed for examinees to respond or other administrative conditions, examiner training or other examiner characteristics, the time intervals separating collection of data on different measures, or conditions that may have changed since the validity evidence was obtained.

Standard 1.14

When validity evidence includes empirical analyses of test responses together with data on other variables, the rationale for selecting the additional variables should be provided. Where appropriate and feasible, evidence concerning the constructs represented by other variables, as well as their technical properties, should be presented or cited. Attention should be drawn to any likely sources of dependence (or lack of independ-ence) among variables other than dependen-cies among the construct(s) they represent.

Comment: The patterns of association between and among scores on the instrument under study and other variables should be consistent with theoretical expectations. The additional variables might be demographic characteristics, indicators of treatment conditions, or scores on other measures. They might include intended measures of the same construct or of different constructs. The reliability of scores from such other measures and the validity of intended interpretations of scores from these measures are an important part of the validity evidence for the instrument under study. If such variables include composite scores, the construction of the composites should be explained. In addition to considering the properties of each variable in isolation, it is important to guard against faulty interpretations arising from spurious sources of dependency among measures, including correlated errors or shared variance due to common methods of measurement or common elements.

Standard 1.15

When it is asserted that a certain level of test performance predicts adequate or inadequate criterion performance, information about the levels of criterion performance associated with given levels of test scores should be provided.

Comment: Regression equations are more useful than correlation coefficients, which are generally insufficient to fully describe patterns of association between tests and other variables. Means, standard deviations, and other statistical summaries are needed, as well as information about the distribution of criterion performances conditional upon a given test score. Evidence of overall association between variables should be supplemented by information about the form of that association and about the variability associated with that association in different ranges of test scores. Note that data collections employing examinees selected for their extreme scores on one or more measures (extreme groups) typically cannot provide adequate information about the association.

Standard 1.16

When validation relies on evidence that test scores are related to one or more criterion variables, information about the suitability and technical quality of the criteria should be reported.

Comment: The description of each criterion variable should include evidence concerning its reliability, the extent to which it represents the intended construct (e.g., job performance), and the extent to which it is likely to be influenced by extraneous sources of variance. Special attention should be given to sources that previous research suggests may introduce extraneous variance that might bias the criterion for or against identifiable groups.

Standard 1.17

If test scores are used in conjunction with other quantifiable variables to predict some outcome or criterion, regression (or equivalent) analyses should include those additional relevant variables along with the test scores.

Comment: In general, if several predictors of some criterion are available, the optimum combination of predictors cannot be determined solely from separate, pairwise examinations of the criterion variable with each separate predictor in turn. It is often informative to estimate the increment in predictive accuracy that may be expected when each variable, including the test score, is introduced in addition to all other available variables. Analyses involving multiple predictors should be verified by cross-validation or equivalent analysis whenever feasible, and the precision of estimated regression coefficients should be reported.

Standard 1.18

When statistical adjustments, such as those for restriction of range or attenuation, are made, both adjusted and unadjusted coefficients, as well as the specific procedure used, and all statistics used in the adjustment, should be reported.

Comment: The correlation between two variables, such as test scores and criterion measures, depends on the range of values on each variable. For example, the test scores and the criterion values of selected applicants will typically have a smaller range than the scores of all applicants. Statistical methods are available for adjusting the correlation to reflect the population of interest rather than the sample available. Such adjustments are often appropriate, as when comparing results across various situations. Reporting an adjusted correlation should be accompanied by a statement of the method and the statistics used in making the adjustment.

Standard 1.19

If a test is recommended for use in assigning persons to alternative treatments or is likely to be so used, and if outcomes from those treatments can reasonably be compared on a common criterion, then, whenever feasible, supporting evidence of differential outcomes should be provided.

Comment: If a test is used for classification into alternative occupational, therapeutic, or educational programs, it is not sufficient just to show that the test predicts treatment outcomes. Support for the validity of the classification procedure is provided by showing that the test is useful in determining which persons are likely to profit differentially from one treatment or another. Treatment categories may have to be combined to assemble sufficient cases for statistical analysis. It is recognized, however, that such research may not be feasible, because ethical and legal constraints on differential assignments may forbid control groups.

Standard 1.20

When a meta-analysis is used as evidence of the strength of a test-criterion relationship, the test and the criterion variables in the local situation should be comparable with those in the studies summarized. If relevant research includes credible evidence that any other features of the testing application may influence the strength of the test-criterion relationship, the correspondence between those features in the local situation and in the meta-analysis should be reported. Any significant disparities that might limit the applicability of the meta-analytic findings to the local situation should be noted explicitly.

Comment: The meta-analysis should incorporate all available studies meeting explicitly stated inclusion criteria. Meta-analytic evidence used in test validation typically is based on a number of tests measuring the same or very similar constructs and criterion measures that likewise measure the same or similar constructs. A meta-analytic study may also be limited to a single test and a single criterion. For each study included in the analysis, the test-criterion relationship is expressed in some common metric, often as an *effect size.* The strength of the test-criterion relationship may be moderated by features of the situation in which the test and criterion measures were obtained (e.g., types of jobs, characteristics of test takers, time interval separating collection of test and criterion measures, year or decade in which the data were collected). If test-criterion relationships vary according to such moderator variables, then, the numbers of studies permitting, the meta-analysis should report separate estimated effect size distributions conditional upon relevant situational features. This might be accomplished, for example, by reporting separate distributions for subsets of studies or by estimating the magnitudes of the influences of situational features on effect sizes.

Standard 1.21

Any meta-analytic evidence used to support an intended test use should be clearly described, including methodological choices in identifying and coding studies, correcting for artifacts, and examining potential moderator variables. Assumptions made in correcting for artifacts such as criterion unreliability and range restriction should be presented, and the consequences of these assumptions made clear.

Comment: Meta-analysis inevitably involves judgments regarding a number of methodological choices. The bases for these judgments should be articulated. In the case of choices involving some degree of uncertainty, such as artifact corrections based on assumed values, the uncertainty should be acknowledged and the degree to which conclusions about validity hinge on these assumptions should be examined and reported.

Standard 1.22

When it is clearly stated or implied that a recommended test use will result in a specific outcome, the basis for expecting that outcome should be presented, together with relevant evidence.

Comment: If it is asserted, for example, that using a given test for employee selection will result in reduced employee errors or training costs, evidence in support of that assertion should be provided. A given claim for the benefits of test use may be supported by logical or theoretical argument as well as empirical data. Due weight should be given to findings in the scientific literature that may be inconsistent with the stated expectation.

Standard 1.23

When a test use or score interpretation is recommended on the grounds that testing or the testing program per se will result in some indirect benefit in addition to the utility of information from the test scores themselves, the rationale for anticipating the indirect benefit should be made explicit. Logical or theoretical arguments and empirical evidence for the indirect benefit should be provided. Due weight should be given to any contradictory findings in the scientific literature, including findings suggesting important indirect outcomes other than those predicted.

Comment: For example, certain educational testing programs have been advocated on the grounds that they would have a salutary influence on classroom instructional practices or would clarify students' understanding of the kind or level of achievement they were expected to attain. To the extent that such claims enter into the justification for a testing program, they become part of the validity argument for test use and so should be examined as part of the validation effort. Due weight should be given to evidence against such predictions, for example, evidence that under some conditions educational testing may have a negative effect on classroom instruction.

Standard 1.24

When unintended consequences result from test use, an attempt should be made to investigate whether such consequences arise from the test's sensitivity to characteristics other than those it is intended to assess or to the test's failure fully to represent the intended construct.

Comment: The validity of test score interpretations may be limited by construct-irrelevant components or construct underrepresentation. When unintended consequences appear to stem, at least in part, from the use of one or more tests, it is especially important to check that these consequences do not arise from such sources of invalidity. Although group differences, in and of themselves, do not call into question the validity of a proposed interpretation, they may increase the salience of plausible rival hypotheses that should be investigated as part of the validation effort.

2. RELIABILITY AND ERRORS OF MEASUREMENT

Background

A test, broadly defined, is a set of tasks designed to elicit or a scale to describe examinee behavior in a specified domain, or a system for collecting samples of an individual's work in a particular area. Coupled with the device is a scoring procedure that enables the examiner to quantify, evaluate, and interpret the behavior or work samples. *Reliability* refers to the consistency of such measurements when the testing procedure is repeated on a population of individuals or groups.

The discussion that follows introduces concepts and procedures that may not be familiar to some readers. It is not expected that the brief definitions and explanations presented here will be sufficient to enable the less sophisticated reader to become adequately conversant with these developments. To achieve a better understanding, such readers may need to consult more comprehensive treatments in the measurement literature.

The usefulness of behavioral measurements presupposes that individuals and groups exhibit some degree of stability in their behavior. However, successive samples of behavior from the same person are rarely identical in all pertinent respects. An individual's performances, products, and responses to sets of test questions vary in their quality or character from one occasion to another, even under strictly controlled conditions. This variation is reflected in the examinee's scores. The causes of this variability are generally unrelated to the purposes of measurement. An examinee may try harder, may make luckier guesses, be more alert, feel less anxious, or enjoy better health on one occasion than another. An examinee may have knowledge, experience, or understanding that is more relevant to some tasks than to others in the domain sampled by the test. Some individuals may exhibit less variation in their scores than others, but no examinee is completely consistent. Because of this variation and, in some instances, because of subjectivity in the scoring process, an individual's obtained score and the average score of a group will always reflect at least a small amount of measurement error.

To say that a score includes a component of error implies that there is a hypothetical error-free value that characterizes an examinee at the time of testing. In classical test theory this error-free value is referred to as the person's *true score* for the test or measurement procedure. It is conceptualized as the hypothetical average score resulting from many repetitions of the test or alternate forms of the instrument. In statistical terms, the true score is a personal parameter and each observed score of an examinee is presumed to estimate this parameter. Under an approach to reliability estimation known as *generalizability theory*, a comparable concept is referred to as an examinee's *universe score*. Under *item response theory (IRT)*, a closely related concept is called an examinee's *ability or trait parameter*, though observed scores and trait parameters may be stated in different units. The hypothetical difference between an examinee's observed score on any particular measurement and the examinee's true or universe score for the procedure is called *measurement error*.

The definition of what constitutes a standardized test or measurement procedure has broadened significantly in recent years. At one time the cardinal features of most standardized tests were consistency of the test materials from examinee to examinee, close adherence to stipulated procedures for test administration, and use of prescribed scoring rules that could be applied with a high degree of consistency. These features were, in fact, what made a test "standardized," and they made meaningful norms possible. In employment settings and certification programs, flexible measurement procedures have been in use for many years. Individualized oral examinations, simulations, analyses of extended case reports, and performance in real-life settings such as clinics are now commonplace. In education, however, large-scale testing programs with a high degree of flexibility in test format and administrative procedures are a relatively recent development. In some programs cumulative portfolios of student work have been substituted for more traditional end-of-year tests of achievement. Other programs now allow examinees to choose their own topics to demonstrate their abilities. Still others permit or encourage small groups of examinees to work cooperatively in completing the test. A science examination, for example, might involve a team of high school students who conduct a study of the sources of pollution in local streams and prepare a report on their findings. Examinations of this kind raise complex issues regarding the domain represented by the test and about the generalizability of individual and group scores. Each step toward greater flexibility almost inevitably enlarges the scope and magnitude of measurement error. However, it is possible that some of the resultant sacrifices in reliability may reduce construct irrelevance or construct underrepresentation in an assessment program.

Characteristics and Implications of Measurement Error

Errors of measurement are generally viewed as random and unpredictable. They are conceptually distinguished from systematic errors, which may also affect performance of individuals or groups, but in a consistent rather than a random manner. For example, a systematic group error would occur as a result of differences in the difficulty of test forms that have not been adequately equated. When one test form is less difficult than another, examinees

who take the easier form may be expected to earn a higher average score than those who take the more difficult form. Such a difference would not be considered an error of measurement under most methods of quantifying and summarizing error, though generalizability theory would permit test form differences to be recognized as an error source.

The systematic factors that may differentially affect the performance of individual test takers are not as easily detected or overridden as those affecting groups. For example, some examinees experience levels of test anxiety that severely impair cognitive efficiency. The presence of such a condition can sometimes be recognized in an examinee, but the effect cannot be overcome by statistical adjustments. The individual systematic errors are not generally regarded as an element that contributes to unreliability. Rather, they constitute a source of construct-irrelevant variance and thus may detract from validity.

Important sources of measurement error may be broadly categorized as those rooted within the examinees and those external to them. Fluctuations in the level of an examinee's motivation, interest, or attention and the inconsistent application of skills are clearly internal factors that may lead to score inconsistencies. Differences among testing sites in their freedom from distractions, the random effects of scorer subjectivity, and variation in scorer standards are examples of external factors. The potency and importance of any particular source depend on the specific conditions under which the measures are taken, how performances are scored, and the interpretations made from the scores. A particular factor, such as the subjectivity in scoring, may be a significant source of measurement error in some assessments and a minor consideration in others.

Some changes in scores from one occasion to another, it should be noted, are not regarded as error, because they result, in part, from an intervention, learning, or maturation that has occurred between the initial and final measures. The difference within an individual indicates, to some extent, the effects of the intervention or the extent of growth. In such settings, change per se constitutes the phenomenon of interest. The difference or the change score then becomes the measure to which reliability pertains.

Measurement error reduces the usefulness of measures. It limits the extent to which test results can be generalized beyond the particulars of a specific application of the measurement process. Therefore, it reduces the confidence that can be placed in any single measurement. Because random measurement errors are inconsistent and unpredictable, they cannot be removed from observed scores. However, their aggregate magnitude can be summarized in several ways, as discussed below.

Summarizing Reliability Data

Information about measurement error is essential to the proper evaluation and use of an instrument. This is true whether the measure is based on the responses to a specific set of questions, a portfolio of work samples, the performance of a task, or the creation of an original product. The ideal approach to the study of reliability entails independent replication of the entire measurement process. However, only a rough or partial approximation of such replication is possible in many testing situations, and investigation of measurement error may require special studies that depart from routine testing procedures. Nevertheless, it should be the goal of test developers to investigate test reliability as fully as practical considerations permit. No test developer is exempt from this responsibility.

The critical information on reliability includes the identification of the major sources of error, summary statistics bearing on the size of such errors, and the degree of generalizability of scores across alternate forms, scorers, administrations, or other relevant dimensions. It also includes a description of the examinee population to whom the foregoing data apply, as the data may accurately reflect what is true of one population but misrepresent what is true of another. For example, a given reliability coefficient or estimated standard error derived from scores of a nationally representative sample may differ significantly from that obtained for a more homogeneous sample drawn from one gender, one ethnic group, or one community.

Reliability information may be reported in terms of variances or standard deviations of measurement errors, in terms of one or more coefficients, or in terms of IRT-based test information functions. The standard error of measurement is the standard deviation of a hypothetical distribution of measurement errors that arises when a given population is assessed via a particular test or procedure. The overall variance of measurement errors is actually a weighted average of the values that hold at various true score levels. The variance at a particular level is called a *conditional error variance* and its square root a *conditional standard error*. Traditionally, three broad categories of reliability coefficients have been recognized: (a) coefficients derived from the administration of parallel forms in independent testing sessions (alternate-form coefficients); (b) coefficients obtained by administration of the same instrument on separate occasions (test-retest or stability coefficients); and (c) coefficients based on the relationships among scores derived from individual items or subsets of the items within a test, all data accruing from a single administration (internal consistency coefficients). Where test scoring involves a high level of judgment, indexes of scorer consistency are commonly obtained. With the development of generalizability theory, the foregoing three categories may now be seen as special cases of a more general classification: generalizability coefficients.

Like traditional reliability coefficients, a *generalizability coefficient* is defined as the ratio of true or universe score variance to observed score variance. Unlike traditional approaches to the study of reliability, however, generalizability theory permits the researcher to specify and estimate the various components of true score variance, error variance, and observed score variance. Estimation is typically accomplished by the application of the techniques of analysis of variance. Of special interest are the separate numerical estimates of the components of overall error variance. Such estimates permit examination of the contribution of each source of error to the overall measurement process. The generalizability approach also makes possible the estimation of coefficients that apply to a wide variety of potential measurement designs.

The test information function, an important result of IRT, efficiently summarizes how well the test discriminates among individuals at various levels of the ability or trait being assessed. Under the IRT conceptualization, a mathematical function called the *item characteristic curve* or *item response function* is used as a model to represent the increasing proportion of correct responses to an item for groups at progressively higher levels of the ability or trait being measured. Given an adequate database, the parameters of the characteristic curve of each item in a test can be estimated. The test information function can then be approximated. This function may be viewed as a mathematical statement of the precision of measurement at each level of the given trait. Precision, in the IRT context, is analogous to the reciprocal of the conditional error variance of classical test theory.

Interpretation of Reliability Data

In general, reliability coefficients are most useful in comparing tests or measurement procedures, particularly those that yield scores in different units or metrics. However, such comparisons are rarely straightforward. Allowance must be made for differences in the variability of the groups on which the coefficients are based, the techniques used to obtain the coefficients, the sources of error reflected in the coefficients, and the lengths of the instruments being compared in terms of testing time.

Generalizability coefficients and the many coefficients included under the traditional categories may appear to be interchangeable, but some convey quite different information from others. A coefficient in any given category may encompass errors of measurement from a highly restricted perspective, a very broad perspective, or some point between these extremes. For example, a coefficient may reflect error due to scorer inconsistencies but not reflect the variation that characterizes a succession of examinee performances or products. A coefficient may reflect only the internal consistency of item responses within an instrument and fail to reflect measurement error associated with day-to-day changes in examinee health, efficiency, or motivation.

It should not be inferred, however, that alternate-form or test-retest coefficients based on test administrations several days or weeks apart are always preferable to internal consistency coefficients. For many tests, internal consistency coefficients do not differ significantly from alternate-form coefficients. Where only one form of a test exists, retesting may result in an inflated correlation between the first and second scores due to idiosyncratic features of the test or to examinee recall of initial responses. Also, an individual's status on some attributes, such as mood or emotional state, may change significantly in a short period of time. In the assessment of such constructs the multiple measures that give rise to reliability estimates should be obtained within the short period in which the attribute remains stable. Therefore, for characteristics of this kind an internal consistency coefficient may be preferred.

The standard error of measurement is generally more relevant than the reliability coefficient once a measurement procedure has been adopted and interpretation of scores has become the user's primary concern. It should be noted that standard errors share some of the ambiguities which characterize reliability coefficients, and estimates may vary in their quality. Information about the precision of measurement at each of several widely spaced score levels—that is, conditional standard errors—is usually a valuable supplement to the single statistic for all score levels combined. Like reliability and generalizability coefficients, standard errors may reflect variation from many sources of error or only a few. For most purposes, a more comprehensive standard error is more informative than a less comprehensive value. However, there are many exceptions to this generalization. Practical constraints often preclude conduct of the kinds of studies that would yield estimates of the preferred standard errors.

Measurements derived from observations of behavior or evaluations of products are especially sensitive to a variety of error factors. These include evaluator biases and idiosyncrasies, scoring subjectivity, and intra-examinee factors that cause variation from one performance or product to another. The methods of generalizability theory are well suited to the investigation of the reliability of the scores on such measures. Estimates of the error variance associated with each specific source and with the interactions between sources indicate the extent to which examinee scores may be generalized to a population of scorers and to a universe of products or performances.

The interpretations of test scores may be broadly categorized as *relative* or *absolute*. Relative interpretations convey the standing of an individual or group within a reference population. Absolute interpretations relate the status of an individual or group to defined standards. These standards may originate in empirical data for one or more populations or be based entirely on authoritative judgment. Different values of the standard error apply to the two types of interpretations.

The test information function can be perceived an alternative to traditional indices of measurement precision, but there are important distinctions that should be noted. Standard errors under classical test theory can be derived by several different approaches. These yield similar, but not identical, results. More significantly, standard errors, like reliability coefficients, may reflect a broad configuration of error factors or a restricted configuration, depending on the design of the reliability study. Test information functions, on the other hand, are limited to the restricted definition of measurement error that is associated with internal consistency reliabilities. In addition, under IRT several different mathematical models have been proposed and accepted as the basic form of the item characteristic curve. Adoption of one model rather than another can have a material effect on the derived test information function.

A final consideration has significant implications for both IRT and classical approaches to quantification of test score precision. It is this: Indices of precision depend on the scale in which they are reported. An index stated in terms of raw scores or the trait level estimates of IRT may convey a radically different perception of reliability than the same index restated in terms of derived scores. This same contrast may hold for conditional standard errors. In terms of the basic score scale, precision may appear to be high at one score level, low at another. But when the conditional standard errors are restated in units of derived scores, such as grade equivalents or standard scores, quite different trends in comparative precision may emerge. Therefore, measurement precision under both theories very strongly depends on the scale in which test scores are reported and interpreted.

Precision and consistency in measurement are always desirable. However, the need for precision increases as the consequences of decisions and interpretations grow in importance. If a decision can and will be corroborated by information from other sources or if an erroneous initial decision can be quickly corrected, scores with modest reliability may suffice. But if a test score leads to a decision that is not easily reversed, such as rejection or admission of a candidate to a professional school or the decision by a jury that a serious injury was sustained, the need for a high degree of precision is much greater.

Where the purpose of measurement is classification, some measurement errors are more serious than others. An individual who is far above or far below the value established for pass/fail or for eligibility for a special program can be mismeasured without serious consequences. Mismeasurement of examinees whose true scores are close to the cut score is a more serious concern. The techniques used to quantify reliability should recognize these circumstances. This can be done by reporting the conditional standard error in the vicinity of the critical value.

Some authorities have proposed that a semantic distinction be made between "reliability of scores" and "degree of agreement in classification." The former term would be reserved for analysis of score variation under repeated measurement. The term *classification consistency* or *inter-rater agreement*, rather than *reliability*, would be used in discussions of consistency of classification. Adoption of such usage would make it clear that the importance of an error of any given size depends on the proximity of the examinee's score to the cut score. However, it should be recognized that the degree of consistency or agreement in examinee classification is specific to the cut score employed and its location within the score distribution.

Average scores of groups, when interpreted as measures of program effectiveness, involve error factors that are not identical to those that operate at the individual level. For large groups, the positive and negative measurement errors of individuals may average out almost completely in group means. However, the sampling errors associated with the random sampling of persons who are tested for purposes of program evaluation are still present. This component of the variation in the mean achievement of school classes from year to year or in the average expressed satisfaction of successive samples of the clients of a program may constitute a potent source of error in program evaluations. It can be a significant source of error in inferences about programs even if there is a high degree of precision in individual test scores. Therefore, when an instrument is used to make group judgments, reliability data must bear directly on the interpretations specific to groups. Standard errors appropriate to individual scores are not appropriate measures of the precision of group averages. A more appropriate statistic is the standard error of the observed score means. Generalizability theory can provide more refined indices when the sources of measurement error are numerous and complex.

Typically, developers and distributors of tests have primary responsibility for obtaining and reporting evidence of reliability or test information functions. The user must have such data to make an informed choice among alternative measurement approaches and will generally be unable to conduct reliability studies prior to operational use of an instrument. In some instances, however, local users of a test or procedure must accept at least partial responsibility for documenting the precision of measurement. This obligation holds when one of the primary purposes of measurement is to rank or classify examinees within the local population. It also holds when users must rely on local scorers who are trained to use the scoring rubrics provided by the test developer. In such settings, local factors may materially affect the magnitude of error variance and observed score variance. Therefore, the reliability of

scores may differ appreciably from that reported by the developer.

The reporting of reliability coefficients alone, with little detail regarding the methods used to estimate the coefficient, the nature of the group from which the data were derived, and the conditions under which the data were obtained constitutes inadequate documentation. General statements to the effect that a test is "reliable" or that it is "sufficiently reliable to permit interpretations of individual scores" are rarely, if ever, acceptable. It is the user who must take responsibility for determining whether or not scores are sufficiently trustworthy to justify anticipated uses and interpretations. Of course, test constructors and publishers are obligated to provide sufficient data to make informed judgments possible.

As the foregoing comments emphasize, there is no single, preferred approach to quantification of reliability. No single index adequately conveys all of the relevant facts. No one method of investigation is optimal in all situations, nor is the test developer limited to a single approach for any instrument. The choice of estimation techniques and the minimum acceptable level for any index remain a matter of professional judgment.

Although reliability is discussed here as an independent characteristic of test scores, it should be recognized that the level of reliability of scores has implications for the validity of score interpretations. Reliability data ultimately bear on the repeatability of the behavior elicited by the test and the consistency of the resultant scores. The data also bear on the consistency of classifications of individuals derived from the scores. To the extent that scores reflect random errors of measurement, their potential for accurate prediction of criteria, for beneficial examinee diagnosis, and for wise decision making is limited. Relatively unreliable scores, in conjunction with other convergent information, may sometimes be of value to a test user, but the level of a score's reliability places limits on its unique contribution to validity for all purposes.

Standard 2.1

For each total score, subscore, or combination of scores that is to be interpreted, estimates of relevant reliabilities and standard errors of measurement or test information functions should be reported.

Comment: It is not sufficient to report estimates of reliabilities and standard errors of measurement only for total scores when subscores are also interpreted. The form-to-form and day-to-day consistency of total scores on a test may be acceptably high, yet subscores may have unacceptably low reliability. For all scores to be interpreted, users should be supplied with reliability data in enough detail to judge whether scores are precise enough for the users' intended interpretations. Composites formed from selected subtests within a test battery are frequently proposed for predictive and diagnostic purposes. Users need information about the reliability of such composites.

Standard 2.2

The standard error of measurement, both overall and conditional (if relevant), should be reported both in raw score or original scale units and in units of each derived score recommended for use in test interpretation.

Comment: The most common derived scores include standard scores, grade or age equivalents, and percentile ranks. Because raw scores on norm-referenced tests are only rarely interpreted directly, standard errors in derived score units are more helpful to the typical test user. A confidence interval for an examinee's true score, universe score, or percentile rank serves much the same purpose as a standard error and can be used as an alternative approach to convey reliability information. The implications of the standard error of measurement are especially important in situations where decisions cannot be postponed and corroborative sources of information are limited.

Standard 2.3

When test interpretation emphasizes differences between two observed scores of an individual or two averages of a group, reliability data, including standard errors, should be provided for such differences.

Comment: Observed score differences are used for a variety of purposes. Achievement gains are frequently the subject of inferences for groups as well as individuals. Differences between verbal and performance scores of intelligence and scholastic ability tests are often employed in the diagnosis of cognitive impairment and learning problems. Psychodiagnostic inferences are frequently drawn from the differences between subtest scores. Aptitude and achievement batteries, interest inventories, and personality assessments are commonly used to identify and quantify the relative strengths and weaknesses or the pattern of trait levels of an examinee. When the interpretation of test scores centers on the peaks and valleys in the examinee's test score profile, the reliability of score differences for all pairs of scores is critical.

Standard 2.4

Each method of quantifying the precision or consistency of scores should be described clearly and expressed in terms of statistics appropriate to the method. The sampling procedures used to select examinees for reliability analyses and descriptive statistics on these samples should be reported.

Comment: Information on the method of subject selection, sample sizes, means, standard deviations, and demographic characteristics of the groups helps users judge the extent to which reported data apply to their own examinee populations. If the test-retest or alternate-form approach is used, the interval between testings should be indicated. Because there are many ways of estimating reliability,

each influenced by different sources of measurement error, it is unacceptable to say simply, "The reliability of test X is .90." A better statement would be, "The reliability coefficient of .90 reported for scores on test X was obtained by correlating scores from forms A and B administered on successive days. The data were based on a sample of 400 10th-grade students from five middle-class suburban schools in New York State. The demographic breakdown of this group was as follows: ...."

Standard 2.5

A reliability coefficient or standard error of measurement based on one approach should not be interpreted as interchangeable with another derived by a different technique unless their implicit definitions of measurement error are equivalent.

Comment: Internal consistency, alternate-form, test-retest, and generalizability coefficients should not be considered equivalent, as each may incorporate a unique definition of measurement error. Error variances derived via item response theory may not be equivalent to error variances estimated via other approaches. Test developers should indicate the sources of error that are reflected in or ignored by the reported reliability indices.

Standard 2.6

If reliability coefficients are adjusted for restriction of range or variability, the adjustment procedure and both the adjusted and unadjusted coefficients should be reported. The standard deviations of the group actually tested and of the target population, as well as the rationale for the adjustment, should be presented.

Comment: Application of a correction for restriction in variability presumes that the available sample is not representative of the test-taker population to which users might be expected to generalize. The rationale for the correction should consider the appropriateness of such a generalization. Adjustment formulas that presume constancy in the standard error across score levels should not be used unless constancy can be defended.

Standard 2.7

When subsets of items within a test are dictated by the test specifications and can be presumed to measure partially independent traits or abilities, reliability estimation procedures should recognize the multifactor character of the instrument.

Comment: The total score on a test that is clearly multifactor in nature should be treated as a composite score. If an internal consistency estimate of total score reliability is obtained by the split-halves procedure, the halves should be parallel in content and statistical characteristics. Stratified coefficient alpha should be used rather than the more familiar nonstratified coefficient.

Standard 2.8

Test users should be informed about the degree to which rate of work may affect examinee performance.

Comment: It is not possible to state, in general, whether reliability coefficients will increase or decrease when rate of work becomes an important source of systematic variance. Rate of work, as an examinee trait, may be more stable or less stable from occasion to occasion than the other factors the test is designed to measure. Because speededness has differential effects on various estimates, information on speededness is helpful in interpreting reported coefficients.

The importance of the speed factor can sometimes be inferred from analyses of item responses and from observations by examiners during test administrations conducted for reliability analyses. The distribution of "last item attempted" and increases in the frequen-

cy of omitted responses toward the end of a test are also highly informative, though not conclusive, evidence regarding speededness. A decline in the proportion of correct responses, beyond that attributable to increasing item difficulty, may indicate that some examinees were responding randomly. With computer-administered tests, abnormally fast item response times, particularly toward the end of the test, may also suggest that examinees were responding randomly. In the case of constructed-response exercises, including essay questions, the completeness of the responses may suggest that time constraints had little effect on early items but a significant effect on later items. Introduction of a speed factor into what might otherwise be a power test may have a marked effect on alternate-form and test-retest reliabilities. A shift from a paper-and-pencil format to a computer-administered format may affect test speededness.

Standard 2.9

When a test is designed to reflect rate of work, reliability should be estimated by the alternate-form or test-retest approach, using separately timed administrations.

Comment: Split-half coefficients based on separate scores from the odd-numbered and even-numbered items are known to yield inflated estimates of reliability for highly speeded tests. Coefficient alpha and other internal consistency coefficients may also be biased, though the size of the bias is not as clear as that for the split-halves coefficient.

Standard 2.10

When subjective judgment enters into test scoring, evidence should be provided on both inter-rater consistency in scoring and within-examinee consistency over repeated measurements. A clear distinction should be made among reliability data based on (a) independent panels of raters scoring the same perform-

ances or products, (b) a single panel scoring successive performances or new products, and (c) independent panels scoring successive performances or new products.

Comment: Task-to-task variations in the quality of an examinee's performance and rater-to-rater inconsistencies in scoring represent independent sources of measurement error. Reports of reliability studies should make clear which of these sources are reflected in the data. Where feasible, the error variances arising from each source should be estimated. Generalizability studies and variance component analyses are especially helpful in this regard. These analyses can provide separate error variance estimates for tasks within examinees, for judges, and for occasions within the time period of trait stability. Information should be provided on the qualifications of the judges used in reliability studies.

Inter-rater or inter-observer agreement may be particularly important for ratings and observational data that involve subtle discriminations. It should be noted, however, that when raters evaluate positively correlated characteristics, a favorable or unfavorable assessment of one trait may color their opinions of other traits. Moreover, high inter-rater consistency does not imply high examinee consistency from task to task. Therefore, internal consistency within raters and inter-rater agreement do not guarantee high reliability of examinee scores.

Standard 2.11

If there are generally accepted theoretical or empirical reasons for expecting that reliability coefficients, standard errors of measurement, or test information functions will differ substantially for various subpopulations, publishers should provide reliability data as soon as feasible for each major population for which the test is recommended.

Comment: If test score interpretation involves inferences within subpopulations as well as within the general population, reliability data should be provided for both the subpopulations and the general population. Test users who work exclusively with a specific cultural group or with individuals who have a particular disability would benefit from an estimate of the standard error for such a subpopulation. Some groups of test takers—pre-school children, for example—tend to respond to test stimuli in a less consistent fashion than do older children.

Standard 2.12

If a test is proposed for use in several grades or over a range of chronological age groups and if separate norms are provided for each grade or each age group, reliability data should be provided for each age or grade population, not solely for all grades or ages combined.

Comment: A reliability coefficient based on a sample of examinees spanning several grades or a broad range of ages in which average scores are steadily increasing will generally give a spuriously inflated impression of reliability. When a test is intended to discriminate within age or grade populations, reliability coefficients and standard errors should be reported separately for each population.

Standard 2.13

If local scorers are employed to apply general scoring rules and principles specified by the test developer, local reliability data should be gathered and reported by local authorities when adequate size samples are available.

Comment: For example, many statewide testing programs depend on local scoring of essays, constructed-response exercises, and performance tests. Reliability analyses bear on the possibility that additional training of scorers is needed and, hence, should be an integral part of program monitoring.

Standard 2.14

Conditional standard errors of measurement should be reported at several score levels if constancy cannot be assumed. Where cut scores are specified for selection or classification, the standard errors of measurement should be reported in the vicinity of each cut score.

Comment: Estimation of conditional standard errors is usually feasible even with the sample sizes that are typically used for reliability analyses. If it is assumed that the standard error is constant over a broad range of score levels, the rationale for this assumption should be presented.

Standard 2.15

When a test or combination of measures is used to make categorical decisions, estimates should be provided of the percentage of examinees who would be classified in the same way on two applications of the procedure, using the same form or alternate forms of the instrument.

Comment: When a test or composite is used to make categorical decisions, such as pass/fail, the standard error of measurement at or near the cut score has important implications for the trustworthiness of these decisions. However, the standard error cannot be translated into the expected percentage of consistent decisions unless assumptions are made about the form of the distributions of measurement errors and true scores. It is preferable that this percentage be estimated directly through the use of a repeated-measurements approach if consistent with the requirements of test security and if adequate samples are available.

Standard 2.16

In some testing situations, the items vary from examinee to examinee—through random selection from an extensive item pool or application of algorithms based on the examinee's level of performance on previous items or preferences with respect to item difficulty. In this type of testing, the preferred approach to reliability estimation is one based on successive administrations of the test under conditions similar to those prevailing in operational test use.

Comment: Varying the set of items presented to each examinee is an acceptable procedure in some settings. If this approach is used, reliability data should be appropriate to this procedure. Estimates of standard errors of ability scores can be computed through the use of IRT and reported routinely as part of the adaptive testing procedure. However, those estimates are not an adequate substitute for estimates based on successive administrations of the adaptive test, nor do they bear on the issue of stability over short intervals. IRT estimates are contingent on the adequacy of both the item parameter estimates and the item response models adopted in the theory. Estimates of reliabilities and standard errors of measurement based on the administration and analysis of alternate forms of an adaptive test reflect errors associated with the entire measurement process. The alternate-form estimates provide an independent check on the magnitude of the errors of measurement specific to the adaptive feature of the testing procedure.

Standard 2.17

When a test is available in both long and short versions, reliability data should be reported for scores on each version, preferably based on an independent administration of each.

Comment: Some tests and test batteries are published in both a "full-length" version and a "survey" or "short" version. In many applications the Spearman-Brown formula will satisfactorily approximate the reliability of one of these from data based on the other. However, context effects are commonplace in tests of maximum performance. Also, the short version of a standardized test often comprises a nonrandom sample of items from the full-length version. Therefore, the shorter version may be more reliable or less reliable than the Spearman-Brown projections from the full-length version. The reliability of scores on each version is best evaluated through an independent administration of each, using the designated time limits.

Standard 2.18

When significant variations are permitted in test administration procedures, separate reliability analyses should be provided for scores produced under each major variation if adequate sample sizes are available.

Comment: To accommodate examinees with disabilities, test publishers might authorize modifications in the procedures and time limits that are specified for the administration of the paper-and-pencil edition of a test. In some cases, modified editions of the test itself may be provided. For example, tape-recorded versions for use in a group setting or with individual equipment may be used to test examinees who exhibit reading disabilities or attention deficits. If such modifications can be employed with test takers who are not disabled, insights can be gained regarding the possible effects on test scores of these nonstandard administrations.

Standard 2.19

When average test scores for groups are used in program evaluations, the groups tested should generally be regarded as a sample from a larger population, even if all examinees available at the time of measurement are tested. In such cases the standard error of the group mean should be reported, as it reflects variability due to sampling of examinees as well as variability due to measurement error.

Comment: The graduating seniors of a liberal arts college, the current clients of a social service agency, and analogous groups exposed to a program of interest typically constitute a sample in a longitudinal sense. Presumably, comparable groups from the same population will recur in future years, given static conditions. The factors leading to uncertainty in conclusions about program effectiveness arise from the sampling of persons as well as measurement error. Therefore, the standard error of the mean observed score, reflecting variation in both true scores and measurement errors, represents a more realistic standard error in this setting. Even this value may underestimate the variability of group means over time. In many settings, the static conditions assumed under random sampling of persons do not prevail.

Standard 2.20

When the purpose of testing is to measure the performance of groups rather than individuals, a procedure frequently used is to assign a small subset of items to each of many subsamples of examinees. Data are aggregated across subsamples and item subsets to obtain a measure of group performance. When such procedures are used for program evaluation or population descriptions, reliability analyses must take the sampling scheme into account.

Comment: This type of measurement program is termed *matrix sampling*. It is designed to reduce the time demanded of individual examinees and to increase the total number of items on which data are obtained. This testing approach provides the same type of information about group performances that would accrue if all examinees could respond to all exercises in the item pool. Reliability statistics must be appropriate to the sampling plan used with respect to examinees and items.

3. TEST DEVELOPMENT AND REVISION

Background

Test development is the process of producing a measure of some aspect of an individual's knowledge, skill, ability, interests, attitudes, or other characteristics by developing items and combining them to form a test, according to a specified plan. Test development is guided by the stated purpose(s) of the test and the intended inferences to be made from the test scores. The test development process involves consideration of content, format, the context in which the test will be used, and the potential consequences of using the test. Test development also includes specifying conditions for administering the test, determining procedures for scoring the test performance, and reporting the scores to test takers and test users. This chapter focuses primarily on the following aspects of test development: stating the purpose(s) of the test, defining a framework for the test, developing test specifications, developing and evaluating items and their associated scoring procedures, assembling the test, and revising the test. The first section describes the test development process that begins with a statement of the purpose(s) of the test and culminates with the assembly of the test. The second section addresses several special considerations in test development, including considerations in delineating the test framework and in developing performance assessments. The chapter concludes with a discussion on test revision. Issues bearing on validity, reliability, and fairness are interwoven within the stages of test development. Each of these topics is addressed comprehensively in other chapters of the *Standards*: validity in chapter 1, reliability in chapter 2, and aspects of fairness in chapters 7, 8, 9, and 10. Additional material on test administration and scoring, and on reporting scores and results, is provided in chapter 5. Chapter 4 discusses score scales, and the focus of chapter 6 is test documents.

Test Development

The process of developing educational and psychological tests commonly begins with a statement of the purpose(s) of the test and the construct or content domain to be measured. Tests of the same construct or domain can differ in important ways, because a number of decisions must be made as the test is developed. It is helpful to consider the four phases leading from the original statement of purpose(s) to the final product: (a) delineation of the purpose(s) of the test and the scope of the construct or the extent of the domain to be measured; (b) development and evaluation of the test specifications; (c) development, field testing, evaluation, and selection of the items and scoring guides and procedures; and (d) assembly and evaluation of the test for operational use. What follows is a description of typical test development procedures, though there may be sound reasons that some of these steps are followed in some settings and not in others.

The first step is to extend the original statement of purpose(s), and the construct or content domain being considered, into a framework for the test that describes the extent of the domain, or the scope of the construct to be measured. The test framework, therefore, delineates the aspects (e.g., content, skills, processes, and diagnostic features) of the construct or domain to be measured. For example, "Does eighth-grade mathematics include algebra?" "Does verbal ability include text comprehension as well as vocabulary?" "Does self-esteem include both feelings and acts?" The delineation of the test framework can be guided by theory or an analysis of the content domain or job requirements as in the case of many licensing and employment tests. The test framework serves as a guide to subsequent test evaluation. The chapter on validity provides a more thorough discussion of the relationships among the construct or content domain, the test framework, and the purpose(s) of the test.

Once decisions have been made about what the test is to measure, and what its scores are intended to convey, the next step is to design the test by establishing test specifications. The test specifications delineate the format of items, tasks, or questions; the response format or conditions for responding; and the type of scoring procedures. The specifications may indicate the desired psychometric properties of items, such as difficulty and discrimination, as well as the desired test properties such as test difficulty, inter-item correlations, and reliability. The test specifications may also include such factors as time restrictions, characteristics of the intended population of test takers, and procedures for administration. All subsequent test development activities are guided by the test specifications.

Test specifications will include, at least implicitly, an indication of whether the test scores will be primarily norm-referenced or criterion-referenced. When scores are norm-referenced, relative score interpretations are of primary interest. A score for an individual or for a definable group is ranked within one or more distributions of scores or compared to the average performance of test takers for various reference populations (e.g., based on age, grade, diagnostic category, or job classification). When scores are criterion-referenced, absolute score interpretations are of primary interest. The meaning of such scores does not depend on rank information. Rather, the test score conveys directly a level of competence in some defined criterion domain. Both relative and absolute interpretations are often used with a given test, but the test developer determines which approach is most relevant for that test.

The nature of the item and response formats that may be specified depends on the purposes of the test and the defined domain of the test. Selected-response formats, such as multiple-choice items, are suitable for many purposes of testing. The test specifications indicate how many alternatives are to be used

for each item. Other purposes may be more effectively served by a short constructed-response format. Short-answer items require a response of no more than a few words. Extended-response formats require the test taker to write a more extensive response of one or more sentences or paragraphs. Performance assessments often seek to emulate the context or conditions in which the intended knowledge or skills are actually applied. One type of performance assessment, for example, is the standardized job or work sample. A task is presented to the test taker in a standardized format under standardized conditions. Job or work samples might include, for example, the assessment of a practitioner's ability to make an accurate diagnosis and recommend treatment for a defined condition, a manager's ability to articulate goals for an organization, or a student's proficiency in performing a science laboratory experiment.

All types of items require some indication of how to score the responses. For selected-response items, one alternative is considered the correct response in some testing programs. In other testing programs, the alternatives may be weighted differentially. For short-answer items, a list of acceptable alternatives may suffice; extended-response items need more detailed rules for scoring, sometimes called *scoring rubrics*. Scoring rubrics specify the criteria for evaluating performance and may vary in the degree of judgment entailed, in the number of score levels, and in other ways. It is common practice for test developers to provide scorers with examples of performances at each of the score levels to help clarify the criteria.

For extended-response items, including performance tasks, two major types of scoring procedures are used: analytic and holistic. Both of the procedures require explicit performance criteria that reflect the test framework. However, the approaches differ in the degree of detail provided in the evaluation report. Under the analytic scoring procedure, each critical dimension of the performance criteria is judged independently, and separate scores are obtained for each of these dimensions in addition to an overall score. Under the holistic scoring procedure, the same performance criteria may implicitly be considered, but only one overall score is provided. Because the analytic procedure provides information on a number of critical dimensions, it potentially provides valuable information for diagnostic purposes and lends itself to evaluating strengths and weaknesses of test takers. In contrast, the holistic procedure may be preferable when an overall judgment is desired and when the skills being assessed are complex and highly interrelated. Regardless of the type of scoring procedure, designing the items and developing the scoring rubrics and procedures is an integrated process.

A participatory approach may be used in the design of items, scoring rubrics, and sometimes the scoring process itself. Many interested persons (e.g., practitioners, teachers) may be involved in developing items and scoring rubrics, and/or evaluating the subsequent performances. If a participatory approach is used, participants' knowledge about the domain being assessed and their ability to apply the scoring rubrics are of critical importance. Equally important, for those involved in developing tests and evaluating performances, is their familiarity with the nature of the population being tested. Relevant characteristics of the population being tested may include the typical range of expected skill levels, their familiarity with the response modes required of them, and the primary language they use.

The test developer usually assembles an item pool that consists of a larger set of items than what is required by the test specifications. This allows for the test developer to select a set of items for the test that meet the test specifications. The quality of the items is usually ascertained through item review procedures and pilot testing. Items are reviewed for content quality, clarity and lack of ambiguity. Items sometimes are reviewed for sensitivity to gender or cultural issues. An attempt is generally made to avoid words and topics

that may offend or otherwise disturb some test takers, if less offensive material is equally useful. Often, a field test is developed and administered to a group of test takers who are somewhat representative of the target population for the test. The field test helps determine some of the psychometric properties of the test items, such as an item's difficulty and ability to discriminate among test takers of different standing on the scale. Ongoing testing programs often pretest items by inserting them into existing tests. Those items are not used in obtaining test scores of the test takers, but the item responses provide useful data for test development.

The next step in test development is to assemble items into a test or to identify an item pool for an adaptive test. The test developer is responsible for ensuring that the items selected for the test meet the requirements of the test specifications. Depending upon the purpose(s) of the test, relevant considerations in item selection may include the content quality and scope, the weighting of items and subdomains, and the appropriateness of the items selected for the intended population of test takers. Often test developers will specify the distribution of psychometric indices of the items to be included in the test. For example, the specified distribution of item difficulty indices for a selection test would differ from the distribution specified for a general achievement test. When psychometric indices of the items are estimated using item response theory (IRT), the fit of the model to the data is also evaluated. This is accomplished by evaluating the extent to which the assumptions underlying the item response model (e.g., unidimensionality, local independence, speededness, and equality of slope parameters) are satisfied.

The test developer is also responsible for ensuring that the scoring procedures are consistent with the purpose(s) of the test and facilitate meaningful score interpretation. The nature of the intended score interpretations will determine the importance of psychometric characteristics of items in the test construction process. For example, indices of item difficulty and discrimination, and inter-item correlations, may be particularly important when relative score interpretations are intended. In the case of relative score interpretations, good discrimination among test takers at all points along the construct continuum is desirable. It is important, however, that the test specifications are not compromised when optimizing the distribution of these indices. In the case of absolute score interpretations, different criteria apply. In this case, the extent to which the relevant domain has been adequately represented is important even if many of the items are relatively easy or nondiscriminating within a relevant population. It is important, however, to assure the quality of the content of relatively easy or nondiscriminating items. If cut scores are necessary for score interpretation in criterion-referenced programs, the level of item discrimination constitutes critical information primarily in the vicinity of the cut scores. Because of these differences in test development procedures, tests designed to facilitate one type of interpretation function less effectively for other types of interpretation. Given appropriate test design and supporting evidence, however, scores arising from some norm-referenced programs may provide reasonable absolute score interpretations and scores arising from some criterion-referenced programs may provide reasonable relative score interpretations.

When evaluating the quality of the items in the item pool and the test itself, test developers often conduct studies of differential item functioning (see chapter 7). Differential item functioning is said to exist when test takers of approximately equal ability on the targeted construct or content domain differ in their responses to an item according to their group membership. In theory, the ultimate goal of such studies is to identify construct-irrelevant aspects of item content, item format, or scoring criteria that may differentially affect test scores of one or more groups of test takers. When differential item functioning is detected, test developers try to identify plausible explanations for the differences, and then they may replace or revise items that give rise to group differences if construct irrelevance is deemed likely. However, at this time, there has been little progress in discerning the cause or substantive themes that account for differential item functioning on a group basis. Items for which the differential item functioning index is significant may constitute valid measures of an element of the intended domain and differ in no way from other items that show nonsignificant indexes. When the differential item functioning index is significant, the test developer must take care that any replacement items or item revisions do not compromise the test specifications.

When multiple forms of a test are prepared, the test specifications govern each of the forms. Also, when an item pool is developed for a computerized adaptive test, the specifications refer both to the item pool and to the rules or procedures by which the individual item sets are created for each test taker. Some of the attractive features of computerized adaptive tests, such as tailoring the difficulty level of the items to the test taker's ability, place additional constraints on the design of such tests. In general, a large number of items is needed for a computerized adaptive test to ensure that each tailored item set meets the requirements of the test specifications. Further, tests often are developed in the context of larger systems or programs. Multiple item sets, for example, may be created for use with different groups of test takers or on different testing dates. Last, when a short form of a test is prepared, the test specifications of the original test govern the short form. Differences in the test specifications and the psychometric properties of the short form and the original test will affect the interpretation of the scores derived from the short form. In any of these cases, the same fundamental methods and principles of test development apply.

Special Considerations in Test Development

This section elaborates on several topics discussed above. First, considerations in delineating the framework for the test are discussed. Following this, considerations in the development of performance assessments and portfolios are addressed.

Delineating the Framework for the Test

The scenario presented above outlines what is often done to develop a test. However, the activities do not always happen in a rigid sequence. There is often a subtle interplay between the process of conceptualizing a construct or content domain and the development of a test of that construct or domain. The framework for the test provides a description of how the construct or domain will be represented. The procedures used to develop items and scoring rubrics and to examine item characteristics may often contribute to clarifying the framework. The extent to which the framework is defined a priori is dependent on the testing application. In many testing applications, a well-defined framework and detailed test specifications guide the development of items and their associated scoring rubrics and procedures. In some areas of psychological measurement, test development may be less dependent on an a priori defined framework and may rely more on a data-based approach that results in an empirically derived definition of the framework. In such instances, items are selected primarily on the basis of their empirical relationship with an external criterion, their relationships with one another, or their power to discriminate among groups of individuals. For example, construction of a selection test for sales personnel might be guided by the correlations of item scores with productivity measures of current sales personnel or a measure of client satisfaction might be assembled from those items in an item pool that correlate most highly with customer loyalty. Similarly, an inventory to help identify different patterns of psychopathology might be developed using patients from different diagnostic subgroups. When test development relies on a data-based approach, it is likely that some items will be selected based on chance occurrences in the data. Cross-validation studies are routinely conducted to determine the tendency to select items by chance, which involves administering the test to a comparable sample.

In many testing applications, the framework for the test is specified initially and this specification subsequently guides the development of items and scoring procedures. Empirical relationships may then be used to inform decisions about retaining, rejecting, or modifying items. Interpretations of scores from tests developed by this process have the advantage of a logical/theoretical and an empirical foundation for the underlying dimensions represented by the test.

PERFORMANCE ASSESSMENTS

One distinction between performance assessments and other forms of tests has to do with the type of response that is required from the test takers. Performance assessments require the test takers to carry out a process such as playing a musical instrument or tuning a car's engine or to produce a product such as a written essay. Performance assessments generally require the test takers to demonstrate their abilities or skills in settings that closely resemble real-life settings. For example, an assessment of a psychologist in training may require the test taker to interview a client, choose appropriate tests, and arrive at diagnosis and plan for therapy. Performance assessments are diverse in nature and can be product-based as well as behavior-based. Because performance assessments typically consist of a small number of tasks, establishing the extent to which the results can be generalized to the broader domain is particularly important. The use of test specifications will contribute to tasks being developed so as to systematically represent the critical dimensions to be assessed, leading to a more comprehensive coverage of the domain than what would occur if test specifications were not used. Further, both logical and empirical evidence are important to document the extent to which performance assessments—tasks as well as scoring criteria—reflect the processes or skills that are specified by the domain definition. When tasks are designed to elicit complex cognitive processes, logical analyses of the tasks and both logical and empirical analyses of the test takers' performances on the tasks provide necessary validity evidence.

Portfolios

A unique type of performance assessment is an individual portfolio. Portfolios are systematic collections of work or educational products typically collected over time. Like other assessment procedures, the design of portfolios is dependent on the purpose. Typical purposes include judgment of the improvement in job or educational performance and evaluation of the eligibility for employment, promotion, or graduation. A well-designed portfolio specifies the nature of the work that is to be put into the portfolio. The portfolio may include entries such as representative products, the best work of the test taker, or indicators of progress. For example, in an employment setting involving promotion, employees may be instructed to include their best work or products. Alternatively, if the purpose is to judge a student's educational growth, students may be asked to provide evidence of improvement with respect to particular competencies or skills. They may also be requested to provide justifications for the choices. Still other methods may include the use of videotapes, exhibitions, demonstrations, simulations, and so on.

In employment settings, employees may be involved in the selection of their work and prod-

ucts that demonstrate their competencies for promotion purposes. Analogously, in educational applications, students may participate in the selection of some of their work and the products to be included in their portfolios as well as in the evaluation of the materials. The specifications for the portfolio indicate who is responsible for selecting its contents. For example, the specifications may state that the test taker, the examiner, or both parties working together should be involved in the selection of the contents of the portfolio. The particular responsibilities of each party are delineated in the specifications. The more standardized the contents and procedures of administration, the easier it is to establish comparability of portfolio-based scores. Regardless of the methods used, all performance assessments are evaluated by the same standards of technical quality as other forms of tests.

Test Revisions

Tests and their supporting documents (e.g., test manuals, technical manuals, user's guides) are reviewed periodically to determine whether revisions are needed. Revisions or amendments are necessary when new research data, significant changes in the domain, or new conditions of test use and interpretation would either improve the validity of interpretations of the test scores or suggest that the test is no longer fully appropriate for its intended use. As an example, tests are revised if the test content or language has become outdated and, therefore, may subsequently affect the validity of the test score interpretations. Revisions to test content are also made to ensure the confidentiality of the test. It should be noted, however, that outdated norms may not have the same implications for revisions as an outdated test. For example, it may be necessary to update the norms for an achievement test after a period of rising or falling achievement in the norming population, or when there are changes in the test-taking population, but the test content itself may continue to be as relevant as it was when the test was developed.

Standard 3.1

Tests and testing programs should be developed on a sound scientific basis. Test developers and publishers should compile and document adequate evidence bearing on test development.

Standard 3.2

The purpose(s) of the test, definition of the domain, and the test specifications should be stated clearly so that judgments can be made about the appropriateness of the defined domain for the stated purpose(s) of the test and about the relation of items to the dimensions of the domain they are intended to represent.

Comment: The adequacy and usefulness of test interpretations depend on the rigor with which the purposes of the test and the domain represented by the test have been defined and explicated. The domain definition should be sufficiently detailed and delimited to show clearly what dimensions of knowledge, skill, processes, attitude, values, emotions, or behavior are included and what dimensions are excluded. A clear description will enhance accurate judgments by reviewers and others about the congruence of the defined domain and the test items.

Standard 3.3

The test specifications should be documented, along with their rationale and the process by which they were developed. The test specifications should define the content of the test, the proposed number of items, the item formats, the desired psychometric properties of the items, and the item and section arrangement. They should also specify the amount of time for testing, directions to the test takers, procedures to be used for test administration and scoring, and other relevant information.

Comment: Professional judgment plays a major role in developing the test specifications. The specific procedures used for developing the specifications depend on the purposes of the test. For example, in developing licensure and certification tests, practice analyses or job analyses usually provide the basis for defining the test specifications, and job analyses primarily serve this function for employment tests. For achievement tests to be given at the end of a course, the test specifications should be based on an outline of course content and goals. Whereas, for placement tests, it may be necessary to examine the required entry knowledge and skills for several courses.

Standard 3.4

The procedures used to interpret test scores, and, when appropriate, the normative or standardization samples or the criterion used should be documented.

Comment: Test specifications may indicate that the intended score interpretations are for absolute or relative score interpretations, or both. In relative score interpretations the status of an individual (or group) is determined by comparing the score (or mean score) to the performance of others in one or more defined populations. In absolute score interpretations, the score or average is assumed to reflect directly a level of competence or mastery in some defined criterion domain. Tests designed to facilitate one type of interpretation function less effectively for other types of interpretations. Given appropriate test design and adequate supporting data, however, scores arising from norm-referenced testing programs may provide reasonable absolute score interpretations and scores arising from criterion-referenced programs may provide reasonable relative score interpretations.

Standard 3.5

When appropriate, relevant experts external to the testing program should review the test specifications. The purpose of the review, the process by which the review is conducted, and the results of the review should be documented. The qualifications, relevant experiences, and demographic characteristics of expert judges should also be documented.

Comment: Expert review of the test specifications may serve many useful purposes such as helping to assure content quality and representativeness. The expert judges may include individuals representing defined populations of concern to the test specifications. For example, if the test is related to ethnic minority concerns, the expert review typically includes members of appropriate ethnic minority groups or experts on minority group issues.

Standard 3.6

The type of items, the response formats, scoring procedures, and test administration procedures should be selected based on the purposes of the test, the domain to be measured, and the intended test takers. To the extent possible, test content should be chosen to ensure that intended inferences from test scores are equally valid for members of different groups of test takers. The test review process should include empirical analyses and, when appropriate, the use of expert judges to review items and response formats. The qualifications, relevant experiences, and demographic characteristics of expert judges should also be documented.

Comment: Expert judges may be asked to identify material likely to be inappropriate, confusing, or offensive for groups in the test-taking population. For example, judges may be asked to identify whether lack of exposure to problem contexts in mathematics word problems may be of concern for some groups of students. Various groups of test takers can be defined by characteristics such as age, ethnicity, culture, gender, disability, or demographic region. There is limited evidence, however, that expert reviews alleviate problems with bias in testing (see chapter 7).

Standard 3.7

The procedures used to develop, review, and try out items, and to select items from the item pool should be documented. If the items were classified into different categories or subtests according to the test specifications, the procedures used for the classification and the appropriateness and accuracy of the classification should be documented.

Comment: Empirical evidence and/or expert judgment are used to classify items according to categories of the test specifications. For example, professional panels may be used for classifying the items or for determining the appropriateness of the developer's classification scheme. The panel and procedures used should be chosen with care as they will affect the accuracy of the classification.

Standard 3.8

When item tryouts or field tests are conducted, the procedures used to select the sample(s) of test takers for item tryouts and the resulting characteristics of the sample(s) should be documented. When appropriate, the sample(s) should be as representative as possible of the population(s) for which the test is intended.

Comment: Conditions which may differentially affect performance on the test items by the sample(s) as compared to the intended population(s) should be documented when appropriate. As an example, test takers may be less motivated when they know their scores will not have an impact on them.

Standard 3.9

When a test developer evaluates the psychometric properties of items, the classical or item response theory (IRT) model used for evaluating the psychometric properties of items should be documented. The sample used for estimating item properties should be described and should be of adequate size and diversity for the procedure. The process by which items are selected and the data used for item selection, such as item difficulty, item discrimination, and/or item information, should also be documented. When IRT is used to estimate item parameters in test development, the item response model, estimation procedures, and evidence of model fit should be documented.

Comment: Although overall sample size is important, it is important also that there be an adequate number of cases in regions critical to the determination of the psychometric properties of items. If the test is to achieve greatest precision in a particular part of the score scale and this consideration affects item selection, the manner in which item statistics are used needs to be carefully described. When IRT is used as the basis of test development, it is important to document the adequacy of fit of the model to the data. This is accomplished by providing information about the extent to which IRT assumptions (e.g., unidimensionality, local item independence, or equality of slope parameters) are satisfied.

Test developers should show that any differences between the administration conditions of the field test and the final form do not affect item performance. Conditions that can affect item statistics include item position, time limits, length of test, mode of testing (e.g., paper-and-pencil versus computer-administered), and use of calculators or other tools. For example, in field testing items, those placed at the end of a test might obtain poorer item statistics than those inserted within the test.

Standard 3.10

Test developers should conduct cross-validation studies when items are selected primarily on the basis of empirical relationships rather than on the basis of content or theoretical considerations. The extent to which the different studies identify the same item set should be documented.

Comment: When data-based approaches to test development are used, items are selected primarily on the basis of their empirical relationships with an external criterion, their relationships with one another, or their power to discriminate among groups of individuals. Under these circumstances, it is likely that some items will be selected based on chance occurrences in the data used. Administering the test to a comparable sample of test takers or a hold-out sample provides a means by which the tendency to select items by chance can be determined.

Standard 3.11

Test developers should document the extent to which the content domain of a test represents the defined domain and test specifications.

Comment: Test developers should provide evidence of the extent to which the test items and scoring criteria represent the defined domain. This affords a basis to help determine whether performance on the test can be generalized to the domain that is being assessed. This is especially important for tests that contain a small number of items such as performance assessments. Such evidence may be provided by expert judges.

Standard 3.12

The rationale and supporting evidence for computerized adaptive tests should be documented. This documentation should include procedures used in selecting subsets of items for administration, in determining the starting point and termination conditions for the test, in scoring the test, and for controlling item exposure.

Comment: It is important to assure that documentation of the procedures does not compromise the security of the test items.

If a computerized adaptive test is intended to measure a number of different content subcategories, item selection procedures are to assure that the subcategories are adequately represented by the items presented to the test taker.

Standard 3.13

When a test score is derived from the differential weighting of items, the test developer should document the rationale and process used to develop, review, and assign item weights. When the item weights are obtained based on empirical data, the sample used for obtaining item weights should be sufficiently large and representative of the population for which the test is intended. When the item weights are obtained based on expert judgment, the qualifications of the judges should be documented.

Comment: Changes in the population of test takers, along with other changes such as changes in instructions, training, or job requirements, may impact the original derived item weights, necessitating subsequent studies after an appropriate period of time.

Standard 3.14

The criteria used for scoring test takers' performance on extended-response items should be documented. This documentation is especially important for performance assessments, such as scorable portfolios and essays, where the criteria for scoring may not be obvious to the user.

Comment: The completeness and clarity of the test specifications, including the definition of the domain, are essential in developing the scoring criteria. The test developer needs to provide a clear description of how the test scores are intended to be interpreted to help ensure the appropriateness of the scoring procedures.

Standard 3.15

When using a standardized testing format to collect structured behavior samples, the domain, test design, test specifications, and materials should be documented as for any other test. Such documentation should include a clear definition of the behavior expected of the test takers, the nature of the expected responses, and any materials or directions that are necessary to carry out the testing.

Comment: In developing a prompt, the age, language, experience, and ability level of test takers should be considered, as should other possible unique sources of difficulty for groups in the population to be tested. Test directions that specify time allowances, nature of the responses expected, and rules regarding use of supplementary materials, such as notes, references, dictionaries, calculators, or manipulatives such as lab equipment, may be established via field testing.

Standard 3.16

If a short form of a test is prepared, for example, by reducing the number of items on the original test or organizing portions of a test into a separate form, the specifications of the short form should be as similar as possible to those of the original test. The procedures used for the reduction of items should be documented.

Comment: The extent to which the specifications of the short form differ from those of the original test, and the implications of such differences for interpreting the scores derived from the short form, should be documented.

Standard 3.17

When previous research indicates that irrelevant variance could confound the domain definition underlying the test, then to the extent feasible, the test developer should investigate sources of irrelevant variance. Where possible, such sources of irrelevant variance should be removed or reduced by the test developer.

Standard 3.18

For tests that have time limits, test development research should examine the degree to which scores include a speed component and evaluate the appropriateness of that component, given the domain the test is designed to measure.

Standard 3.19

The directions for test administration should be presented with sufficient clarity and emphasis so that it is possible for others to replicate adequately the administration conditions under which the data on reliability and validity, and, where appropriate, norms were obtained.

Comment: Because all people administering tests, including those in schools, industry, and clinics, need to follow test administration conditions carefully, it is essential that test administrators receive detailed instructions on test administration guidelines and procedures.

Standard 3.20

The instructions presented to test takers should contain sufficient detail so that test takers can respond to a task in the manner that the test developer intended. When appropriate, sample material, practice or sample questions, criteria for scoring, and a representative item identified with each major area in the test's classification or domain should be provided to the test takers prior to the administration of the test or included in the testing material as part of the standard administration instructions.

Comment: For example, in a personality inventory it may be intended that test takers give the first response that occurs to them. Such an expectation should be made clear in the inventory directions. As another example, in directions for interest or occupational inventories, it may be important to specify whether test takers are to mark the activities they would like ideally or whether they are to consider both their opportunity and their ability realistically.

The extent and nature of practice materials and directions depend on expected levels of knowledge among test takers. For example, in using a novel test format, it may be very important to provide the test taker a practice opportunity as part of the test administration. In some testing situations, it may be important for the instructions to address such matters as the effects that guessing and time limits have on test scores. If expansion or elaboration of the test instructions is permitted, the condi-

tions under which this may be done should be stated clearly in the form of general rules and by giving representative examples. If no expansion or elaboration is to be permitted, this should be stated explicitly. Publishers should include guidance for dealing with typical questions from test takers. Users should be instructed how to deal with questions that may arise during the testing period.

Standard 3.21

If the test developer indicates that the conditions of administration are permitted to vary from one test taker or group to another, permissible variation in conditions for administration should be identified, and a rationale for permitting the different conditions should be documented.

Comment: In deciding whether the conditions of administration can vary, the test developer needs to consider and study the potential effects of varying conditions of administration. If conditions of administration vary from the conditions studied by the test developer or from those used in the development of norms, the comparability of the test scores may be weakened and the applicability of the norms can be questioned.

Standard 3.22

Procedures for scoring and, if relevant, scoring criteria should be presented by the test developer in sufficient detail and clarity to maximize the accuracy of scoring. Instructions for using rating scales or for deriving scores obtained by coding, scaling, or classifying constructed responses should be clear. This is especially critical if tests can be scored locally.

Standard 3.23

The process for selecting, training, and qualifying scorers should be documented by the test developer. The training materials, such as the scoring rubrics and examples of test takers' responses that illustrate the levels on the score scale, and the procedures for training scorers should result in a degree of agreement among scorers that allows for the scores to be interpreted as originally intended by the test developer. Scorer reliability and potential drift over time in raters' scoring standards should be evaluated and reported by the person(s) responsible for conducting the training session.

Standard 3.24

When scoring is done locally and requires scorer judgment, the test user is responsible for providing adequate training and instruction to the scorers and for examining scorer agreement and accuracy. The test developer should document the expected level of scorer agreement and accuracy.

Comment: A common practice of test developers is to provide examples of training materials (e.g., scoring rubrics, test takers' responses at each score level) and procedures when scoring is done locally and requires scorer judgment.

Standard 3.25

A test should be amended or revised when new research data, significant changes in the domain represented, or newly recommended conditions of test use may lower the validity of test score interpretations. Although a test that remains useful need not be withdrawn or revised simply because of the passage of time, test developers and test publishers are responsible for monitoring changing conditions and for amending, revising, or withdrawing the test as indicated.

Comment: Test developers need to consider a number of factors that may warrant the revision of a test, including outdated test content and language. If an older version of a test is used when a newer version has been published or made available, test users are responsible for

providing evidence that the older version is as appropriate as the new version for that particular test use.

Standard 3.26

Tests should be labeled or advertised as "revised" only when they have been revised in significant ways. A phrase such as "with minor modification" should be used when the test has been modified in minor ways. The score scale should be adjusted to account for these modifications, and users should be informed of the adjustments made to the score scale.

Comment: It is the test developer's responsibility to determine whether revisions to a test would influence test score interpretations. If test score interpretations would be affected by the revisions, it would then be appropriate to label the test "revised." When tests are revised, the nature of the revisions and their implications on test score interpretations should be documented.

Standard 3.27

If a test or part of a test is intended for research use only and is not distributed for operational use, statements to this effect should be displayed prominently on all relevant test administration and interpretation materials that are provided to the test user.

Comment: This standard refers to tests that are intended for research use only and does not refer to standard test development functions that occur prior to the operational use of a test (e.g., field testing).

4. SCALES, NORMS, AND SCORE COMPARABILITY

Background

Test scores are reported on scales designed to assist score interpretation. Typically, scoring begins with responses to separate test items, which are often coded using 0 or 1 to represent wrong/right or negative/positive, but sometimes using numerical values to indicate finer response gradations. Then the item scores are combined, often by addition but sometimes by a more elaborate procedure, to obtain a *raw score*. Raw scores are determined, in part, by features of a test such as test length, choice of time limit, item difficulties, and the circumstances under which the test is administered. This makes raw scores difficult to interpret in the absence of further information. Interpretation and statistical analyses may be facilitated by converting raw scores into an entirely different set of values called *derived scores* or *scale scores*. The various scales used for reporting scores on college admissions tests, the standard scores often used to report results for intelligence scales or vocational interest and personality inventories, and the grade equivalents reported for achievement tests in the elementary grades are examples of scale scores. The process of developing such a score scale is called *scaling* a test. Scale scores may aid interpretation by indicating how a given score compares to those of other test takers, by enhancing the comparability of scores obtained using different forms of a test, or in other ways.

Another way of assisting score interpretation is to establish *standards* or *cut scores* that distinguish different score ranges. In some cases, a single cut score may define the boundary between passing and failing. In other cases, a series of cut scores may define distinct proficiency levels. Cut scores may be established for either raw or scale scores. Both scale scores and standards or cut scores can be central to the use and interpretation of test scores. For

that reason, their defensibility is an important consideration in test validation. There is a close connection between standards or cut scores and certain scale scores. If the successive score ranges defined by a series of cut scores are relabeled, say 0, 1, 2, and so on, then a scale score has been created.

In addition to facilitating interpretations of a single test form considered in isolation, scale scores are often created to enhance comparability across different forms of the same test, across test formats or administration conditions, or even across tests designed to measure different constructs (e.g., related subtests in a battery). Equated scores from alternate forms of a test can often be interpreted more easily when expressed in scale score units rather than raw score units. Scaling may be used to place scores from different levels of an achievement test on a continuous scale and thereby facilitate inferences about growth or development. Scaling can also enhance the comparability of scores derived from tests in different areas, as in subtests within an aptitude, interest, or achievement battery.

Norm-Referenced and Criterion-Referenced Score Interpretations

Individual raw scores or scale scores are often referred to the distribution of scores for one or more comparison groups to draw useful inferences about an individual's performance. Test score interpretations based on such comparisons are said to be *norm-referenced*. Percentile rank norms, for example, indicate the standing of an individual or group within a defined population of individuals or groups. An example of such a comparison group might be fourth-grade students in the United States, tested in the last 2 months of a recent school year. Percentiles, averages, or other statistics for such reference groups are called *norms*. By showing how the test score of a given examinee compares to those of others, norms assist in the classification or description of examinees.

Other test score interpretations make no direct reference to the performance of other examinees. These interpretations may take a variety of forms; most are collectively referred to as *criterion-referenced* interpretations. Derived scores supporting such interpretations may indicate the likely proportion of correct responses on some larger domain of items, or the probability of an examinee's answering particular sorts of items correctly. Other criterion-referenced interpretations may indicate the likelihood that some psychopathology is present. Still other criterion-referenced interpretations indicate the probability that an examinee's level of tested knowledge or skill is adequate to perform successfully in some other setting; such probabilities may be summarized in an expectancy table. Scale scores to support such criterion-referenced score interpretations are often developed on the basis of statistical analyses of the relationships of test scores to other variables.

Some scale scores are developed primarily to support norm-referenced interpretations and others, criterion-referenced interpretations. In practice, however, there is not always a sharp distinction. Both criterion-referenced and norm-referenced scales may be developed and used for the same test scores. Moreover, a norm-referenced score scale originally developed, for example, to indicate performance relative to some specific reference population might, over time, also come to support criterion-referenced interpretations. This could happen as research and experience brought increased understanding of the capabilities implied by different scale score levels. Conversely, results of an educational assessment might be reported on a scale consisting of several ordered proficiency levels, defined by descriptions of the kinds of tasks students at each level were able to perform. That would be a criterion-referenced scale, but once the

distribution of scores over levels was reported, say, for all eighth-grade students in a given state, individual students' scores would also convey information about their standing relative to that tested population.

Interpretations based on cut scores may likewise be either criterion-referenced or norm-referenced. If qualitatively different descriptions are attached to successive score ranges, a criterion-referenced interpretation is supported. For example, the descriptions of performance levels in some assessment task scoring rubrics can enhance score interpretation by summarizing the capabilities that must be demonstrated to merit a given score. In other cases, criterion-referenced interpretations may be based on empirically determined relationships between test scores and other variables. But when tests are used for selection, it may be appropriate to rank-order examinees according to their test performance and establish a cut score so as to select a prespecified number or proportion of examinees from one end of the distribution, if the selection use is otherwise supported by relevant reliability and validity evidence. In such cases, the cut score interpretation is norm-referenced; the labels *reject* or *fail* versus *accept* or *pass* are determined solely by an examinee's standing relative to others tested.

Criterion-referenced interpretations based on cut scores are sometimes criticized on the grounds that there is very rarely a sharp distinction of any kind between those just below versus just above a cut score. A neuropsychological test may be helpful in diagnosing some particular impairment, for example, but the probability that the impairment is present is likely to increase continuously as a function of the test score. Cut scores may nonetheless aid in formulating rules for reaching decisions on the basis of test performance. It should be recognized, however, that the probability of misclassification will generally be relatively high for persons with scores close to the cut points.

Norms

The validity of norm-referenced interpretations depends in part on the appropriateness of the reference group to which test scores are compared. Norms based on hospitalized patients, for example, might be inappropriate for some interpretations of nonhospitalized patients' scores. Thus, it is important that reference populations be carefully defined and clearly described. Validity of such interpretations also depends on the accuracy with which norms summarize the performance of the reference population. That population may be small enough that essentially the entire population can be tested (e.g., all pupils at a given grade level in a given district tested on the same occasion). Often, however, only a sample of examinees from the reference population is tested. It is then important that the norms be based on a technically sound, representative, scientific sample of sufficient size. Patients in a few hospitals in a small geographic region are unlikely to be representative of all patients in the United States, for example. Moreover, the appropriateness of norms based on a given sample may diminish over time. Thus, for tests that have been in use for a number of years, periodic review is generally required to assure the continued utility of norms. Renorming may be required to maintain the validity of norm-referenced test score interpretations.

More than one reference population may be appropriate for the same test. For example, achievement test performance might be interpreted by reference to local norms based on sampling from a particular school district, norms for a state or type of community, or national norms. For other tests, norms might be based on occupational or educational classifications. Descriptive statistics for all examinees who happen to be tested during a given period of time (sometimes called *user norms* or *program norms*) may be useful for some purposes, such as describing trends over time. But there must be sound reason to regard that group of test takers as an appropriate basis for such inferences. When there is a suitable rationale for using such a group, the descriptive statistics should be clearly characterized as being based on a sample of persons routinely tested as part of an ongoing program.

Comparability and Equating

Many test uses involve different versions of the same test, which yield scores that can be used interchangeably even though they are based on different sets of items. In testing programs that offer a choice of examination dates, for example, test security may be compromised if the same form is used repeatedly. Other testing applications may entail repeated measurements of the same individuals, perhaps to measure change in levels of psychological dysfunction, change in attitudes, or educational progress. In such contexts, reuse of the same set of test items may result in correlated errors of measurement and biased estimates of change. When distinct forms of a test are constructed to the same explicit content and statistical specifications and administered under identical conditions, they are referred to as *alternate forms* or sometimes *parallel* or *equivalent* forms. The process of placing scores from such alternate forms on a common scale is called *equating*. Equating is analogous to the calibration of different balances so that they all indicate the same weight for any given object. However, the equating process for test scores is more complex. It involves small statistical adjustments to account for minor differences in the difficulty and statistical properties of the alternate forms.

In theory, equating should provide accurate score conversions for any set of persons drawn from the examinee population for which the test is designed. Furthermore, the same score conversion should be appropriate regardless of the score interpretation or use intended. It is not possible to construct conversions with these ideal properties between scores on tests that measure different constructs; that differ materially in difficulty, reliability, time limits, or other conditions of administration; or that are designed to different specifications.

There is another assessment approach that may provide interchangeable scores based on responses to different items using different methods, not referred to as equating. This is the use of *adaptive tests.* It has long been recognized that little is learned from examinees' responses to items that are much too easy or much too difficult for them. Consequently, some testing procedures use only a subset of the available items with each examinee in order to avoid boredom or frustration, or to shorten testing time. An adaptive test consists of a pool of items together with rules for selecting a subset of those items to be administered to an individual examinee, and a procedure for placing different examinees' scores on a common scale. The selection of successive items is based in part on the examinee's responses to previous items. The item pool and item selection rules may be designed so that each examinee receives a representative set of items, of appropriate difficulty. The selection rules generally assure that an acceptable degree of precision is attained before testing is terminated. At one time, such tailored testing was limited to certain individually administered psychological tests. With advances in item response theory (IRT) and in computer technology, however, adaptive testing is becoming more sophisticated. With some adaptive tests, it may happen that two examinees rarely if ever respond to precisely the same set of items. Moreover, two examinees taking the same adaptive test may be given sets of items that differ markedly in difficulty. Nevertheless, when certain statistical and content conditions are met, test scores produced by an adaptive testing system can function like scores from equated alternate forms.

Scaling to Achieve Comparability

The term *equating* is properly reserved only for score conversions derived for alternate forms of the same test. It is often useful, however, to compare scores from tests that cannot, in theory, be equated. For example, it may be desirable to interpret scores from a shortened (and hence less reliable) form of a test by first converting them to corresponding scores on the full-length version. For the evaluation of examinee growth over time, it may be desirable to develop scales that span a broad range of developmental or educational levels. Test revision often brings a need for some linkage between scores obtained using newer and older editions. International comparative studies or use with hearing-impaired examinees may require test forms in different languages. In still other cases, linkages or alignments may be created between tests measuring different constructs, perhaps comparing an aptitude with a form of behavior, or linking measures of achievement in several content areas. Scores from such tests may sometimes be aligned or presented in a concordance table to aid users in estimating relative performance on one test from performance on another.

Score conversions to facilitate such comparisons may be described using terms like linkage, calibration, concordance, projection, moderation, or anchoring. These weaker score linkages may be technically sound and may fully satisfy desired goals of comparability for one purpose or for one subgroup of examinees, but they cannot be assumed to be stable over time or invariant across multiple subgroups of the examinee population nor is there any assurance that scores obtained using different tests will be equally accurate. Thus, their use for other purposes or with other populations than originally intended may require additional research. For example, a score conversion that was accurate for a group of native speakers might systematically overpredict or underpredict the scores of a group of nonnative speakers.

Cut Scores

A critical step in the development and use of some tests is to establish one or more cut points dividing the score range to partition the distribution of scores into categories. These categories may be used just for descriptive purposes or may be used to distinguish among examinees for whom different programs are deemed desirable or different predictions are warranted. An employer may determine a cut score to screen potential employees or promote current employees; a school may use test scores to decide which of several alternative instructional programs would be most beneficial for a student; in granting a professional license, a state may specify a minimum passing score on a licensure test.

These examples differ in important respects, but all involve delineating categories of examinees on the basis of test scores. Such cut scores embody the rules according to which tests are used or interpreted. Thus, in some situations the validity of test interpretations may hinge on the cut scores. There can be no single method for determining cut scores for all tests or for all purposes, nor can there be any single set of procedures for establishing their defensibility. These examples serve only as illustrations.

The first example, that of an employer hiring all those who earn scores above a given level on an employment test, is most straightforward. Assuming that the employment test is valid for its intended use, average job performance would typically be expected to rise steadily, albeit slowly, with each increment in test score, at least for some range of scores surrounding the cut point. In such a case the designation of the particular value for the cut point may be largely determined by the number of persons to be hired or promoted. There is no sharp difference between those just below the cut point and those just above it, and the use of the cut score does not entail any criterion-referenced interpretation. This method

of establishing a cut score may be subject to legal requirements with respect to the nature of the validity and reliability evidence needed to support the use of rank-order selections and the unavailability of effective alternative selection methods, if it has a disproportionate effect on one or more subgroups of employees or prospective employees.

In the second example, a school district might structure its courses in writing around three categories of needs. For children whose proficiency is least developed, instruction might be provided in small groups, with considerable individual attention to assist them in creating meaningful written stories grounded in their own experience. For children whose proficiency was further developed, more emphasis might be placed on systematic exploration of the stages of the writing process. Instruction for children at the highest proficiency level might emphasize mastery of specific writing genres or prose structures used in more formal writing. In an appropriate implementation of such a program, children could easily be transferred from one level to another if their original placement was in error or as their proficiency increased. Ideally, cut scores delineating categories in this application would be based on research demonstrating empirically that pupils in successive score ranges did most often benefit more from the respective treatments to which they were assigned than from the alternatives available. It would typically be found that between those score ranges in which one or another instructional treatment was clearly superior, there was an intermediate region in which neither treatment was clearly preferred. The cut score might be located somewhere in that intermediate region.

In the final example, that of a professional licensure examination, the cut score represents an informed judgment that those scoring below it are likely to make serious errors for want of the knowledge or skills tested. Little evidence apart from errors made on the test itself may document the need to deny the right to practice the profession. No test is perfect, of course, and regardless of the cut score chosen, some examinees with inadequate skills are likely to pass and some with adequate skills are likely to fail. The relative probabilities of such false positive and false negative errors will vary depending on the cut score chosen. A given probability of exposing the public to potential harm by issuing a license to an incompetent individual (false positive) must be weighed against some corresponding probability of denying a license to, and thereby disenfranchising, a qualified examinee (false negative). Changing the cut score to reduce either probability will increase the other, although both kinds of errors can be minimized through sound test design that anticipates the role of the cut score in test use and interpretation. Determining cut scores in such situations cannot be a purely technical matter, although empirical studies and statistical models can be of great value in informing the process.

Cut scores embody value judgments as well as technical and empirical considerations. Where the results of the standard-setting process have highly significant consequences, and especially where large numbers of examinees are involved, those responsible for establishing cut scores should be concerned that the process by which cut scores are determined be clearly documented and defensible. The qualifications of any judges involved in standard setting and the process by which they are selected are part of that documentation. Care must be taken to assure that judges understand what they are to do. The process must be such that well-qualified judges can apply their knowledge and experience to reach meaningful and relevant judgments that accurately reflect their understandings and intentions. A sufficiently large and representative group of judges should be involved to provide reasonable assurance that results would not vary greatly if the process were replicated.

Standard 4.1

Test documents should provide test users with clear explanations of the meaning and intended interpretation of derived score scales, as well as their limitations.

Comment: All scales (raw score or derived) may be subject to misinterpretation. Sometimes scales are extrapolated beyond the range of available data or are interpolated without sufficient data points. Grade- and age-equivalent scores have been criticized in this regard, but percentile ranks and standard score scales are also subject to misinterpretation. If the nature or intended uses of a scale are novel, it is especially important that its uses, interpretations, and limitations be clearly described. Illustrations of appropriate versus inappropriate interpretations may be helpful, especially for types of scales or interpretations that may be unfamiliar to most users. This standard pertains to score scales intended for criterion-referenced as well as for norm-referenced interpretation.

Standard 4.2

The construction of scales used for reporting scores should be described clearly in test documents.

Comment: When scales, norms, or other interpretive systems are provided by the test developer, technical documentation should enable users to judge the quality and precision of the resulting derived scores. This standard pertains to score scales intended for criterion-referenced as well as for norm-referenced interpretation.

Standard 4.3

If there is sound reason to believe that specific misinterpretations of a score scale are likely, test users should be explicitly forewarned.

Comment: Test publishers and users can reduce misinterpretations of grade-equivalent scores, for example, by ensuring that such scores are accompanied by instructions that make clear that grade-equivalent scores do not represent a standard of growth per year or grade and that roughly 50% of the students tested in the standardization sample should by definition fall below grade level. As another example, a score scale point originally defined as the mean of some reference population should no longer be interpreted as representing average performance if the scale is held constant over time and the examinee population changes.

Standard 4.4

When raw scores are intended to be directly interpretable, their meanings, intended interpretations, and limitations should be described and justified in the same manner as is done for derived score scales.

Comment: In some cases the items in a test are a representative sample of a well-defined domain of items. The proportion correct on the test may then be interpreted as an estimate of the proportion of items in the domain that could be answered correctly. In other cases, different interpretations may be attached to scores above or below one or another cut score. Support should be offered for any such interpretations recommended by the test developer.

Standard 4.5

Norms, if used, should refer to clearly described populations. These populations should include individuals or groups to whom test users will ordinarily wish to compare their own examinees.

Comment: It is the responsibility of test developers to describe norms clearly and the responsibility of test users to employ norms appropriately. Users need to know the applicability of a test to different groups. Differentiated norms or sum-

mary information about differences between gender, ethnic, language, disability, grade, or age groups, for example, may be useful in some cases. The permissible uses of such differentiated norms and related information may be limited by law. Users also need to be made alert to situations in which norms are less appropriate for some groups or individuals than others. On an occupational interest inventory, for example, norms for persons actually engaged in an occupation may be inappropriate for interpreting the scores of persons not so engaged. As another example, the appropriateness of norms for personality inventories or relationship scales may differ depending upon an examinee's sexual orientation.

Standard 4.6

Reports of norming studies should include precise specification of the population that was sampled, sampling procedures and participation rates, any weighting of the sample, the dates of testing, and descriptive statistics. The information provided should be sufficient to enable users to judge the appropriateness of the norms for interpreting the scores of local examinees. Technical documentation should indicate the precision of the norms themselves.

Comment: Scientific sampling is important if norms are to be representative of intended populations. For example, schools already using a given published test and volunteering to participate in a norming study for that test should not be assumed to be representative of schools in general. In addition to sampling procedures, participation rates should be reported, and the method of calculating participation rates should be clearly described. Studies that are designed to be nationally representative often use weights so that the weighted sample better represents the nation than does the unweighted sample. When weights are used, it is important that the procedure for deriving the weights be described and that the demographic representation of both the weighted and the unweighted samples be given. If norming data are collected under conditions in which student motivation in completing the test is likely to differ from that expected during operational use, this should be clearly documented. Likewise, if the instructional histories of students in the norming sample differ systematically from those to be expected during operational test use, that fact should be noted. Norms based on samples cannot be perfectly precise. Even though the imprecision of norm-referenced interpretations due to imperfections in the norms themselves may be small compared to that due to measurement error, estimates of the precision of norms should be available in technical documentation. For example, standard errors based on the sample design might be presented. In some testing applications, norms based on all examinees tested over a given period of time may be useful for some purposes. Such norms should be clearly characterized as being based on a sample of persons routinely tested as part of an ongoing testing program.

Standard 4.7

If local examinee groups differ materially from the populations to which norms refer, a user who reports derived scores based on the published norms has the responsibility to describe such differences if they bear upon the interpretation of the reported scores.

Comment: In employment settings, the qualifications of local examinee groups may fluctuate depending on recruitment or referral procedures as well as market conditions. In such cases, appropriate test use and interpretation may not require documentation or cautions concerning departures from characteristics of the norming population.

Standard 4.8

When norms are used to characterize examinee groups, the statistics used to summarize each group's performance and the norms to which those statistics are referred should be clearly defined and should support the intended use or interpretation.

Comment: Group means are distributed differently from individual scores. For example, it is not possible to determine the percentile rank of a school's average test score if all that is known are the percentile ranks of each of that school's students. It may sometimes be useful to develop special norms for group means, but when the sizes of the groups differ materially or when some groups are much more heterogeneous than others, the construction and interpretation of group norms is problematical. One common and acceptable procedure is to report the percentile rank of the median group member, for example, the median percentile rank of the pupils tested in a given school.

Standard 4.9

When raw score or derived score scales are designed for criterion-referenced interpretation, including the classification of examinees into separate categories, the rationale for recommended score interpretations should be clearly explained.

Comment: Criterion-referenced interpretations are score-based descriptions or inferences that do not take the form of comparisons to the test performance of other examinees. Examples include statements that some psychopathology is likely present, that a prospective employee possesses specific skills required in a given position, or that a child scoring above a certain score point can successfully apply a given set of skills. Such interpretations may refer to the absolute levels of test scores or to patterns of scores for an individual examinee. Whenever the test developer recommends such interpretations, the rationale and empirical basis should be clearly presented. Serious efforts should be made whenever possible to obtain independent

evidence concerning the soundness of such score interpretations. Criterion-referenced and norm-referenced scales are not mutually exclusive. Given adequate supporting data, scores may be interpreted by both approaches, not necessarily just one or the other.

Standard 4.10

A clear rationale and supporting evidence should be provided for any claim that scores earned on different forms of a test may be used interchangeably. In some cases, direct evidence of score equivalence may be provided. In other cases, evidence may come from a demonstration that the theoretical assumptions underlying procedures for establishing score comparability have been sufficiently satisfied. The specific rationale and the evidence required will depend in part on the intended uses for which score equivalence is claimed.

Comment: Support should be provided for any assertion that scores obtained using different items or testing materials, or different testing procedures, are interchangeable for some purpose. This standard applies, for example, to alternate forms of a paper-and-pencil test or to alternate sets of items taken by different examinees in computerized adaptive testing. It also applies to test forms administered in different formats (e.g., paper-and-pencil and computerized tests) or test forms designed for individual versus group administration. Score equivalence is easiest to establish when different forms are constructed following identical procedures and then equated statistically. When that is not possible, for example, in cases where different test formats are used, additional evidence may be required to establish the requisite degree of score equivalence for the intended context and purpose. When recommended inferences or actions are based solely on classifications of examinees into one of two or more categories, the rationale and evidence should address consistency of classification. If the only

score reported and used is a pass-fail decision, for example, then the form-to-form equivalence of measurements for examinees far above or far below the cut score is of no concern. Some testing accommodations may only affect the dependence of test scores on capabilities irrelevant to the construct the test is intended to measure. Use of a large-print edition, for example, assures that performance does not depend on the ability to perceive standard-size print. In such cases, relatively modest studies or professional judgment may be sufficient to support claims of score equivalence.

Standard 4.11

When claims of form-to-form score equivalence are based on equating procedures, detailed technical information should be provided on the method by which equating functions or other linkages were established and on the accuracy of equating functions.

Comment: The fundamental concern is to show that equated scores measure essentially the same construct, with very similar levels of reliability and conditional standard errors of measurement. Technical information should include the design of equating studies, the statistical methods used, the size and relevant characteristics of examinee samples used in equating studies, and the characteristics of any anchor tests or linking items. Standard errors of equating functions should be estimated and reported whenever possible. Sample sizes permitting, it may be informative to determine equating functions independently for identifiable subgroups of examinees. It may also be informative to use two anchor forms and to conduct the equating using each of the anchors. In some cases, equating functions may be determined independently using different statistical methods. The correspondence of separate functions obtained by such methods can lend support to the adequacy of the equating results. Any substantial disparities found by such methods should be resolved or reported. To be most useful, equating error should be presented in units of the reported score scale. For testing programs with cut scores, equating error near the cut score is of primary importance. The degree of scrutiny of equating functions should be commensurate with the extent of test use anticipated and the importance of the decisions the test scores are intended to inform.

Standard 4.12

In equating studies that rely on the statistical equivalence of examinee groups receiving different forms, methods of assuring such equivalence should be described in detail.

Comment: Certain equating designs rely on the random equivalence of groups receiving different forms. Often, one way to assure such equivalence is to systematically mix different test forms and then distribute them in a random fashion so that roughly equal numbers of examinees in each group tested receive each form.

Standard 4.13

In equating studies that employ an anchor test design, the characteristics of the anchor test and its similarity to the forms being equated should be presented, including both content specifications and empirically determined relationships among test scores. If anchor items are used, as in some IRT-based and classical equating studies, the representativeness and psychometric characteristics of anchor items should be presented.

Comment: Tests or test forms may be linked via common items embedded within each of them, or a common test administered together with each of them. These common items or tests are referred to as linking items, anchor items, or anchor tests. With such methods, the quality of the resulting equating depends strongly on the adequacy of the anchor tests or items used.

Standard 4.14

When score conversions or comparison procedures are used to relate scores on tests or test forms that are not closely parallel, the construction, intended interpretation, and limitations of those conversions or comparisons should be clearly described.

Comment: Various score conversions or concordance tables have been constructed relating tests at different levels of difficulty, relating earlier to revised forms of published tests, creating score concordances between different tests of similar or different constructs, or for other purposes. Such conversions are often useful, but they may also be subject to misinterpretation. The limitations of such conversions should be clearly described.

Standard 4.15

When additional test forms are created by taking a subset of the items in an existing test form or by rearranging its items and there is sound reason to believe that scores on these forms may be influenced by item context effects, evidence should be provided that there is no undue distortion of norms for the different versions or of score linkages between them.

Comment: Some tests and test batteries are published in both a full-length version and a survey or short version. In other cases, multiple versions of a single test form may be created by rearranging its items. It should not be assumed that performance data derived from the administration of items as part of the initial version can be used to approximate norms or construct conversion tables for alternative intact tests. Due caution is required in cases where context effects are likely, including speeded tests, long tests where fatigue may be a factor, and so on. In many cases, adequate psychometric data may only be obtainable from independent administrations of the alternate forms.

Standard 4.16

If test specifications are changed from one version of a test to a subsequent version, such changes should be identified in the test manual, and an indication should be given that converted scores for the two versions may not be strictly equivalent. When substantial changes in test specifications occur, either scores should be reported on a new scale or a clear statement should be provided to alert users that the scores are not directly comparable with those on earlier versions of the test.

Comment: Major shifts sometimes occur in the specifications of tests that are used for substantial periods of time. Often such changes take advantage of improvements in item types or of shifts in content that have been shown to improve validity and, therefore, are highly desirable. It is important to recognize, however, that such shifts will result in scores that cannot be made strictly interchangeable with scores on an earlier form of the test.

Standard 4.17

Testing programs that attempt to maintain a common scale over time should conduct periodic checks of the stability of the scale on which scores are reported.

Comment: In some testing programs, items are introduced into and retired from item pools on an ongoing basis. In other cases, the items in successive test forms may overlap very little, or not at all. In either case, if a fixed scale is used for reporting, it is important to assure that the meaning of the scaled scores does not change over time.

Standard 4.18

If a publisher provides norms for use in test score interpretation, then so long as the test remains in print, it is the publisher's responsibility to assure that the test is renormed with sufficient frequency to permit continued accurate and appropriate score interpretations.

Comment: Test publishers should assure that up-to-date norms are readily available, but it remains the test user's responsibility to avoid inappropriate use of norms that are out of date and to strive to assure accurate and appropriate test interpretations.

Standard 4.19

When proposed score interpretations involve one or more cut scores, the rationale and procedures used for establishing cut scores should be clearly documented.

Comment: Cut scores may be established to select a specified number of examinees (e.g., to fill existing vacancies), in which case little further documentation may be needed concerning the specific question of how the cut scores are established, though attention should be paid to legal requirements that may apply. In other cases, however, cut scores may be used to classify examinees into distinct categories (e.g., diagnostic categories, or passing versus failing) for which there are no preestablished quotas. In these cases, the standard-setting method must be clearly documented. Ideally, the role of cut scores in test use and interpretation is taken into account during test design. Adequate precision in regions of score scales where cut points are established is prerequisite to reliable classification of examinees into categories. If standard setting employs data on the score distributions for criterion groups or on the relation of test scores to one or more criterion variables, those data should be summarized in technical documentation. If a judgmental standard-setting process is followed, the method employed should be clearly described, and the precise nature of the judgments called for should be presented, whether those are judgments of persons, of item or test performances, or of other criterion performances predicted by test scores. Documentation should also include the selection and qualification of judges, training provided, any feedback to judges concerning the implications of their provisional judgments, and any opportunities for judges to confer with one another. Where applicable, variability over judges should be reported. Whenever feasible, an estimate should be provided of the amount of variation in cut scores that might be expected if the standard-setting procedure were replicated.

Standard 4.20

When feasible, cut scores defining categories with distinct substantive interpretations should be established on the basis of sound empirical data concerning the relation of test performance to relevant criteria.

Comment: In employment settings, although it is important to establish that test scores are related to job performance, the precise relation of test and criterion may have little bearing on the choice of a cut score. However, in contexts where distinct interpretations are applied to different score categories, the empirical relation of test to criterion assumes greater importance. Cut scores used in interpreting diagnostic tests may be established on the basis of empirically determined score distributions for criterion groups. With achievement or proficiency tests, such as those used in licensure, suitable criterion groups (e.g., successful versus unsuccessful practitioners) are often unavailable. Nonetheless, it is highly desirable, when appropriate and feasible, to investigate the relation between test scores and performance in relevant practical settings. Note that a carefully designed and implemented procedure based solely on judgments of content relevance and item difficulty may be preferable to an empirical study with an inadequate criterion measure or other deficiencies. Professional judgment is required to determine an appropriate standard-setting approach (or combination of approaches) in any given situation. In general, one would not expect to find a sharp difference in levels of the criterion variable between those just below versus just above the cut score, but evidence should be provided where feasible of a relationship between test and criterion performance over a score interval that includes or approaches the cut score.

Standard 4.21

When cut scores defining pass-fail or proficiency categories are based on direct judgments about the adequacy of item or test performances or performance levels, the judgmental process should be designed so that judges can bring their knowledge and experience to bear in a reasonable way.

Comment: Cut scores are sometimes based on judgments about the adequacy of item or test performances (e.g., essay responses to a writing prompt) or performance levels (e.g., the level that would characterize a borderline examinee). The procedures used to elicit such judgments should result in reasonable, defensible standards that accurately reflect the judges' values and intentions. Reaching such judgments may be most straightforward when judges are asked to consider kinds of performances with which they are familiar and for which they have formed clear conceptions of adequacy or quality. When the responses elicited by a test neither sample nor closely simulate the use of tested knowledge or skills in the actual criterion domain, judges are not likely to approach the task with such clear understandings. Special care must then be taken to assure that judges have a sound basis for making the judgments requested. Thorough familiarity with descriptions of different proficiency categories, practice in judging task difficulty with feedback on accuracy, the experience of actually taking a form of the test, feedback on the failure rates entailed by provisional standards, and other forms of information may be beneficial in helping judges to reach sound and principled decisions.

5. TEST ADMINISTRATION, SCORING, AND REPORTING

Background

The usefulness and interpretability of test scores require that a test be administered and scored according to the developer's instructions. When directions to examinees, testing conditions, and scoring procedures follow the same detailed procedures, the test is said to be standardized. Without such standardization, the accuracy and comparability of score interpretations would be reduced. For tests designed to assess the examinee's knowledge, skills, or abilities, standardization helps to ensure that all examinees have the same opportunity to demonstrate their competencies. Maintaining test security also helps to ensure that no one has an unfair advantage.

Occasionally, however, situations arise in which modifications of standardized procedures may be advisable or legally mandated. Persons of different backgrounds, ages, or familiarity with testing may need nonstandard modes of test administration or a more comprehensive orientation to the testing process, in order that all test takers can come to the same understanding of the task. Standardized modes of presenting information or of responding may not be suitable for specific individuals, such as persons with some kinds of disability, or persons with limited proficiency in the language of the test, so that accommodations may be needed (see chapters 9 and 10). Large-scale testing programs generally have established specific procedures to be used in considering and granting accommodations. Some test users feel that any accommodation not specifically required by law could lead to a charge of unfair treatment and discrimination. Although accommodations are made with the intent of maintaining score comparability, the extent to which that is possible may not be known. Comparability of scores may be compromised, and the test may then not measure the same constructs for all test takers.

Tests and assessments differ in their degree of standardization. In many instances different examinees are given not the same test form, but equivalent forms that have been shown to yield comparable scores. Some assessments permit examinees to choose which tasks to perform or which pieces of their work are to be evaluated. A degree of standardization can be maintained by specifying the conditions of the choice and the criteria of evaluation of the products. When an assessment permits a certain kind of collaboration, the limits of that collaboration can be specified. With some assessments, test administrators may be expected to tailor their instructions to help assure that all examinees understand what is expected of them. In all such cases, the goal remains the same: to provide accurate and comparable measurement for everyone, and unfair advantage to no one. The degree of standardization is dictated by that goal, and by the intended use of the test.

Standardized directions to test takers help to ensure that all test takers understand the mechanics of test taking. Directions generally inform test takers how to make their responses, what kind of help they may legitimately be given if they do not understand the question or task, how they can correct inadvertent responses, and the nature of any time constraints. General advice is sometimes given about omitting item responses. Many tests, including computer-administered tests, require special equipment. Practice exercises are often presented in such cases to ensure that the test taker understands how to operate the equipment. The principle of standardization includes orienting test takers to materials with which they may not be familiar. Some equipment may be provided at the testing site, such as shop tools or balances. Opportunity for test takers to practice with the equipment will often be appropriate, unless using the equipment is the purpose of the test.

Tests are sometimes administered by computer, with test responses made by keyboard, computer mouse, or similar device. Although many test takers are accustomed to computers, some are not and may need some brief explanation. Even those test takers who use computers will need to know about some details. Special issues arise in managing the testing environment, such as the arrangement of illumination so that light sources do not reflect on the computer screen, possibly interfering with display legibility. Maintaining a quiet environment can be challenging when candidates are tested separately, starting at different times and finishing at different times from neighboring test takers. Those who administer computer-based tests require training in the hardware and software used for the test, so that they can deal with problems that may arise in human-computer interactions.

Standardized scoring procedures help to ensure accurate scoring and reporting, which are essential in all circumstances. When scoring is done by machine, the accuracy of the machine is at issue, including any scoring algorithm. When scoring is done by human judges, scorers require careful training. Regular monitoring can also help to ensure that every test protocol is scored according to the same standardized criteria and that the criteria do not change as the test scorers progress through the submitted test responses.

Test scores, per se, are not readily interpreted without other information, such as norms or standards, indications of measurement error, and descriptions of test content. Just as a temperature of 50° in January is warm for Minnesota and cool for Florida, a test score of 50 is not meaningful without some context. When the scores are to be reported to persons who are not technical specialists, interpretive material can be provided that is readily understandable to those receiving the report. Often, the test user provides an interpretation of the results for the test taker, suggesting the limitations of the results and the relationship of any reported scores to other information. Scores on some tests are not designed to be released to test takers; only broad test interpretations, or dichotomous classifications, such as pass/fail, are intended to be reported.

Interpretations of test results are sometimes prepared by computer systems. Such interpretations are generally based on a combination of empirical data and expert judgment and experience. In some professional applications of individualized testing, the computer-prepared interpretations are communicated by a professional, possibly with modifications for special circumstances. Such test interpretations require validation. Consistency with interpretations provided by nonalgorithmic approaches is clearly a concern.

In some large-scale assessments, the primary target of assessment is not the individual test taker but is a larger unit, such as a school district or an industrial plant. Often, different test takers are given different sets of items, following a carefully balanced matrix sampling plan, to broaden the range of information that can be obtained in a reasonable time period. The results acquire meaning when aggregated over many individuals taking different samples of items. Such assessments may not furnish enough information to support even minimally valid, reliable scores for individuals, as each individual may take only an incomplete test.

Some further issues of administration and scoring are discussed in chapter 3, "Test Development and Revision."

Standard 5.1

Test administrators should follow carefully the standardized procedures for administration and scoring specified by the test developer, unless the situation or a test taker's disability dictates that an exception should be made.

Comment: Specifications regarding instructions to test takers, time limits, the form of item presentation or response, and test materials or equipment should be strictly observed. In general, the same procedures should be followed as were used when obtaining the data for scaling and norming the test scores. A test taker with a disabling condition may require special accommodation. Other special circumstances may require some flexibility in administration. Judgments of the suitability of adjustments should be tempered by the consideration that departures from standard procedures may jeopardize the validity of the test score interpretations.

Standard 5.2

Modifications or disruptions of standardized test administration procedures or scoring should be documented.

Comment: Information about the nature of modifications of administration should be maintained in secure data files, so that research studies or case reviews based on test records can take this into account. This includes not only special accommodations for particular test takers, but also disruptions in the testing environment that may affect all test takers in the testing session. A researcher may wish to use only the records based on standardized administration. In other cases, research studies may depend on such information to form groups of respondents. Test users or test sponsors should establish policies concerning who keeps the files and who may have access to the files. Whether the information about

modifications is reported to users of test data, such as admissions officers, depends on different considerations (see chapters 8 and 10). If such reports are made, certain cautions may be appropriate.

Standard 5.3

When formal procedures have been established for requesting and receiving accommodations, test takers should be informed of these procedures in advance of testing.

Comment: When large-scale testing programs have established strict procedures to be followed, administrators should not depart from these procedures.

Standard 5.4

The testing environment should furnish reasonable comfort with minimal distractions.

Comment: Noise, disruption in the testing area, extremes of temperature, poor lighting, inadequate work space, illegible materials, and so forth are among the conditions that should be avoided in testing situations. The testing site should be readily accessible. Testing sessions should be monitored where appropriate to assist the test taker when a need arises and to maintain proper administrative procedures. In general, the testing conditions should be equivalent to those that prevailed when norms and other interpretative data were obtained.

Standard 5.5

Instructions to test takers should clearly indicate how to make responses. Instructions should also be given in the use of any equipment likely to be unfamiliar to test takers. Opportunity to practice responding should be given when equipment is involved, unless use of the equipment is being assessed.

Comment: When electronic calculators are provided for use, examinees may need practice in using the calculator. Examinees may need practice responding with unfamiliar tasks, such as a numeric grid, which is sometimes used with mathematics performance items. In computer-administered tests, the method of responding may be unfamiliar to some test takers. Where possible, the practice responses should be monitored to ensure that the test taker is making acceptable responses. In some performance tests that involve tools or equipment, instructions may be needed for unfamiliar tools, unless accommodating to unfamiliar tools is part of what is being assessed. If a test taker is unable to use the equipment or make the responses, it may be appropriate to consider alternative testing modes.

Standard 5.6

Reasonable efforts should be made to assure the integrity of test scores by eliminating opportunities for test takers to attain scores by fraudulent means.

Comment: In large-scale testing programs where the results may be viewed as having important consequences, efforts to assure score integrity should include, when appropriate and practicable, stipulating requirements for identification, constructing seating charts, assigning test takers to seats, requiring appropriate space between seats, and providing continuous monitoring of the testing process. Test developers should design test materials and procedures to minimize the possibility of cheating. Test administrators should note and report any significant instances of testing irregularity. A local change in the date or time of testing may offer an opportunity for fraud. In general, steps should be taken to minimize the possibility of breaches in test security. In any evaluation of work products (e.g., portfolios) steps should be taken to ensure that the product represents the candidate's own work, and that the amount and kind of assistance provided should be consistent with the intent of

the assessment. Ancillary documentation, such as the date when the work was done, may be useful.

Standard 5.7

Test users have the responsibility of protecting the security of test materials at all times.

Comment: Those who have test materials under their control should, with due consideration of ethical and legal requirements, take all steps necessary to assure that only individuals with a legitimate need for access to test materials are able to obtain such access before the test administration, and afterwards as well, if any part of the test will be reused at a later time. Test users must balance test security with the rights of all test takers and test users. When sensitive test documents are challenged, it may be appropriate to employ an independent third party, using a closely supervised secure procedure to conduct a review of the relevant materials. Such secure procedures are usually preferable to placing tests, manuals, and an examinee's test responses in the public record.

Standard 5.8

Test scoring services should document the procedures that were followed to assure accuracy of scoring. The frequency of scoring errors should be monitored and reported to users of the service on reasonable request. Any systematic source of scoring errors should be corrected.

Comment: Clerical and mechanical errors should be examined. Scoring errors should be minimized and, when they are found, steps should be taken promptly to minimize their recurrence.

Standard 5.9

When test scoring involves human judgment, scoring rubrics should specify criteria for scor-

ing. Adherence to established scoring criteria should be monitored and checked regularly. Monitoring procedures should be documented.

Comment: Human scorers may be provided with scoring rubrics listing acceptable alternative responses, as well as general criteria. Consistency of scoring is often checked by rescoring randomly selected test responses and by rescoring some responses from earlier administrations. Periodic checks of the statistical properties (e.g., means, standard deviations) of scores assigned by individual scorers during a scoring session can provide feedback for the scorers, helping them to maintain scoring standards. Lack of consistent scoring may call for retraining or dismissing some scorers or for reexamining the scoring rubrics.

Standard 5.10

When test score information is released to students, parents, legal representatives, teachers, clients, or the media, those responsible for testing programs should provide appropriate interpretations. The interpretations should describe in simple language what the test covers, what scores mean, the precision of the scores, common misinterpretations of test scores, and how scores will be used.

Comment: Test users should consult the interpretive material prepared by the test developer or publisher and should revise or supplement the material as necessary to present the local and individual results accurately and clearly. Score precision might be depicted by error bands, or likely score ranges, showing the standard error of measurement.

Standard 5.11

When computer-prepared interpretations of test response protocols are reported, the sources, rationale, and empirical basis for these interpretations should be available, and their limitations should be described.

Comment: Whereas computer-prepared interpretations may be based on expert judgment, the interpretations are of necessity based on accumulated experience and may not be able to take into consideration the context of the individual's circumstances. Computer-prepared interpretations should be used with care in diagnostic settings, because they may not take into account other information about the individual test taker, such as age, gender, education, prior employment, and medical history, that provide context for test results.

Standard 5.12

When group-level information is obtained by aggregating the results of partial tests taken by individuals, validity and reliability should be reported for the level of aggregation at which results are reported. Scores should not be reported for individuals unless the validity, comparability, and reliability of such scores have been established.

Comment: Large-scale assessments often achieve efficiency by "matrix sampling" of the content domain by asking different test takers different questions. The testing then requires less time from each test taker, while the aggregation of individual results provides for domain coverage that can be adequate for meaningful group- or program-level interpretations, such as schools, or grade levels within a locality or particular subject-matter areas. Because the individual receives only an incomplete test, an individual score would have limited meaning. If individual scores are provided, comparisons between scores obtained by different individuals are based on responses to items that may cover different material. Some degree of calibration among incomplete tests can sometimes be made. Such calibration is essential to the comparisons of individual scores.

Standard 5.13

Transmission of individually identified test scores to authorized individuals or institutions should be done in a manner that protects the confidential nature of the scores.

Comment: Care is always needed when communicating the scores of identified test takers, regardless of the form of communication. Face-to-face communication, as well as telephone and written communication present well-known problems. Transmission by electronic media, including computer networks and facsimile, presents modern challenges to confidentiality.

Standard 5.14

When a material error is found in test scores or other important information released by a testing organization or other institution, a corrected score report should be distributed as soon as practicable to all known recipients who might otherwise use the erroneous scores as a basis for decision making. The corrected report should be labeled as such.

Comment: A material error is one that could change the interpretation of the test score. Innocuous typographical errors would be excluded. Timeliness is essential for decisions that will be made soon after the test scores are received.

Standard 5.15

When test data about a person are retained, both the test protocol and any written report should also be preserved in some form. Test users should adhere to the policies and record-keeping practice of their professional organizations.

Comment: The protocol may be needed to respond to a possible challenge from a test taker. The protocol would ordinarily be accompanied by testing materials and test scores. Retention of more detailed records of responses would depend on circumstances and should be covered in a retention policy (see the following standard). Record keeping may be subject to legal and professional requirements. Policy for the release of any test information for other than research purposes is discussed in chapter 8.

Standard 5.16

Organizations that maintain test scores on individuals in data files or in an individual's records should develop a clear set of policy guidelines on the duration of retention of an individual's records, and on the availability, and use over time, of such data.

Comment: In some instances, test scores become obsolete over time, no longer reflecting the current state of the test taker. Outdated scores should generally not be used or made available, except for research purposes. In other cases, test scores obtained in past years can be useful as, for example, in longitudinal assessment. The key issue is the valid use of the information. Score retention and disclosure may be subject to legal and professional requirements.

6. SUPPORTING DOCUMENTATION FOR TESTS

Background

The provision of supporting documents for tests is the primary means by which test developers, publishers, and distributors communicate with test users. These documents are evaluated on the basis of their completeness, accuracy, currency, and clarity and should be available to qualified individuals as appropriate. A test's documentation typically specifies the nature of the test; its intended use; the processes involved in the test's development; technical information related to scoring, interpretation, and evidence of validity and reliability; scaling and norming if appropriate to the instrument; and guidelines for test administration and interpretation. The objective of the documentation is to provide test users with the information needed to make sound judgments about the nature and quality of the test, the resulting scores, and the interpretations based on the test scores. The information may be reported in documents such as test manuals, technical manuals, user's guides, specimen sets, examination kits, directions for test administrators and scorers, or preview materials for test takers.

Test documentation is most effective if it communicates information to multiple user groups. To accommodate the breadth of training of professionals who use tests, separate documents or sections of documents may be written for identifiable categories of users such as practitioners, consultants, administrators, researchers, and educators. For example, the test user who administers the tests and interprets the results needs interpretive information or guidelines. On the other hand, those who are responsible for selecting tests need to be able to judge the technical adequacy of the test. Therefore, some combination of technical manuals, user's guides, test manuals, test supplements, examination kits, or specimen sets ordinarily is published to provide a potential test user or test reviewer with sufficient information to evaluate the appropriateness and technical adequacy of the test. The types of information presented in these documents typically include a description of the intended test-taking population, stated purpose of the test, test specifications, item formats, scoring procedures, and the test development process. Technical data, such as psychometric indices of the items, reliability and validity evidence, normative data, and cut scores or configural rules including those for computer-generated interpretations of test scores also are summarized.

An essential feature of the documentation for every test is a discussion of the known appropriate and inappropriate uses and interpretations of the test scores. The inclusion of illustrations of score interpretations, as they relate to the test developer's intended applications, also will help users make accurate inferences on the basis of the test scores. When possible, illustrations of improper test uses and inappropriate test score interpretations will help guard against the misuse of the test.

Test documents need to include enough information to allow test users and reviewers to determine the appropriateness of the test for its intended purposes. References to other materials that provide more details about research by the publisher or independent investigators should be cited and should be readily obtainable by the test user or reviewer. This supplemental material can be provided in any of a variety of published or unpublished forms; when demand is likely to be low, it may be maintained in archival form, including electronic storage. Test documentation is useful for all test instruments, including those that are developed exclusively for use within a single organization.

In addition to technical documentation, descriptive materials are needed in some settings to inform examinees and other interested parties about the nature and content of the test. The amount and type of information will depend on the particular test and application. For example, in situations requiring informed consent, information should be sufficient to develop a reasoned judgment. Such information should be phrased in nontechnical language and should be as inclusive as is consistent with the use of the test scores. The materials may include a general description and rationale for the test; sample items or complete sample tests; and information about conditions of test administration, confidentiality, and retention of test results. For some applications, however, the true nature and purpose of a test are purposely hidden or disguised to prevent faking or response bias. In these instances, examinees may be motivated to reveal more or less of the characteristics intended to be assessed. Under these circumstances, hiding or disguising the true nature or purpose of the test is acceptable provided this action is consistent with legal principles and ethical standards.

This chapter provides general standards for the preparation and publication of test documentation. The other chapters contain specific standards that will be useful to test developers, publishers, and distributors in the preparation of materials to be included in a test's documentation.

Standard 6.1

Test documents (e.g., test manuals, technical manuals, user's guides, and supplemental material) should be made available to prospective test users and other qualified persons at the time a test is published or released for use.

Comment: The test developer or publisher should judge carefully which information should be included in first editions of the test manual, technical manual, or user's guides and which information can be provided in supplements. For low-volume, unpublished tests, the documentation may be relatively brief. When the developer is also the user, documentation and summaries are still necessary.

Standard 6.2

Test documents should be complete, accurate, and clearly written so that the intended reader can readily understand the content.

Comment: Test documents should provide sufficient detail to permit reviewers and researchers to judge or replicate important analyses published in the test manual. For example, reporting correlation matrices in the test document may allow the test user to judge the data upon which decisions and conclusions were based, or describing in detail the sample and the nature of any factor analyses that were conducted will allow the test user to replicate reported studies.

Standard 6.3

The rationale for the test, recommended uses of the test, support for such uses, and information that assists in score interpretation should be documented. Where particular misuses of a test can be reasonably anticipated, cautions against such misuses should be specified.

Comment: Test publishers make every effort to caution test users against known misuses of tests. However, test publishers are not required to anticipate all possible misuses of a test. If publishers do know of persistent test misuse by a test user, extraordinary educational efforts may be appropriate.

Standard 6.4

The population for whom the test is intended and the test specifications should be documented. If applicable, the item pool and scale development procedures should be described in the relevant test manuals. If normative data are provided, the norming population should be described in terms of relevant demographic variables, and the year(s) in which the data were collected should be reported.

Comment: Known limitations of a test for certain populations also should be clearly delineated in the test documents. In addition, if the test is available in more than one language, test documents should provide information on the translation or adaptation procedures, on the demographics of each norming sample, and on score interpretation issues for each language into which the test has been translated.

Standard 6.5

When statistical descriptions and analyses that provide evidence of the reliability of scores and the validity of their recommended interpretations are available, the information should be included in the test's documentation. When relevant for test interpretation, test documents ordinarily should include item level information, cut scores and configural rules, information about raw scores and derived scores, normative data, the standard errors of measurement, and a description of the procedures used to equate multiple forms.

Standard 6.6

When a test relates to a course of training or study, a curriculum, a textbook, or packaged

instruction, the documentation should include an identification and description of the course or instructional materials and should indicate the year in which these materials were prepared.

Standard 6.7

Test documents should specify qualifications that are required to administer a test and to interpret the test scores accurately.

Comment: Statements of user qualifications need to specify the training, certification, competencies, or experience needed to have access to a test.

Standard 6.8

If a test is designed to be scored or interpreted by test takers, the publisher and test developer should provide evidence that the test can be accurately scored or interpreted by the test takers. Tests that are designed to be scored and interpreted by the test taker should be accompanied by interpretive materials that assist the individual in understanding the test scores and that are written in language that the test taker can understand.

Standard 6.9

Test documents should cite a representative set of the available studies pertaining to general and specific uses of the test.

Comment: Summaries of cited studies—excluding published works, dissertations, or proprietary documents—should be made available on request to test users and researchers by the publisher.

Standard 6.10

Interpretive materials for tests, that include case studies, should provide examples illustrating the diversity of prospective test takers.

Comment: For some instruments, the presentation of case studies that are intended to assist the user in the interpretation of the test scores and profiles also will be appropriate for inclusion in the test documentation. For example, case studies might cite as appropriate examples of women and men of different ages; individuals differing in sexual orientation; persons representing various ethnic, cultural, or racial groups; and individuals with special needs. The inclusion of examples illustrating the diversity of prospective test takers is not intended to promote interpretation of test scores in a manner inconsistent with legal requirements that may restrict certain practices in some contexts, such as employee selection.

Standard 6.11

If a test is designed so that more than one method can be used for administration or for recording responses—such as marking responses in a test booklet, on a separate answer sheet, or on a computer keyboard— then the manual should clearly document the extent to which scores arising from these methods are interchangeable. If the results are not interchangeable, this fact should be reported, and guidance should be given for the interpretation of scores obtained under the various conditions or methods of administration.

Standard 6.12

Publishers and scoring services that offer computer-generated interpretations of test scores should provide a summary of the evidence supporting the interpretations given.

Comment: The test user should be informed of any cut scores or configural rules necessary for understanding computer-generated score interpretations. A description of both the samples used to derive cut scores or configural rules and the methods used to derive the cut scores should be provided. When proprietary interests result in the withholding of cut scores or configural rules, the owners of the intellectual

property are responsible for documenting evidence in support of the validity of computer-generated score interpretations. Such evidence might be provided, for example, by reporting the finding of an independent review of the algorithms by qualified professionals.

Standard 6.13

When substantial changes are made to a test, the test's documentation should be amended, supplemented, or revised to keep information for users current and to provide useful additional information or cautions.

Standard 6.14

Every test form and supporting document should carry a copyright date or publication date.

Comment: During the operational life of a test, new or revised test forms may be published, and manuals and other materials may be added or revised. Users and potential users are entitled to know the publication dates of various documents that include test norms. Communication among researchers is hampered when the particular test documents used in experimental studies are ambiguously referenced in research reports.

Standard 6.15

Test developers, publishers, and distributors should provide general information for test users and researchers who may be required to determine the appropriateness of an intended test use in a specific context. When a particular test use cannot be justified, the response to an inquiry from a prospective test user should indicate this fact clearly. General information also should be provided for test takers and legal guardians who must provide consent prior to a test's administration.

PART II

Fairness
in Testing

7. FAIRNESS IN TESTING AND TEST USE

Background

This chapter addresses overriding issues of fairness in testing. It is intended both to emphasize the importance of fairness in all aspects of testing and assessment and to serve as a context for the technical standards. Later chapters address in greater detail some fairness issues involving the responsibilities of test users, the rights and responsibilities of test takers, the testing of individuals of diverse linguistic backgrounds, and the testing of those with disabilities. Chapters 12 through 15 also address some fairness issues specific to psychological, educational, employment and credentialing, and program evaluation applications of testing and assessment.

Concern for fairness in testing is pervasive, and the treatment accorded the topic here cannot do justice to the complex issues involved. A full consideration of fairness would explore the many functions of testing in relation to its many goals, including the broad goal of achieving equality of opportunity in our society. It would consider the technical properties of tests, the ways test results are reported, and the factors that are validly or erroneously thought to account for patterns of test performance for groups and individuals. A comprehensive analysis would also examine the regulations, statutes, and case law that govern test use and the remedies for harmful practices. The *Standards* cannot hope to deal adequately with all these broad issues, some of which have occasioned sharp disagreement among specialists and other thoughtful observers. Rather, the focus of the *Standards* is on those aspects of tests, testing, and test use that are the customary responsibilities of those who make, use, and interpret tests, and that are characterized by some measure of professional and technical consensus.

Absolute fairness to every examinee is impossible to attain, if for no other reasons than the facts that tests have imperfect reliability and that validity in any particular context is a matter of degree. But neither is any alternative selection or evaluation mechanism perfectly fair. Properly designed and used, tests can and do further societal goals of fairness and equality of opportunity. Serious technical deficiencies in test design, use, or interpretation should, of course, be addressed, but the fairness of testing in any given context must be judged relative to that of feasible test and nontest alternatives. It is general practice that large-scale tests are subjected to careful review and empirical checks to minimize bias. The amount of explicit attention to fairness in the design of well-made tests compares favorably to that of many alternative selection or evaluation methods.

It is also crucial to bear in mind that test settings are interpersonal. The interaction of examiner with examinee should be professional, courteous, caring, and respectful. In most testing situations, the roles of examiner and examinee are sharply unequal in status. A professional's inferences and reports from test findings may markedly impact the life of the person who is examined. Attention to these aspects of test use and interpretation is no less important than more technical concerns.

As is emphasized in professional education and training, users of tests should be alert to the possibility that human issues involving examiner and examinee may sometimes affect test fairness. Attention to interpersonal issues is always important, perhaps especially so when examinees have a disability or differ from the examiner in ethnic, racial, or religious background; in gender or sexual orientation; in socioeconomic status; in age; or in other respects that may affect the examinee-examiner interaction.

Varying Views of Fairness

The term *fairness* is used in many different ways and has no single technical meaning. It is possible that two individuals may endorse fairness in testing as a desirable social goal, yet reach quite different conclusions about the fairness of a given testing program. Outlined below are four principal ways in which the term fairness is used. It should be noted, however, that many additional interpretations may be found in the technical and popular literature.

The first two characterizations presented here relate fairness to absence of bias and to equitable treatment of all examinees in the testing process. There is broad consensus that tests should be free from bias (as defined below) and that all examinees should be treated fairly in the testing process itself (e.g., afforded the same or comparable procedures in testing, test scoring, and use of scores). The third characterization of test fairness addresses the equality of testing outcomes for examinee subgroups defined by race, ethnicity, gender, disability, or other characteristics. The idea that fairness requires equality in overall passing rates for different groups has been almost entirely repudiated in the professional testing literature. A more widely accepted view would hold that examinees of equal standing with respect to the construct the test is intended to measure should on average earn the same test score, irrespective of group membership. Unfortunately, because examinees' levels of the construct are measured imperfectly, this requirement is rarely amenable to direct examination. The fourth definition of fairness relates to equity in opportunity to learn the material covered in an achievement test. There would be general agreement that adequate opportunity to learn is clearly relevant to some uses and interpretations of achievement tests and clearly irrelevant to others, although disagreement might arise as to the relevance of opportunity to learn to test fairness in some specific situations.

FAIRNESS AS LACK OF BIAS

Bias is used here as a technical term. It is said to arise when deficiencies in a test itself or the manner in which it is used result in different meanings for scores earned by members of different identifiable subgroups. When evidence of such deficiencies is found at the level of item response patterns for members of different groups, the terms *item bias* or *differential item functioning* (DIF) are often used. When evidence is found by comparing the patterns of association for different groups between test scores and other variables, the term *predictive bias* may be used. The concept of bias and techniques for its detection are discussed below and are also discussed in other chapters of the *Standards*. There is general consensus that consideration of bias is critical to sound testing practice.

FAIRNESS AS EQUITABLE TREATMENT IN THE TESTING PROCESS

There is consensus that just treatment throughout the testing process is a necessary condition for test fairness. There is also consensus that fair treatment of all examinees requires consideration not only of a test itself, but also the context and purpose of testing and the manner in which test scores are used. A well-designed test is not intrinsically fair or unfair, but the use of the test in a particular circumstance or with particular examinees may be fair or unfair. Unfairness can have individual and collective consequences.

Regardless of the purpose of testing, fairness requires that all examinees be given a comparable opportunity to demonstrate their standing on the construct(s) the test is intended to measure. Just treatment also includes such factors as appropriate testing conditions and equal opportunity to become familiar with the test format, practice materials, and so forth. In situations where individual or group test results are reported, just treatment also implies that such reporting should be accurate and fully informative.

Fairness also requires that all examinees be afforded appropriate testing conditions. Careful standardization of tests and administration conditions generally helps to assure that examinees have comparable opportunity to demonstrate the abilities or attributes to be measured. In some cases, however, aspects of the testing process that pose no particular challenge for most examinees may prevent specific groups or individuals from accurately demonstrating their standing with respect to the construct of interest (e.g., due to disability or language background). In some instances, greater comparability may sometimes be attained if standardized procedures are modified. There are contexts in which some such modifications are forbidden by law and other contexts in which some such modifications are required by law. In all cases, standardized procedures should be followed for all examinees unless explicit, documented accommodations have been made.

Ideally, examinees would also be afforded equal opportunity to prepare for a test. Examinees should in any case be afforded equal access to materials provided by the testing organization and sponsor which describe the test content and purpose and offer specific familiarization and preparation for test taking. In addition to assuring equity in access to accepted resources for test preparation, this principle covers test security for nondisclosed tests. If some examinees were to have prior access to the contents of a secure test, for example, basing decisions upon the relative performance of different examinees would be unfair to others who did not have such access. On tests that have important individual consequences, all examinees should have a meaningful opportunity to provide input to relevant decision makers if procedural irregularities in testing are alleged, if the validity of the individual's score is challenged or may not be reported, or if similar special circumstances arise.

Finally, the conception of fairness as equitable treatment in the testing process extends to the reporting of individual and group test results. Individual test score information is entitled to confidential treatment in most circumstances. Confidentiality should be respected; scores should be disclosed only as appropriate. When test scores are reported, either for groups or individuals, score reports should be accurate and informative. It may be especially important when reporting results to nonprofessional audiences to use appropriate language and wording and to try to design reports to reduce the likelihood of inappropriate interpretations. When group achievement differences are reported, for example, including additional information to help the intended audience understand confounding factors such as unequal educational opportunity may help to reduce misinterpretation of test results and increase the likelihood that tests will be used wisely.

FAIRNESS AS EQUALITY IN OUTCOMES OF TESTING

The idea that fairness requires overall passing rates to be comparable across groups is not generally accepted in the professional literature. Most testing professionals would probably agree that while group differences in testing outcomes should in many cases trigger heightened scrutiny for possible sources of test bias, outcome differences across groups do not in themselves indicate that a testing application is biased or unfair. It might be argued that when tests are used for selection, persons who all would perform equally well on the criterion measure if selected should have an equal chance of being chosen regardless of group membership. Unfortunately, there is rarely any direct procedure for determining whether this ideal has been met. Moreover, if score distributions differ from one group to another, it is generally impossible to satisfy this ideal using any test that has a less than perfect correlation with the criterion measure.

Many testing professionals would agree that if a test is free of bias and examinees have received fair treatment in the testing process, then the conditions of fairness have been met. That is, given evidence of the validity of intended test uses and interpretations, including evidence of lack of bias and attention to issues of fair treatment, fairness has been established regardless of group-level outcomes. This view need not imply that unequal testing outcomes should be ignored altogether. They may be important in generating new hypotheses about bias and fair treatment. But in this view, unequal outcomes at the group level have no direct bearing on questions of test fairness. There may be legal requirements to investigate certain differences in outcomes of testing among subgroups. Those requirements further may provide that, other things being equal, a testing alternative that minimizes outcome differences across relevant subgroups should be used. The standards in this chapter are intended to be applied in a manner consistent with legal and regulatory standards.

Fairness as Opportunity to Learn

This final conception of fairness arises in connection with educational achievement testing. In many contexts, achievement tests are intended to assess what a test taker knows or can do as a result of formal instruction. When some test takers have not had the opportunity to learn the subject matter covered by the test content, they are likely to get low scores. The test score may accurately reflect what the test taker knows and can do, but low scores may have resulted in part from not having had the opportunity to learn the material tested as well as from having had the opportunity and having failed to learn. When test takers have not had the opportunity to learn the material tested, the policy of using their test scores as a basis for withholding a high school diploma, for example, is viewed as unfair. This issue is further discussed in chapter 13, on educational testing.

At least three important difficulties arise with this conception of fairness. First, the definition of *opportunity to learn* is difficult in practice, especially at the level of individuals. Opportunity is a matter of degree. Moreover, the measurement of some important learning outcomes may require students to work with material they have not seen before. Second, even if it is possible to document the topics included in the curriculum for a group of students, specific content coverage for any one student may be impossible to determine. Finally, there is a well-founded desire to assure that credentials attest to certain proficiencies or capabilities. Granting a diploma to a low-scoring examinee on the grounds that the student had insufficient opportunity to learn the material tested means certificating someone who has not attained the degree of proficiency the diploma is intended to signify.

It should be noted that opportunity to learn ordinarily plays no role in determining the fairness of tests used for employment and credentialing, which are covered in chapter 14, nor of admissions testing. In those circumstances, it is deemed fair that the test should cover the full range of requisite knowledge and skills. However, there are situations in which the agency that determines the contents of a test used for employment or credentialing also sets the curriculum that must be followed in preparing to take the test. In such cases, it is the responsibility of that agency to assure that what is to be tested is fully included in the specification of what is to be taught.

Bias Associated With Test Content and Response Processes

The term *bias* in tests and testing refers to construct-irrelevant components that result in systematically lower or higher scores for identifiable groups of examinees. Such construct-irrelevant score components may be introduced due to inappropriate sampling of test content or lack of clarity in test instructions. They may also arise if scoring criteria fail to credit fully some correct problem approaches or solutions that are more typical of one group than another. Evidence of these potential sources of bias may be sought in the content of the tests, in comparisons of the internal structure of test responses for different groups, and in comparisons of the relationships of test scores to other measures, although none of these types of evidence is unequivocal.

CONTENT-RELATED SOURCES OF TEST BIAS

Bias due to inappropriate selection of test content may sometimes be detected by inspection of the test itself. In some testing contexts, it is common for test developers to engage an independent panel of diverse experts to review test content for language that might be interpreted differently by members of different groups and for material that might be offensive or emotionally disturbing to some test takers. For performance assessments, panels are often engaged to review the scoring rubric as well. A test intended to measure verbal analogical reasoning, for example, should include words in general use, not words and expressions associated with particular disciplines, occupations, ethnic groups, or locations. Where material likely to be differentially interesting or relevant to some examinees is included, it may be balanced by material that may be of particular interest to the remaining examinees.

In educational achievement testing, alignment with curriculum may bear on questions of content-related test bias. One may ask how well a test represents some content domain and also whether that domain is appropriate given intended score interpretations. A test of 19th-century United States history might give considerable emphasis to the War of 1812, the Mexican War, the Civil War, and the Spanish American War. If some state's curriculum framework dealt relatively

lightly with these wars, devoting more attention instead, say, to social and industrial developments, then that state's test takers might be relatively disadvantaged.

Bias may also result from a lack of clarity in test instructions or from scoring rubrics that credit responses more typical of one group than another. For example, cognitive ability tests often require test takers to classify objects according to an unspecified rule. If a given task credits classification on the basis of the stimulus objects' functions, but an identifiable subgroup of examinees tends to classify the objects on the basis of their physical appearance, faulty test interpretations are likely. Similarly, if the scoring rubric for a constructed response item reserves the highest score level for those examinees who in fact provide more information or elaboration than was actually requested, then less test-wise examinees who simply follow instructions will earn lower scores. In this case, testwiseness becomes a construct-irrelevant component of test scores.

Judgmental methods for the review of tests and test items are often supplemented by statistical procedures for identifying items on tests that function differently across identifiable subgroups of examinees. Differential item functioning (DIF) is said to exist when examinees of equal ability differ on average, according to their group membership, in their responses to a particular item. If examinees from each group are divided into subgroups according to the tested ability and subgroups at the same ability level have unequal probabilities of answering a given item correctly, then there is evidence that that item may not be functioning as intended. It may be measuring something different from the remainder of the test or it may be measuring with different levels of precision for different subgroups of examinees. Such an item may offer a valid measurement of some narrow element of the intended construct, or it may tap some construct-irrelevant component that advantages or disadvantages members of one group. Although DIF procedures may hold some promise for improving test quality, there has been little progress in identifying the causes or substantive themes that characterize items exhibiting DIF. That is, once items on a test have been statistically identified as functioning differently from one examinee group to another, it has been difficult to specify the reasons for the differential performance or to identify a common deficiency among the identified items.

RESPONSE-RELATED SOURCES OF TEST BIAS

In some cases, construct-irrelevant score components may arise because test items elicit varieties of responses other than those intended or can be solved in ways that were not intended. For example, clients responding to a diagnostic inventory may attempt to provide the answers they think the test administrator expects as opposed to the answers that best describe themselves. To the extent that such response acquiescence is more typical of some groups than others, bias may result. Bias may also be associated with test response formats that pose particular difficulties for one group or another. For example, test performance may rely on some capability (e.g., English language proficiency or fine-motor coordination) that is irrelevant to the intent of the measurement but nonetheless poses impediments for some examinees. A test of quantitative reasoning that makes inappropriately heavy demands on verbal ability would probably be biased against examinees whose first language is other than that of the test.

In addition to content reviews and DIF analyses, evidence of bias related to response processes may be provided by comparisons of the internal structure of the test responses for different groups of examinees. If an analysis of the factors or dimensions underlying test performance reveals different internal structures for different groups, it may be that different constructs are being measured or it

may simply be that groups differ in their variability with respect to the same underlying dimensions. When there is evidence that tests, including personality tests, measure different constructs in different gender, racial, or cultural groups, it is important to determine that the internal structure of the test supports inferences made for clients from these distinct subgroups of the client population. In situations where internal test structure varies markedly across ethnically diverse cultures, it may be inappropriate to make direct comparisons of scores of members of these different cultural groups.

Bias may also be indicated by patterns of association between test scores and other variables. Perhaps the most familiar form such evidence may take is a difference across groups in the regression equations relating selection test performance to criterion performance. This case is discussed at greater length in the following section. However, evidence of bias based on relations to other variables may also take many other forms. The relationship between two tests of the same cognitive ability might be found to differ from one group to another, for example. Such a difference might indicate bias in one or both tests. As another instance, a higher than expected association between reading and mathematics achievement test scores among students who might well have limited English proficiency could trigger an investigation to determine whether language proficiency was influencing some examinees' mathematics scores. Patterns of score averages or other distributional summaries might also point to potential sources of test bias. If males outperformed females on one measure of academic performance and, in the same population, females outperformed males on another, it would follow that the two measures could not both be linearly related to the identical underlying construct. Note, however, that if the tested populations differed, if the content domains sampled differed, or if the constructs tested otherwise differed due to varying motivational contexts or other effects, two reliable tests, each valid for its intended purpose, might show such a pattern. Association need not imply any direct or causal linkage, and alternative explanations for patterns of association should usually be considered. In some cases, a test-criterion correlation may arise because the test and criterion both depend on the same construct-irrelevant ability. If identifiable subgroups differ with respect to that extraneous ability, then bias may result.

Fairness in Selection and Prediction

When tests are used for selection and prediction, evidence of bias or lack of bias is generally sought in the relationships between test and criterion scores for the respective groups. Under one broadly accepted definition, no bias exists if the regression equations relating the test and the criterion are indistinguishable for the groups in question. (Some formulations may hold that not only regression slopes and intercepts but also standard errors of estimate must be equal.) If test-criterion relationships differ, different decision rules may be followed depending on the group to which the person belongs.

If fitting a common prediction equation for all groups combined suggests that the criterion performance of persons in any one group is systematically overpredicted or underpredicted, and if bias in the criterion measure has been set aside as a possible explanation, one possibility is to generate a separate prediction formula for each group. Another possibility is to seek predictor variables that may be used in lieu of or in addition to the initial predictor score to reduce differential prediction without reducing overall predictive accuracy. If separate regression equations are employed, the effect of their use on the distribution of predicted criterion

scores for the different groups should be examined. Note that in the United States, the use of different selection rules for identifiable subgroups of examinees is legally proscribed in some contexts. There may, however, be legal requirements to consider alternative selection procedures in some such situations.

There is often tension between the perspective that equates fairness with lack of bias, in the technical sense, and the perspective that focuses on testing outcomes. A test that is valid for its intended purpose might be considered fair if a given test score predicts the same performance level for members of all groups. It might nonetheless be regarded by some as unfair, however, if average test scores differ across groups. This is because a given selection score and criterion threshold will often result in proportionately more false negative decisions in groups with lower mean test scores. In other words, a lower-scoring group will usually have a higher proportion of examinees who are rejected on the basis of their test scores even though they would have performed successfully if they had been selected. This seeming paradox is a statistical consequence of the imperfect correlation between test and criterion. It does not occur because of any other property of the test and has no direct relationship to group demographics. It is a purely statistical phenomenon that occurs as a function of lower test scores, regardless of group membership. For example, it usually occurs when the top and bottom test score halves of the majority group are compared. The fairness of a test or another predictor should be evaluated relative to that of nontest alternatives that might be used instead.

GROUP OUTCOME DIFFERENCES DUE TO CHOICE OF PREDICTORS

Success in virtually all real-world endeavors requires multiple skills and abilities, which may interact in complex ways. Testing programs typically address only a subset of these. Some skills and abilities are excluded because they are assessed in other components of the selection process (e.g., completion of course work or an interview); others may be excluded because reliable and valid measurement is economically, logistically, or administratively infeasible. Success in college, for example, requires perseverance, motivation, good study habits, and a host of other factors in addition to verbal and quantitative reasoning ability. Even if each of the criteria employed in a selection process is demonstrably valid and appropriate for that purpose, issues of fairness may arise in the choice of which factors are measured. If identifiable groups differ in their average levels of measured versus unmeasured job-relevant characteristics, then fairness becomes a concern at the group level as well as the individual level.

Can Consensus Be Achieved?

It is unlikely that consensus in society at large or within the measurement community is imminent on all matters of fairness in the use of tests. As noted earlier, fairness is defined in a variety of ways and is not exclusively addressed in technical terms; it is subject to different definitions and interpretations in different social and political circumstances. According to one view, the conscientious application of an unbiased test in any given situation is fair, regardless of the consequences for individuals or groups. Others would argue that fairness requires more than satisfying certain technical requirements. It bears repeating that while the *Standards* will provide more specific guidance on matters of technical adequacy, matters of values and public policy are crucial to responsible test use.

Standard 7.1

When credible research reports that test scores differ in meaning across examinee subgroups for the type of test in question, then to the extent feasible, the same forms of validity evidence collected for the examinee population as a whole should also be collected for each relevant subgroup. Subgroups may be found to differ with respect to appropriateness of test content, internal structure of test responses, the relation of test scores to other variables, or the response processes employed by individual examinees. Any such findings should receive due consideration in the interpretation and use of scores as well as in subsequent test revisions.

Comment: Scores differ in meaning across subgroups when the same score produces systematically different inferences about examinees who are members of different subgroups. In those circumstances where credible research reports differences in score meaning for particular subgroups for the type of test in question, this standard calls for separate, parallel analyses of data for members of those subgroups, sample sizes permitting. Relevant examinee subgroups may be defined by race or ethnicity, culture, language, gender, disability, age, socioeconomic status, or other classifications. Not all forms of evidence can be examined separately for members of all such groups. The validity argument may rely on existing research literature, for example, and such literature may not be available for some populations. For some kinds of evidence, some separate subgroup analyses may not be feasible due to the limited number of cases available. Data may sometimes be accumulated so that these analyses can be performed after the test has been in use for a period of time. This standard is not satisfied by assuring that such groups are represented within larger, pooled samples, although this may also be important. In giving "due consideration in the interpretation and use of scores," pursuant to this standard, test users should be mindful of legal restrictions that may prohibit or limit within-group scoring and other practices.

Standard 7.2

When credible research reports differences in the effects of construct-irrelevant variance across subgroups of test takers on performance on some part of the test, the test should be used if at all only for those subgroups for which evidence indicates that valid inferences can be drawn from test scores.

Comment: An obvious reason why a test may not measure the same constructs across subgroups is that different components come into play from one subgroup to another. Alternatively, an irrelevant component may have a more significant effect on the performance of examinees in one subgroup than in another. Such intrusive elements are rarely entirely absent for any subgroup but are seldom present to any great extent. The decision whether or not to use a test with any given examinee subgroup necessarily involves a careful analysis of the validity evidence for different subgroups, as called for in Standard 7.1, and the exercise of thoughtful professional judgment regarding the significance of the irrelevant components.

A conclusion that a test is not appropriate for a particular subgroup requires an alternative course of action. This may involve a search for a test that can be used for all groups or, in circumstances where it is feasible to use different construct-equivalent tests for different groups, for an alternative test for use in the subgroup for which the intended construct is not well measured by the current test. In some cases multiple tests may be used in combination,

and a composite that permits valid inferences across subgroups may be identified. In some circumstances, such as employment testing, there may be legal or other constraints on the use of different tests for different subgroups.

It is acknowledged that there are occasions where examinees may request or demand to take a version of the test other than that deemed most appropriate by the developer or user. An individual with a disability may decline an alternate form and request the standard form. Acceding to this request, after ensuring that the examinee is fully informed about the test and how it will be used, is not a violation of this standard.

Standard 7.3

When credible research reports that differential item functioning exists across age, gender, racial/ethnic, cultural, disability, and/or linguistic groups in the population of test takers in the content domain measured by the test, test developers should conduct appropriate studies when feasible. Such research should seek to detect and eliminate aspects of test design, content, and format that might bias test scores for particular groups.

Comment: Differential item functioning exists when examinees of equal ability differ, on average, according to their group membership in their responses to a particular item. In some domains, existing research may indicate that differential item functioning occurs infrequently and does not replicate across samples. In others, research evidence may indicate that differential item functioning occurs reliably at meaningful above-chance levels for some particular groups; it is to such circumstances that the standard applies. Although it may not be possible prior to first release of a test to study the question of differential item functioning for some such groups, continued operational use of a test may afford opportunities to check for differential item functioning.

Standard 7.4

Test developers should strive to identify and eliminate language, symbols, words, phrases, and content that are generally regarded as offensive by members of racial, ethnic, gender, or other groups, except when judged to be necessary for adequate representation of the domain.

Comment: Two issues are involved. The first deals with the inadvertent use of language that, unknown to the test developer, has a different meaning or connotation in one subgroup than in others. Test publishers often conduct sensitivity reviews of all test material to detect and remove sensitive material from the test. The second deals with settings in which sensitive material is essential for validity. For example, history tests may appropriately include material on slavery or Nazis. Tests on subjects from the life sciences may appropriately include material on evolution. A test of understanding of an organization's sexual harassment policy may require employees to evaluate examples of potentially offensive behavior.

Standard 7.5

In testing applications involving individualized interpretations of test scores other than selection, a test taker's score should not be accepted as a reflection of standing on the characteristic being assessed without consideration of alternate explanations for the test taker's performance on that test at that time.

Comment: Many test manuals point out variables that should be considered in interpreting test scores, such as clinically relevant history, school record, vocational status, and test-taker motivation. Influences associated with variables such as socioeconomic status, ethnicity, gender, cultural background, language, or age may also be relevant. In addition, medication, visual impairments, or other disabilities may affect a test taker's performance on, for example, a paper-and-pencil test of mathematics.

Standard 7.6

When empirical studies of differential prediction of a criterion for members of different subgroups are conducted, they should include regression equations (or an appropriate equivalent) computed separately for each group or treatment under consideration or an analysis in which the group or treatment variables are entered as moderator variables.

Comment: Correlation coefficients provide inadequate evidence for or against a differential prediction hypothesis if groups or treatments are found not to be approximately equal with respect to both test and criterion means and variances. Considerations of both regression slopes and intercepts are needed. For example, despite equal correlations across groups, differences in intercepts may be found.

Standard 7.7

In testing applications where the level of linguistic or reading ability is not part of the construct of interest, the linguistic or reading demands of the test should be kept to the minimum necessary for the valid assessment of the intended construct.

Comment: When the intent is to assess ability in mathematics or mechanical comprehension, for example, the test should not contain unusual words or complicated syntactic conventions unrelated to the mathematical or mechanical skill being assessed.

Standard 7.8

When scores are disaggregated and publicly reported for groups identified by characteristics such as gender, ethnicity, age, language proficiency, or disability, cautionary statements should be included whenever credible research reports that test scores may not have comparable meaning across these different groups.

Comment: Comparisons across groups are only meaningful if scores have comparable meaning across groups. The standard is intended as applicable to settings where scores are implicitly or explicitly presented as comparable in score meaning across groups.

Standard 7.9

When tests or assessments are proposed for use as instruments of social, educational, or public policy, the test developers or users proposing the test should fully and accurately inform policymakers of the characteristics of the tests as well as any relevant and credible information that may be available concerning the likely consequences of test use.

Standard 7.10

When the use of a test results in outcomes that affect the life chances or educational opportunities of examinees, evidence of mean test score differences between relevant subgroups of examinees should, where feasible, be examined for subgroups for which credible research reports mean differences for similar tests. Where mean differences are found, an investigation should be undertaken to determine that such differences are not attributable to a source of construct underrepresentation or construct-irrelevant variance. While initially the responsibility of the test developer, the test user bears responsibility for uses with groups other than those specified by the developer.

Comment: Examples of such test uses include situations in which a test plays a dominant role in a decision to grant or withhold a high school diploma or to promote a student or retain a student in grade. Such an investigation might include a review of the cumulative research literature or local studies, as appropriate. In some domains, such as cognitive ability testing in employment, a substantial relevant research base may preclude the need for local studies. In educational settings, as discussed in chapter 13, potential differences in opportunity to learn may be relevant as a possible source of mean differences.

Standard 7.11

When a construct can be measured in different ways that are approximately equal in their degree of construct representation and freedom from construct-irrelevant variance, evidence of mean score differences across relevant subgroups of examinees should be considered in deciding which test to use.

Comment: Mean score differences, while important, are but one factor influencing the choice between one test and another. Cost, testing time, test security, and logistic issues (e.g., an application where very large numbers of examinees must be screened in a very short time) are among the issues also entering into the professional judgment about test use.

Standard 7.12

The testing or assessment process should be carried out so that test takers receive comparable and equitable treatment during all phases of the testing or assessment process.

Comment: For example, should a person administering a test or interpreting test results recognize a personal bias for or against an examinee, or for or against any subgroup of which the examinee is a member, the person could take a variety of steps ranging from seeking a review of test interpretations from a colleague to withdrawal from the testing process.

8. THE RIGHTS AND RESPONSIBILITIES OF TEST TAKERS

Background

This chapter addresses fairness issues unique to the interests of the individual test taker. Fair treatment of test takers is not only a matter of equity, but also promotes the validity and reliability of the inferences made from the test performance. The standards presented in this chapter reflect widely accepted principles in the field of measurement. The standards address the responsibilities of test takers with regard to test security, their access to test results, and their rights when irregularities in their testing are claimed. Other issues of fairness are treated in other chapters: general principles in chapter 7; the testing of linguistic minorities in chapter 9; the testing of persons with disabilities in chapter 10. General considerations concerning reports of test results are covered in chapter 5.

Test takers have the right to be assessed with tests that meet current professional standards, including standards of technical quality, fairness, administration, and reporting of results. Fair and equitable treatment of test takers involves providing, in advance of testing, information about the nature of the test, the intended use of test scores, and the confidentiality of the results. Test takers, or their legal representatives when appropriate, need enough information about the test and the intended use of test results to reach a competent decision about participating in testing. In some instances, formal informed consent for testing is required by law or by other standards of professional practice, such as those governing research on human subjects. The greater the consequences to the test taker, the greater the importance of ensuring that the test taker is fully informed about the test and voluntarily consents to participate, except when testing without consent is permitted by law. If a test is optional, the test taker has the right to know the consequences of taking or not taking the test. The test taker has the right to acceptable opportunities for asking questions or expressing concerns, and may expect timely responses to legitimate questions.

Where consistent with the purposes and nature of the assessment, general information is usually provided about the test's content and purposes. Some programs, in the interests of fairness, provide all test takers with helpful materials, such as study guides, sample questions, or complete sample tests, when such information does not jeopardize the validity of the results from future test administration. Advice may also be provided about test-taking strategies, including time management, and the advisability of omitting an item response, when it is permitted. Information is made known about the availability of special accommodations for those who need them. The policy on retesting may be stated, in case the test taker feels that the present performance does not appropriately reflect his/her best performance.

As participants in the assessment, test takers have responsibilities as well as rights. Their responsibilities include preparing themselves for the test, following the directions of the test administrator, representing themselves honestly on the test, and informing appropriate persons if they believe the test results do not adequately reflect them. In group testing situations, test takers are expected not to interfere with the performance of other test takers.

Test validity rests on the assumption that a test taker has earned fairly a particular score or pass/fail decision. Any form of cheating, or other behavior that reduces the fairness and validity of a test, is irresponsible, is unfair to other test takers and may lead to sanctions. It is unfair for a test taker to use aids that are prohibited. It is unfair for a test taker to arrange for someone else to take the test in his/her place. The test taker is obligated to respect the copyrights of the test publisher or sponsor on all test materials. This means that the test taker will not reproduce the items without authorization nor disseminate, in any form, material that is clearly analogous to the reproduction of the items. Test takers, as well as test administrators, have the responsibility not to compromise security by divulging any details of the test items to others nor may they request such details from others. Failure to honor these responsibilities may compromise the validity of test score interpretations for themselves and for others.

Sometimes, testing programs use special scores, statistical indicators, and other indirect information about irregularities in testing to help ensure that the test scores are obtained fairly. Unusual patterns of responses, large changes in test scores upon retesting, speed of responding, and similar indicators may trigger careful scrutiny of certain testing protocols. The details of these procedures are generally kept secure to avoid compromising their use. However, test takers can be made aware that in special circumstances, such as response or test score anomalies, their test responses may get special scrutiny. If evidence of impropriety or fraud so warrants, the test taker's score may be canceled, or other action taken.

Because these *Standards* are directed to test providers, and not to test takers, standards about test-taker responsibilities are phrased in terms of providing information to test takers about their rights and responsibilities. Providing this information is the joint responsibility of the test developer, the test administrator, the test proctor, if any, and the test user and may be apportioned according to particular circumstances.

Standard 8.1

Any information about test content and purposes that is available to any test taker prior to testing should be available to *all* test takers. Important information should be available free of charge and in accessible formats.

Comment: The intent of this standard is equal treatment for all. Important information would include that necessary for testing, such as when and where the test is given, what material should be brought, the purpose of the test, and so forth. More detailed information, such as practice materials, is sometimes offered for a fee. Such offerings should be made to all test takers.

Standard 8.2

Where appropriate, test takers should be provided, in advance, as much information about the test, the testing process, the intended test use, test scoring criteria, testing policy, and confidentiality protection as is consistent with obtaining valid responses.

Comment: Where appropriate, test takers should be informed, possibly by a test bulletin or similar procedure, about test content, including subject area, topics covered, and item formats. They should be informed about the advisability of omitting responses. They should be aware of any imposed time limits, so that they can manage their time appropriately. General advice should be given about test-taking strategy. In computer administrations, they should be told about any provisions for review of items they have previously answered or omitted. Test takers should understand the intended use of test scores and the confidentiality of test results. They should be advised whether they will have access to their results. They should be informed about the policy concerning taking the test again and about the possibility that some test protocols may receive special scrutiny for security reasons. Test takers should be informed about the consequences of misconduct or improper behavior, such as cheating, that could result in their being prohibited from completing the test, receiving test scores, or other sanctions.

Standard 8.3

When the test taker is offered a choice of test format, information about the characteristics of each format should be provided.

Comment: Test takers sometimes have to choose between a paper-and-pencil administration and a computer-administered test, which may be adaptive. Some tests are offered in several different languages. Sometimes an alternative assessment is offered in lieu of the ordinary test. Test takers need to know the characteristics of each alternative so that they can make an informed choice.

Standard 8.4

Informed consent should be obtained from test takers, or their legal representatives when appropriate, before testing is done except (a) when testing without consent is mandated by law or governmental regulation, (b) when testing is conducted as a regular part of school activities, or (c) when consent is clearly implied.

Comment: Informed consent implies that the test takers or representatives are made aware, in language that they can understand, of the reasons for testing, the type of tests to be used, the intended use, and the range of material consequences of the intended use. If written, video, or audio records are made of the testing session, or other records are kept, test takers

are entitled to know what testing information will be released and to whom. Consent is not required when testing is legally mandated, such as a court-ordered psychological assessment, but there may be legal requirements for providing information. When testing is required for employment or for educational admissions, applicants, by applying, have implicitly given consent to the testing. Nevertheless, test takers and/ or their legal representatives should be given appropriate information about a test when it is in their interest to be informed. Young test takers should receive an explanation of the reasons for testing. Even a child as young as two or three, as well as older test takers of limited cognitive ability, can understand a simple explanation as to why they are being tested (such as, "I'm going to ask you to try to do some things so that I can see what you know how to do and what things you could use some more help with").

Standard 8.5

Test results identified by the names of individual test takers, or by other personally identifying information, should be released only to persons with a legitimate, professional interest in the test taker or who are covered by the informed consent of the test taker or a legal representative, unless otherwise required by law.

Comment: Scores of individuals identified by name, or by some other means by which a person can be readily identified, such as social security number, should be kept confidential. In some situations, information may be provided on a confidential basis to other practitioners with a legitimate interest in the particular case, consistent with legal and ethical considerations. Information may be provided to researchers if a test taker's anonymity is maintained and the intended use is consistent with accepted research practice and is not inconsistent with the conditions of the test taker's informed consent.

Standard 8.6

Test data maintained in data files should be adequately protected from improper disclosure. Use of facsimile transmission, computer networks, data banks, and other electronic data processing or transmittal systems should be restricted to situations in which confidentiality can be reasonably assured.

Comment: When facsimile or computer communication is used to transmit a test protocol to another site for scoring, or if scores are similarly transmitted, special provisions should be made to keep the information confidential. See Standard 5.13.

Standard 8.7

Test takers should be made aware that having someone else take the test for them, disclosing confidential test material, or any other form of cheating is inappropriate and that such behavior may result in sanctions.

Comment: Although the standards cannot regulate the behavior of test takers, test takers should be made aware of their personal and legal responsibilities. Arranging for someone else to impersonate the nominal test taker constitutes fraud. Disclosure of confidential testing material for the purpose of giving other test takers pre-knowledge is unfair and may constitute copyright infringement. In licensure and certification tests, such actions may compromise public health and safety. The validity of test score interpretations is compromised by inappropriate test disclosure.

Standard 8.8

When score reporting includes assigning individuals to categories, the categories should be chosen carefully and described precisely. The least stigmatizing labels, consistent with accurate representation, should always be assigned.

Comment: When labels are associated with test results, care should be taken to be precise in the meanings associated with the labels and to avoid unnecessarily stigmatizing consequences associated with a label. For example, in an assessment designed to aid in determining whether an individual is competent to stand trial, the label "incompetent" is appropriate for individuals who perform poorly on the assessment. However, in a test of basic literacy skills, it is more appropriate to use a label such as "not proficient" rather than "incompetent," because the latter term has a more global and derogatory meaning.

Standard 8.9

When test scores are used to make decisions about a test taker or to make recommendations to a test taker or a third party, the test taker or the legal representative is entitled to obtain a copy of any report of test scores or test interpretation, unless that right has been waived or is prohibited by law or court order.

Comment: In some cases a test taker may be adequately informed when the test report is given to an appropriate third party (treating psychologist or psychiatrist) who can interpret the findings to the test taker. In professional applications of individualized testing, when the test taker is given a copy of the test report, the examiner or a knowledgeable third party should be available to interpret it, even if it is clearly written, as the test taker may misunderstand or raise questions not specifically answered in the report. In employment testing situations, where test results are used solely for the purpose of aiding selection decisions, waivers of access are often a condition of employment, although access to test information may often be appropriately required in other circumstances.

Standard 8.10

In educational testing programs and in licensing and certification applications, when an individual score report is expected to be delayed beyond a brief investigative period, because of possible irregularities such as suspected misconduct, the test taker should be notified, the reason given, and reasonable efforts made to expedite review and to protect the interests of the test taker. The test taker should be notified of the disposition, when the investigation is closed.

Standard 8.11

In educational testing programs and in licensing and certification applications, when it is deemed necessary to cancel or withhold a test taker's score because of possible testing irregularities, including suspected misconduct, the type of evidence and procedures to be used to investigate the irregularity should be explained to all test takers whose scores are directly affected by the decision. Test takers should be given a timely opportunity to provide evidence that the score should not be canceled or withheld. Evidence considered in deciding upon the final action should be made available to the test taker on request.

Comment: Any form of cheating or behavior that reduces the validity and fairness of test results should be investigated promptly, and

appropriate action taken. Withholding or canceling a test score may arise because of suspected misconduct by the test taker, or because of some anomaly involving others, such as theft, or administrative mishap. An avenue of appeal should be available and made known to candidates whose scores may be amended or withheld. Some testing organizations offer the option of a prompt and free retest or arbitration of disputes.

Standard 8.12

In educational testing programs and in licensing and certification applications, when testing irregularities are suspected, reasonably available information bearing directly on the assessment should be considered, consistent with the need to protect the privacy of test takers.

Comment: Unless allegations of misconduct are made by associates of the test taker, the information to be collected would ordinarily be limited to that obtainable without invading the privacy of the test taker or his/her associates.

Standard 8.13

In educational testing programs and in licensing and certification applications, test takers are entitled to fair consideration and reasonable process, as appropriate to the particular circumstances, in resolving disputes about testing. Test takers are entitled to be informed of any available means of recourse.

Comment: When a test taker's score may be questioned and may be invalidated, or when a test taker seeks a review or revision of his/her score or some other aspect of the testing, scoring, or reporting process, the test taker is entitled to some orderly process for effective input into or review of the decision making of the test administrator or test user. Depending upon the magnitude of the consequences associated with the test, this can range from an internal review of all relevant data by a test administrator, to an informal conversation with an examinee, to a full administrative hearing. The greater the consequences, the greater the extent of procedural protections that should be made available. Test takers should also be made aware of procedures for recourse, fees, expected time for resolution, and any possible consequences for the test taker. Some testing programs advise that the test taker may be represented by an attorney, although possibly at the test taker's expense.

9. TESTING INDIVIDUALS OF DIVERSE LINGUISTIC BACKGROUNDS

Background

For all test takers, any test that employs language is, in part, a measure of their language skills. This is of particular concern for test takers whose first language is not the language of the test. Test use with individuals who have not sufficiently acquired the language of the test may introduce construct-irrelevant components to the testing process. In such instances, test results may not reflect accurately the qualities and competencies intended to be measured. In addition, language differences are almost always associated with concomitant cultural differences that need to be taken into account when tests are used with individuals whose dominant language is different from that of the test. Whether a certain dialect of a language should be considered a different language cannot be resolved here, although some aspects of the present discussion are relevant to the debate. In either case, special attention to issues related to language and culture may be needed when developing, administering, scoring, and interpreting test scores and making decisions based on test scores. Language proficiency tests, if appropriately designed and used, are an obvious exception to this concern because they are intended to measure familiarity with the language of the test as required in educational and other settings.

Individuals who are bilingual can vary considerably in their ability to speak, write, comprehend aurally, and read in each language. These abilities are affected by the social or functional situations of communication. Some people develop socially and culturally acceptable ways of speaking that combine two or more languages simultaneously. Other individuals familiar with two languages may perform more slowly, less efficiently, and at times less accurately on problem-solving tasks that are administered in the less familiar language. Language dominance is not necessarily an indicator of language competence in taking a test, and some accommodation may be necessary even when administering the test in the more familiar language. Therefore it is important to consider language background in developing, selecting, and administering tests and in interpreting test performance. Consequently, for example, test norms based on native speakers of English either should not be used with individuals whose first language is not English or such individuals' test results should be interpreted as reflecting in part current level of English proficiency rather than ability, potential, aptitude or personality characteristics or symptomatology. In cases where a language-oriented test is inappropriate due to the test takers' limited proficiency in that language, a nonverbal test may be a suitable alternative.

Where effective job performance requires the ability to communicate in the language of the test, persons who do not have adequate proficiency in that language may perform poorly on the test, on the job, or both. In that case, the tests used for prediction of future job performance appropriately would be administered in the language of the job, as long as the language level needed for the test did not exceed the level needed to meet work requirements. Test users should understand that poor test performance, as well as poor job performance, may result from poor language proficiency rather than other deficiencies.

Many issues addressed in this chapter are also relevant to testing individuals who have unique linguistic characteristics due to disabilities such as deafness and/or blindness. For example, issues regarding test translation and adaptation are applicable to American Sign Language (ASL) versions of traditional tests. It should be noted, however, that ASL is not only a different language but is also a different mode of communication. Also, individuals with disabilities may require modifications in test administration procedures similar to those required by non-native speakers. A more specific discussion of testing individuals with disabilities is provided in chapter 10.

Issues discussed in earlier chapters, in particular chapters 1-5, including validity of test score inferences, test reliability, and test development and administration are germane to this chapter. The present chapter extends these discussions, emphasizing the importance of recognizing the possible impact of language abilities and skills on test performance. There may be legal requirements relevant to the testing of individuals with different language backgrounds. The standards in this chapter are intended to be applied in a manner consistent with those requirements.

Test Translation, Adaptation, and Modification

Testing test takers in their primary language may be necessary in order to draw valid inferences based on their test scores. Thus, language modifications are often needed. Translating a test to the primary language represents one such modification. However, a number of hazards need to be avoided when doing this sort of translation. One cannot simply assume that such a translation produces a version of the test that is equivalent in content, difficulty level, reliability, and validity to the original untranslated version. Further, one cannot assume that test takers' relevant acculturation experiences are comparable across the two versions. Also, many words have different frequency rates or difficulty levels in various languages. Therefore, words in two languages that appear to be close in meaning may differ significantly in ways that seriously impact the translated test for the intended test use. Additionally, the test content of the translated version may not be equivalent to

that of the original version. For example, a test of reading skills in language A that is translated to serve as a test of reading skills in language B may include content not equally meaningful or appropriate for people who read only language B.

For the purposes of test translation and adaptation for use with test takers whose first language is not the language of the test, back translation is not recommended as a standalone procedure. It may provide an artificial similarity of meaning across languages but not the best version in the new language. In most situations, an iterative process more akin to test development and validation is suggested to ensure that similar constructs are measured across versions. When test forms in two or more languages are developed concurrently, it is generally desirable that some items originate in each of the languages involved. The decision as to whether to use the standard original language test or an adapted version is a complex matter. Issues that may have an impact on this decision are discussed in the next section.

Other strategies of test modification may be appropriate when the test taker's primary language is not the language of the test. These include modifying aspects of the test or the test administration procedure such as the presentation format, the response format, the time allowed to complete the test, the test setting (individual administration instead of group testing), and the use of only those portions of the test that are appropriate for the level of language proficiency of the test taker. If modifications are made to the presentation or response format of the test, it may sometimes be appropriate for the modified test to be field tested with an adequate population sample prior to use with its intended population.

Issues of Equivalence

The term *equivalence*, as used here, refers to the degree to which test scores can be used to make comparable inferences for different examinees. When tests are designed for and used with linguistically homogeneous populations, issues of equivalence are relatively straightforward (for example, see chapters 1 and 4). If an individual examinee can be demonstrated to belong to the population for which the test was designed, then adhering to standard procedures of test administration and interpretation is expected to lead to reliable and valid inferences based on the examinee's test score. When a test is intended for use with test takers who differ linguistically from those for whom the test was designed, establishing equivalence poses a greater challenge. In general, the linguistic and cultural characteristics of the intended examinee population should be reflected in examinee samples used throughout the processes of test design, validation, and norming. At each of these stages of test development and standardization, distinct linguistic groups should receive the same level of specific attention. The inclusion of proportional representation of linguistic subgroups in aggregate standardization and validation samples may be insufficient to assure equivalence across linguistic groups.

Issues associated with construct equivalence are perhaps most fundamental. One may question whether the test score for a particular individual represents that individual's standing with respect to the same construct as is measured in the target population. For example, among non-native speakers of the language of the test, one may not know whether a test designed to measure primarily academic achievement becomes in whole or in part a measure of proficiency in the language of the test. There are several psychometric techniques that can be used to determine the equivalence of constructs across groups, including confirmatory factor analysis, analysis of data contained in multi-method-multitrait matrices and the equivalence of responsiveness of the groups to experimental manipulations. These tech-

niques may be supplemented with logical analyses of the results based on knowledge of the linguistic characteristics of the test taker's population of origin.

Other types of equivalence also need to be considered when testing individuals from different linguistic backgrounds. Functional equivalence addresses the question of whether similar activities or behaviors measured by a test have the same meaning in different cultural or linguistic groups. Translation equivalence requires that the translated or adapted test be comparable in content to the original test; it was addressed above in the discussion of test translation and adaptation. Metric equivalence concerns the issue of whether scores from the same test administered in different languages have comparable psychometric properties. For example, with metric equivalence, a score of 50 on test X in language A is interpretable in the same way as a score of 50 on test X in language B. In general, metric equivalence will be limited to particular contexts, examinee groups, and types of interpretations.

Language Proficiency Testing

Consideration of relevant within-linguistic group differences is crucial in determining appropriate test interpretation and decision making in educational programs and in some professional applications of individualized tests. For example, individuals whose first language is not the language of the test may vary considerably in their proficiency along a continuum from those who have no knowledge of the language of the test to those who are fluent in it and knowledgeable of the corresponding culture. Further, a demographic proxy such as Mexican or German is likely to prove insufficient in determining the language of test administration because members of the same cultural group may vary widely in their degree of acculturation, proficiency in the language of the test, familiarity with words and syntax in their native languages, educational background, familiarity with tests and test-taking skills, and other factors that may significantly affect the reliability and validity of inferences drawn from test scores. Thus, it is essential that individual differences that may affect test performance be taken into account when testing individuals of differing linguistic backgrounds.

The need exists to consider both language dominance and language proficiency. Standardized tests that assess multiple domains in a given language can be helpful in determining language dominance and proficiency. The person conducting the testing first should obtain information about the language in which the examinee is dominant (i.e., the preferred or salient language). Following this determination of dominance, the examinee's level of proficiency in the dominant language should be established. If the languages are similarly dominant, then proficiency should be established for both (or all) languages. Then the test should be administered in the most proficient language if available (unless the purpose of the testing is to determine proficiency in the language of the test). However, testing individuals in their dominant language alone is no panacea because, as suggested above, a bilingual individual's two languages are likely to be specialized by domain (e.g., the first language is used in the context of home, religious practices, and native culture, whereas the second language is used in the context of school, work, television, and mainstream culture). Thus, a test in either language by itself will likely measure some domains and miss out on others. In such situations, testing in both languages (i.e., the dominant language and the language in which the test taker is most proficient) may be necessary, provided appropriate tests are available. If assessment in both languages is carried out, careful consideration should be given to the possibility of order effects.

Because students are expected to acquire proficiency in the language used in schools that is appropriate to their ages and educational levels, tests suitable for assessing their progress in that language are needed. For example, some tests, especially paper-and-pencil measures, that are prepared for students of English as a foreign language may not be particularly useful if they place insufficient emphasis on the assessment of important listening and speaking skills. Measures of competency in all relevant English language skills (e.g., communicative competence, literacy, grammar, pronunciation, and comprehension) are likely to be most valuable in the school context.

Observing students' speech in naturalistic situations can provide additional information about their proficiency in a language. However, findings from naturalistic observations may not be sufficient to judge students' ability to function in that language in formal, academically oriented situations (e.g., classrooms). For example, it is not appropriate to base judgments of a child's ability to benefit from instruction in one language solely on language fluency observed in speech use on the playground. Nor is it appropriate to base judgments of a person's ability to perform a job on assessments of formal language usage, if formal language usage is not linked to job performance.

In general, there are special difficulties attendant upon the use of a test with individuals who have not had an adequate opportunity to learn the language used by the test. When a test is used to inform a decision process that has a broad impact, it may be important for the test user to review the test itself and to consider the possible use of alternative information-gathering tools (e.g., additional tests, sources of observational information, modified forms of the chosen test) to ensure that the information obtained is adequate to the intended purpose. Reviews of this kind may sometimes reveal the need to create a formal adaptation of a test or to develop a new test that is suitable for the specific linguistic characteristics of the individuals being tested.

Testing Bilingual Individuals

Test use with examinees who are bilingual also poses special challenges. An individual who knows two languages may not test well in either language. As an example, children from homes where parents speak Spanish may be able to understand Spanish but express themselves best in English. In addition, some persons who are bilingual use their native language in most social situations and use English primarily for academic and work-related activities; the use of one or both languages depends on the nature of the situation. As another example, proficiencies in conversational English and written English can often differ. Non-native English speakers who may give the impression of being fluent in conversational English may not be competent in taking tests that require English literacy skills. Thus, an understanding of an individual's type and degree of bilingualism is important to proper test use.

Administration and Examiner Variables

When an examinee cannot be assumed to belong to the cultural or linguistic population upon which the test was standardized, then use of standardized administration procedures may not provide a comparable administration of the test for that examinee. In this situation, the fundamental principle of sound practice is that examinees, regardless of background, should be provided with an adequate opportunity to complete the test and demonstrate their level of competence on the attributes the test is intended to measure. There may be, however, complex interactions among examiner, examinee, and situational variables

that require careful attention on the part of the practitioner administering the test. Factors that may affect the performance of the examinee include the cultural and linguistic background of both the examiner and examinee; the gender and testing style of the examiner; the level of acculturation of the examinee and examiner; whether the test is administered in the original language of the test, the examinee's primary language, or whether both languages are used (and if so in what order); the time limits of the testing; and whether a bilingual interpreter is used.

Use of Interpreters in Testing

Ideally, when an adequately translated version of the test or a suitable nonverbal test is unavailable, assessment of individuals with limited proficiency in the language of the test should be conducted by a professionally trained bilingual examiner. The bilingual examiner should be proficient in the language of the examinee at the level of a professional trained in that language. When a bilingual examiner is not available, an alternative is to use an interpreter in the testing process and administer the test in the examinee's native language. Although a commonly used procedure, this practice has some inherent difficulties. For example, there may be a lack of linguistic and cultural equivalence between the translation and the original test, the translator or the interpreter may not be adequately trained to work in the testing situation, and representative norms may not be available to score and interpret the test results appropriately. These difficulties may pose significant threats to the validity of inferences based on test results.

When the need for an interpreter arises for a particular testing situation, it is important to obtain a fully qualified interpreter to assist the examiner in administering the test. The most important consideration in testing with the services of an interpreter is the interpreter's ability and preparedness in carrying out the required duties during testing. The interpreter obviously needs to be fluent in both the language of the test and the examinee's native language and have general familiarity with the process of translating. To be effective, the interpreter also needs to have a basic understanding of the process of psychological and educational assessment, including the importance of following standardized procedures, the importance of accurately conveying to the examiner an examinee's actual responses, and the role and responsibilities of the interpreter in testing. Additionally, it is inappropriate for the interpreter to have any prior personal relationship with the test taker that is likely to jeopardize the objectivity of the test administration. However, in small linguistic or cultural communities, speakers of the alternate languages are often known to each other. Therefore, in such cases, it is the responsibility of the test user or examiner to ensure that the interpreter has received adequate instruction in the principles of objective test administration and to assess preexisting biases so that test interpretations can take such factors into account. If clear biases are evident and cannot be ameliorated, then the examiner should make arrangements to obtain another interpreter.

Whenever proficiency in the language of the test is essential to job performance, use of a translator to assist a candidate with licensure, certification, or civil service examinations should be permitted only when it will not compromise standards designed to protect public health, safety, and welfare. When a translator is permitted, it also is essential that the candidate not receive help interpreting the content of the test or any other assistance that would compromise the integrity of the licensure or certification decision. Creation of audio tapes that enable a candidate to listen to each question being read in the language of the test may be more appropriate when such an accommodation is justified.

In educational and psychological testing, it may be appropriate for an interpreter to become familiar with all details of test content and administration prior to the testing. Also, time needs to be provided for the interpreter to translate test instructions and items, if necessary. In psychological testing, it is often desirable for the examiner to demonstrate for the interpreter how certain test items are administered and explain what to expect during testing. In addition, it is important that, prior to the testing, the examiner and the interpreter become familiar with each other's style of speaking and the speed at which they work. Immediately prior to the assessment, the role of the interpreter needs to be explained clearly to the examinee. It is essential that the interpreter make all efforts to provide accurate information in translation. The interpreter must reflect a professional attitude and maintain objectivity throughout the testing process (e.g., not interject subjective opinions, not give cues to the examinee). Once the testing is completed, the examiner is responsible for reviewing the test responses with the assistance of the interpreter. Responses that are difficult to interpret (e.g., vocabulary words), nontest behaviors that might have special meanings (e.g., body language), as well as language factors (e.g., mixed use of two languages) and cultural factors that might have an effect on testing results need to be discussed fully. This information is to be used then by the examiner in carefully evaluating the test results and drawing inferences from the results.

Cultural Differences and Individual Testing

Linguistic behavior that may appear eccentric or be judged to be less appropriate in one culture may be seen as more appropriate in another culture and may need to be taken into account during the testing process. For example, children or adults from some cultures may be reluctant to speak in elaborate language to adults or people in higher status roles and instead may be encouraged to speak to such persons only in response to specific questions or with formulaic utterances. Thus, when tested, such test takers may respond to an examiner probing for elaborate speech with only short phrases or by shrugging their shoulders. Interpretations of scores resulting from such testing may prove to be inaccurate if this tendency is not properly taken into consideration. At the same time, the examiner should not presume that their reticence is necessarily a cultural characteristic. Additional information (e.g., prior observations or a family member's consultation) may be needed to discuss the extent of culture's possible influence on linguistic performance.

The values associated with the nature and degree of verbal output also may differ across cultures. One cultural group may judge verbosity or rapid speech as rude, whereas another may regard those speech patterns as indications of high mental ability or friendliness. An individual from one culture who is evaluated with values appropriate to another culture may be considered taciturn, withdrawn, or of low mental ability. Resulting interpretations and prescriptions of treatment may be invalid and potentially harmful to the individual being tested.

Standard 9.1

Testing practice should be designed to reduce threats to the reliability and validity of test score inferences that may arise from language differences.

Comment: Some tests are inappropriate for use with individuals whose knowledge of the language of the test is questionable. Assessment methods together with careful professional judgment are required to determine when language differences are relevant. Test users can judge how best to address this standard in a particular testing situation.

Standard 9.2

When credible research evidence reports that test scores differ in meaning across subgroups of linguistically diverse test takers, then to the extent feasible, test developers should collect for each linguistic subgroup studied the same form of validity evidence collected for the examinee population as a whole.

Comment: Linguistic subgroups may be found to differ with respect to appropriateness of test content, the internal structure of their test responses, the relation of their test scores to other variables, or the response processes employed by individual examinees. Any such findings need to receive due consideration in the interpretation and use of scores as well as in test revisions. There may also be legal or regulatory requirements to collect subgroup validity evidence. Not all forms of evidence can be examined separately for members of all linguistic groups. The validity argument may rely on existing research literature, for example, and such literature may not be available for some populations. For some kinds of evidence, separate linguistic subgroup analyses may not be feasible due to the limited number of cases available. Data may sometimes be accumulated so that these analyses can be performed after the test has been in use for a period of time. It is important to note that this standard calls for more than representativeness in the selection of samples used for validation or norming studies. Rather, it calls for separate, parallel analyses of data for members of different linguistic groups, sample sizes permitting. If a test is being used while such data are being collected, then cautionary statements are in order regarding the limitations of interpretations based on test scores.

Standard 9.3

When testing an examinee proficient in two or more languages for which the test is available, the examinee's relative language proficiencies should be determined. The test generally should be administered in the test taker's most proficient language, unless proficiency in the less proficient language is part of the assessment.

Comment: Unless the purpose of the testing is to determine proficiency in a particular language or the level of language proficiency required for the test is a work requirement, test users need to take into account the linguistic characteristics of examinees who are bilingual or use multiple languages. This may require the sole use of one language or use of multiple languages in order to minimize the introduction of construct-irrelevant components to the measurement process. For example, in educational settings, testing in both the language used in school and the native language of the examinee may be necessary in order to determine the optimal kind of instruction required by the examinee. Professional judgement needs to be used to determine the most appropriate procedures for establishing relative language proficiencies. Such procedures may range from self-identification by examinees through formal proficiency testing.

Standard 9.4

Linguistic modifications recommended by test publishers, as well as the rationale for the modifications, should be described in detail in the test manual.

Comment: Linguistic modifications may be recommended for the original test in the primary language or for an adapted version in a secondary language, or both. In any case, the test manual should provide appropriate information regarding the recommended modifications, their rationales, and the appropriate use of scores obtained using these linguistic modifications.

Standard 9.5

When there is credible evidence of score comparability across regular and modified tests or administrations, no flag should be attached to a score. When such evidence is lacking, specific information about the nature of the modification should be provided, if permitted by law, to assist test users properly to interpret and act on test scores.

Comment: The inclusion of a flag on a test score where a linguistic modification was provided may conflict with legal and social policy goals promoting fairness in the treatment of individuals of diverse linguistic backgrounds. If a score from a modified administration is comparable to a score from a nonmodified administration, there is no need for a flag. Similarly, if a modification is provided for which there is no reasonable basis for believing that the modification would affect score comparability, there is no need for a flag. Further, reporting practices that use asterisks or other non-specific symbols to indicate that a test's administration has been modified provide little useful information to test users.

Standard 9.6

When a test is recommended for use with linguistically diverse test takers, test developers and publishers should provide the information necessary for appropriate test use and interpretation.

Comment: Test developers should include in test manuals and in instructions for score interpretation explicit statements about the applicability of the test with individuals who are not native speakers of the original language of the test. However, it should be recognized that test developers and publishers seldom will find it feasible to conduct studies specific to the large number of linguistic groups found in certain countries.

Standard 9.7

When a test is translated from one language to another, the methods used in establishing the adequacy of the translation should be described, and empirical and logical evidence should be provided for score reliability and the validity of the translated test's score inferences for the uses intended in the linguistic groups to be tested.

Comment: For example, if a test is translated into Spanish for use with Mexican, Puerto Rican, Cuban, Central American, and Spanish populations, score reliability and the validity of test score inferences should be established with members of each of these groups separately where feasible. In addition, the test translation methods used need to be described in detail.

Standard 9.8

In employment and credentialing testing, the proficiency level required in the language of the test should not exceed that appropriate to the relevant occupation or profession.

Comment: Many occupations and professions require a suitable facility in the language of the test. In such cases, a test that is used as a part of selection, advancement, or credentialing may appropriately reflect that aspect of performance. However, the level of language proficiency required on the test should be no greater than the level needed to meet work requirements. Similarly, the modality in which language proficiency is assessed should be comparable to that on the job. For example, if the job requires only that employees understand verbal instructions in the language used on the job, it would be inappropriate for a selection test to require proficiency in reading and writing that particular language.

Standard 9.9

When multiple language versions of a test are intended to be comparable, test developers should report evidence of test comparability.

Comment: Evidence of test comparability may include but is not limited to evidence that the different language versions measure equivalent or similar constructs, and that score reliability and the validity of inferences from scores from the two versions are comparable.

Standard 9.10

Inferences about test takers' general language proficiency should be based on tests that measure a range of language features, and not on a single linguistic skill.

Comment: For example, a multiple-choice, pencil-and-paper test of vocabulary does not indicate how well a person understands the language when spoken nor how well the person speaks the language. However, the test score might be helpful in determining how well a person understands some aspects of the written language. In making educational placement decisions, a more complete range of communicative abilities (e.g., word knowledge, syntax) will typically need to be assessed.

Standard 9.11

When an interpreter is used in testing, the interpreter should be fluent in both the language of the test and the examinee's native language, should have expertise in translating, and should have a basic understanding of the assessment process.

Comment: Although individuals with limited proficiency in the language of the test should ideally be tested by professionally trained bilingual examiners, the use of an interpreter may be necessary in some situations. If an interpreter is required, the professional examiner is responsible for ensuring that the interpreter has the appropriate qualifications, experience, and preparation to assist appropriately in the administration of the test. It is necessary for the interpreter to understand the importance of following standardized procedures, how testing is conducted typically, the importance of accurately conveying to the examiner an examinee's actual responses, and the role and responsibilities of the interpreter in testing.

10. TESTING INDIVIDUALS WITH DISABILITIES

Background

With the advancement of scientific knowledge, medical practices, and social policies, increasing numbers of individuals with disabilities are participating more fully in educational, employment, and social activities. This increased participation has resulted in a greater need for the testing and assessment of individuals with disabilities for a variety of purposes. Individuals with disabilities are defined as persons possessing a physical, mental, or developmental impairment that substantially limits one or more of their major life activities. Although the *Standards* focus on technical and professional issues regarding the testing of individuals with disabilities, test developers and users are encouraged to become familiar with federal, state, and local laws, and court and administrative rulings that regulate the testing and assessment of individuals with disabilities.

Tests are administered to individuals with disabilities in various settings and for diverse purposes. For example, tests are used for diagnostic purposes to determine the existence and nature of a test taker's disabilities. Testing is also conducted for prescriptive purposes to determine intervention plans. In addition, tests are administered to persons who have been diagnosed with identified disabilities for educational and employment purposes to make placement, selection, or other similar decisions, or for monitoring performance as a tool for educational accountability. These uses of tests for persons with disabilities occur in a variety of contexts including school, clinical, counseling, forensic, employment, and credentialing.

Issues Regarding Accommodation When Testing Individuals With Disabilities

A major issue when testing individuals with disabilities concerns the use of accommoda-

tions, modifications, or adaptations. The purpose of these accommodations or modifications is to minimize the impact of test-taker attributes that are not relevant to the construct that is the primary focus of the assessment. The terms *accommodation* and *modification* have varying connotations in different subfields. Here accommodation is used as the general term for any action taken in response to a determination that an individual's disability requires a departure from established testing protocol. Depending on circumstances, such accommodation may include modification of test administration processes or modification of test content. No connotation that modification implies a change in the construct(s) being measured is intended.

A standardized test that has been designed for use with the general population may be inappropriate for use for individuals with specific disabilities if the test requires the use of sensory, motor, language, or psychological skills that are affected by the disability and that are not relevant to the focal construct. For example, a person who is blind may read only in Braille format, and an individual with hemiplegia may be unable to hold a pencil and thus would have difficulty completing a standard written exam. In addition, some individuals with disabilities may possess other attendant characteristics (e.g., a person with a physical disability may fatigue easily), causing them to be further challenged by some standardized testing situations. In these examples, if reading, use of a pencil, and fatigue are incidental to the construct intended to be measured by the test, modifications of tests and test administration procedures may be necessary for an accurate assessment.

Note also that accommodations are not needed or appropriate under a variety of circumstances. First, the disability may, in fact, be directly relevant to the focal construct. For example, no accommodation is appropriate for a person who is completely blind if the test is designed to measure visual spatial ability. Similarly, in employment testing it would be inappropriate to make test modifications if the test is designed to assess essential skills required for the job and the modifications would fundamentally alter the constructs being measured. Second, an accommodation for a particular disability is inappropriate when the purpose of a test is to diagnose the presence and degree of that disability. For example, allowing extra time on a timed test to assess the existence of a specific learning disability would make it very difficult to determine if a processing difficulty actually exists. Third, it is important to note that not all individuals with disabilities require special provisions when taking all tests. Many individuals have disabilities that would not influence their performance on a particular test, and hence no modification is needed.

Professional judgment necessarily plays a substantial role in decisions about test accommodations. Judgment comes into play in determining whether a particular individual needs accommodation and the nature and extent of such accommodation. In some circumstances, individuals with disabilities request testing accommodations and provide appropriate documentation in support of the request. Generally the request is reviewed by the agency sponsoring the assessment or an outside source knowledgeable about the assessment process and the type of disability. In either case, a conclusion is drawn as to what constitutes reasonable accommodation. Disagreement may arise between the accommodation requested by an individual with a disability and the granted accommodation. In these situations, and to the extent permitted by law, the overarching concern is the validity of the inference made from the score on the modified test: fairness to all parties is best served by a decision about test modification that results in the most accurate measure possible of the construct of interest. The role of professional judgment is further complicated by the fact that empirical research on test accommodations is often lacking.

When modifying tests it is also important to recognize that individuals with the same type of disability may differ considerably in their need for accommodation. A central consideration in determining a test modification for a disability is to recognize that the modifications should be tailored directly to the specific needs of individual test takers. As an example, it would be incorrect to make the assumption that all individuals with visual impairments would be successfully accommodated by providing testing materials in Braille format. Depending on the extent of the disability, it may be more appropriate for some individuals to receive testing materials written in large print, while others might need a tape cassette or reader.

As test modifications involve altering some aspect of a test originally developed for use with a target population, it is important to recognize that making these alterations has the potential to affect the psychometric qualities of the test. There have been few empirical investigations into the effects of various accommodations on the reliability of test scores or the validity of inferences drawn from modified tests. Due to a number of practical limitations (e.g., small sample size, nonrandom selection of test takers with disabilities), there is no precise, technical solution available for equating modified tests to the original form of these tests. Thus it is difficult to compare scores from a test modified for persons with disabilities with scores from the original test.

Modifications designed to accommodate persons with disabilities also may change the construct measured by the test, or the extent to which it is fully measured. For example, a test of oral comprehension may become a test of reading comprehension when administered in written format to a person who is deaf or hard of hearing. Such a change in test administration may alter the construct being measured by the original test. When this occurs, the scores on the standard and modified versions of the test will not have the same meaning. Similarly, modification of test administration may also alter the predictive value of test scores. For example, when a speed test is administered with relaxed time requirements to a person with a disability, the relationship of test scores to criteria such as job performance may be affected. Appropriate professional judgment should be exercised in interpreting and using scores on modified tests.

Some modified tests, with accompanying research to support the appropriate modifications, have been available for a number of years. Although the development of tests and testing procedures for individuals with disabilities is encouraged by the *Standards*, it should be noted that all relevant individual standards given elsewhere in this document are fully applicable to the testing applications and modifications or accommodations considered in this chapter. Issues of validity and reliability are critical whenever modifications or accommodations occur.

Strategies of Test Modification

A variety of test modification strategies have been implemented in various settings to accommodate the needs of test takers with disabilities. Some require modifying test administration procedures (e.g., instructions, response format) while others alter test medium, timing, settings, or content. Depending on the nature and extent of the disability, one or more test modification procedures may be appropriate for a particular individual. The listing here of a variety of modification strategies should not suggest that the full array of strategies is routinely available or appropriate; the decision to modify rests on a determination that modification is needed to make valid inferences about the individual's standing on the construct in question.

MODIFYING PRESENTATION FORMAT

One modification option is to alter the medium used to present the test instructions and items to the test takers. For example, a test booklet may be produced in Braille or large print for individuals with visual impairments. When tests are computer-administered, larger fonts or oversized computer screens may be used. Individuals with a hearing disability may receive test instructions through the use of sign communication or writing.

MODIFYING RESPONSE FORMAT

Modifications also can be made to allow individuals with disabilities to respond to test items using their preferred communication modality. For example, an individual with severe language deficits might be allowed to point to the preferred response. A test taker who cannot manually record answers to test items or questions may be assisted by an aide who would mark the answer. Other ways of obtaining a response include having the respondent use a tape recorder, a computer keyboard, or a Braillewriter.

MODIFYING TIMING

Another modification available is to alter the timing of tests. This may include extended time to complete the test, more breaks during testing, or extended testing sessions over several days. Many national testing programs (e.g., achievement, certification) allow persons with disabilities additional time to take the test. Reading Braille, using a cassette recorder, or having a reader may take longer than reading regular print. Reading large type may or may not be more time-consuming, depending on the layout of the material and on the nature and severity of the impairment.

MODIFYING TEST SETTING

Tests normally administered in group settings may be administered individually for a variety of purposes. Individual administration may avoid interference with others taking a test in a group. Some disabilities (e.g., attention deficit disorder) make it impractical to test in a group setting. Other alterations may include changing the testing location if it is not wheelchair accessible, providing tables or chairs that provide greater physical support, or altering the lighting conditions for individuals who are visually impaired.

Using Only Portions of a Test

Another strategy of test accommodation involves the use of portions of a test in assessing persons with disabilities. These procedures are sometimes used in clinical testing when certain subparts of a test require physical, sensory, language, or other capabilities that a test taker with disabilities does not have. This approach is commonly used in cognitive and achievement testing when the physical or sensory limitations of an individual interfere with the ability to perform on a test. For example, if a cognitive ability test includes items presented orally combined with items presented in a written fashion, the orally-presented items might be omitted when the test is given to an individual with a hearing disability as they will not provide an adequate assessment of that individual's cognitive ability. Results on such items are more likely to reflect the individual's hearing difficulty rather than his or her true cognitive ability. Although omitting test items may represent an effective accommodation technique, it may also prevent the test from adequately measuring the intended skills or abilities, especially if those skills or abilities are of central interest. For example, it should be noted that eliminating a portion of the test may not be appropriate in situations such as certification testing and employment testing where the construct measured by the each portion may represent a separate and necessary job or occupational requirement.

Using Substitute Tests or Alternate Assessments

One additional modification is to replace a test standardized on the general population with a test or alternate assessment that has been specially designed for individuals with disabilities. More valid results may be obtained through the use of a test specifically designed for use with individuals with disabilities. Although a substitute test may represent a desirable accommodation solution, it may be difficult to find an adequate replacement that measures the same construct with comparable technical quality,

and for which scores can be placed on the same scale as the original test.

Using Modifications in Different Testing Contexts

There are important contextual differences between the individualized use of tests, as in the case of clinical diagnosis, and group or large-scale testing, as in the case of testing for academic achievement, employment, credentialing, or admissions.

Individual diagnostic testing is conducted typically for clinical or educational purposes. In these contexts a highly qualified test professional (e.g., a licensed or certified psychologist) is responsible for the entire assessment process of test selection, administration, interpretation, and reporting of results. The test professional seeks to gather appropriate information about the client's specific disability and preferred modality of communication and uses this information to determine the accommodations appropriate for the test taker. During the assessment process, any modified tests are used along with other assessment methods to collect data about the client's functioning in relevant areas. Inferences are then made based on this multitude of information. Test modifications may be used during assessment not only out of necessity but also as a source of clinical insight about the client's functioning. For example, a test taker with obsessive compulsive disorder may be allowed to continue to complete a test item, subtest, or a total test beyond the standardized time limits. Although in such cases the performance of the test taker cannot be judged according to the standardized scoring standards, the fact that the test taker could produce a successful performance with extra time often aids clinical interpretation.

The use of test modifications in large-scale testing is different, however. Large-scale testing is used for purposes such as measurement of academic achievement, program evaluation, credentialing, licensure, and employment. In these contexts, a standardized test usually is administered to all test participants. Large numbers of test takers are not uncommon, and decisions may in some cases be made solely on the basis of test information, as in the case of a test used as an initial screening device in an employment context. In some cases, decision making requires the comparison of test takers, as in selection or admission contexts where the number of applicants may greatly exceed the number of available openings. This context highlights the need for concern for fairness to all parties, as comparisons must be made between test scores obtained by individuals with disabilities taking modified tests and scores obtained by individuals under regular conditions. While test takers should not be disadvantaged due to a disability not relevant to the construct the test is intended to assess, the resulting accommodation should not put those taking a modified test at an undue advantage over those tested under regular conditions. As research on the comparability of scores under regular and modified conditions is sometimes limited, decisions about appropriate accommodation in these contexts involve important and difficult professional judgments.

Reporting Scores on Modified Tests

The practice of reporting scores on modified tests varies in different contexts. In individual testing, the test professional commonly reports when tests have been administered in a nonstandardized fashion when providing test scores. Typically, the steps used in making test accommodations or modifications are described in the test report, and the validity of the inferences resulting from the modified test scores is discussed. This practice of reporting the nature of modifications is consistent with implied requirements to communicate information as to the nature of the assessment process if the modifications impact the reliability of test scores or the validity of inferences drawn from test scores.

On the other hand, the reporting of test scores from modified tests in large-scale test-

ing has created considerable debate. Often when scores from a nonstandardized version of a test are reported, the score report contains an asterisk next to the score or some other designation, often called a *flag*, to indicate that the test administration was modified. Sometimes recipients of these special designations are informed of the meaning of the designation; many times no information is provided about the nature of the modification made. Some argue that reporting scores from nonstandard test administrations without special identification misleads test users and perhaps even harms test takers with disabilities, whose scores may not accurately reflect their abilities. Others, however, argue that identifying scores of test takers with disabilities as resulting from nonstandard administrations unfairly labels these test takers as persons with disabilities, stigmatizes them, and may deny them the opportunity to compete equally with test takers without disabilities when they might otherwise be able to do so. Federal laws and the laws of most states bar discrimination against persons with disabilities, require individualized reasonable accommodations in testing, and limit practices that could stigmatize persons with disabilities, particularly in educational, admissions, credentialing, and employment testing.

The fundamental principles relevant here are that important information about test score meaning should not be withheld from test users who interpret and act on the test scores, and that irrelevant information should not be provided. When there is sufficient evidence of score comparability across regular and modified administrations, there is no need for any sort of flagging. When such evidence is lacking, an undifferentiated flag provides only very limited information to the test user, and specific information about the nature of the modification is preferable, if permitted by law.

Standard 10.1

In testing individuals with disabilities, test developers, test administrators, and test users should take steps to ensure that the test score inferences accurately reflect the intended construct rather than any disabilities and their associated characteristics extraneous to the intent of the measurement.

Comment: Chapter 1 (Validity) deals more broadly with the critical requirement that a test score reflects the intended construct. The need to attend to the possibility of construct-irrelevant variance resulting from a test taker's disability is an example of this general principle. In some settings, test users are prohibited from inquiring about a test taker's disability, making the standard contingent on test taker self-report of a disability or a need for accommodation.

Standard 10.2

People who make decisions about accommodations and test modification for individuals with disabilities should be knowledgeable of existing research on the effects of the disabilities in question on test performance. Those who modify tests should also have access to psychometric expertise for so doing.

Comment: In some areas there may be little known about the effects of a particular disability on performance on a particular type of test.

Standard 10.3

Where feasible, tests that have been modified for use with individuals with disabilities should be pilot tested on individuals who have similar disabilities to investigate the appropriateness and feasibility of the modifications.

Comment: Although useful guides for modifying tests are available, they do not provide a universal substitute for trying out a modified test. Even when such tryouts are conducted

on samples inadequate to produce norm data, they are useful for checking the mechanics of the modifications. In many circumstances, however, lack of ready access to individuals with similar disabilities, or an inability to postpone decision making, make this unfeasible.

Standard 10.4

If modifications are made or recommended by test developers for test takers with specific disabilities, the modifications as well as the rationale for the modifications should be described in detail in the test manual and evidence of validity should be provided whenever available. Unless evidence of validity for a given inference has been established for individuals with the specific disabilities, test developers should issue cautionary statements in manuals or supplementary materials regarding confidence in interpretations based on such test scores.

Comment: When test developers and users intend that a modified version of a test should be interpreted as comparable to an unmodified one, evidence of test score comparability should be provided.

Standard 10.5

Technical material and manuals that accompany modified tests should include a careful statement of the steps taken to modify the tests to alert users to changes that are likely to alter the validity of inferences drawn from the test score.

Comment: If empirical evidence of the nature and effects of changes resulting from modifying standard tests is lacking, it is impossible to assess the impact of significant modifications. Documentation of the procedures used to modify tests will not only aid in the administration and interpretation of the given test but will also inform others who are modifying tests for people with spe-

cific disabilities. This standard should apply to both test developers and test users.

Standard 10.6

If a test developer recommends specific time limits for people with disabilities, empirical procedures should be used, whenever possible, to establish time limits for modified forms of timed tests rather than simply allowing test takers with disabilities a multiple of the standard time. When possible, fatigue should be investigated as a potentially important factor when time limits are extended.

Comment: Such empirical evidence is likely only in the limited settings where a sufficient number of individuals with similar disabilities are tested. Not all individuals with the same disability, however, necessarily require the same accommodation. In most cases, professional judgment based on available evidence regarding the appropriate time limits given the nature of an individual's disability will be the basis for decisions. Legal requirements may be relevant to any decision on absolute time limits.

Standard 10.7

When sample sizes permit, the validity of inferences made from test scores and the reliability of scores on tests administered to individuals with various disabilities should be investigated and reported by the agency or publisher that makes the modification. Such investigations should examine the effects of modifications made for people with various disabilities on resulting scores, as well as the effects of administering standard unmodified tests to them.

Comment: In addition to modifying tests and test administration procedures for people who have disabilities, evidence of validity for inferences drawn from these tests is needed. Validation is the only way to amass knowledge about the usefulness of modified tests

for people with disabilities. The costs of obtaining validity evidence should be considered in light of the consequences of not having usable information regarding the meanings of scores for people with disabilities. This standard is feasible in the limited circumstances where a sufficient number of individuals with the same level or degree of a given disability is available.

Standard 10.8

Those responsible for decisions about test use with potential test takers who may need or may request specific accommodations should (a) possess the information necessary to make an appropriate selection of measures, (b) have current information regarding the availability of modified forms of the test in question, (c) inform individuals, when appropriate, about the existence of modified forms, and (d) make these forms available to test takers when appropriate and feasible.

Standard 10.9

When relying on norms as a basis for score interpretation in assessing individuals with disabilities, the norm group used depends upon the purpose of testing. Regular norms are appropriate when the purpose involves the test taker's functioning relative to the general population. If available, normative data from the population of individuals with the same level or degree of disability should be used when the test taker's functioning relative to individuals with similar disabilities is at issue.

Standard 10.10

Any test modifications adopted should be appropriate for the individual test taker, while maintaining all feasible standardized features. A test professional needs to consider reasonably available information about each test taker's experiences, characteristics, and capabilities that might impact test performance, and document the grounds for the modification.

Standard 10.11

When there is credible evidence of score comparability across regular and modified administrations, no flag should be attached to a score. When such evidence is lacking, specific information about the nature of the modification should be provided, if permitted by law, to assist test users properly to interpret and act on test scores.

Comment: The inclusion of a flag on a test score where an accommodation for a disability was provided may conflict with legal and social policy goals promoting fairness in the treatment of individuals with disabilities. If a score from a modified administration is comparable to a score from a nonmodified administration, there is no need for a flag. Similarly, if a modification is provided for which there is no reasonable basis for believing that the modification would affect score comparability, there is no need for a flag. Further, reporting practices that use asterisks or other nonspecific symbols to indicate that a test's administration has been modified provide little useful information to test users. When permitted by law, if a nonstandardized administration is to be reported because evidence does not exist to support score comparability, then this report should avoid referencing the existence or nature of the test taker's disability and should instead report only the nature of the accommodation provided, such as extended time for testing, the use of a reader, or the use of a tape recorder.

Standard 10.12

In testing individuals with disabilities for diagnostic and intervention purposes, the test should not be used as the sole indicator of the test taker's functioning. Instead, multiple sources of information should be used.

Comment: For example, when assessing the intellectual functioning of persons with mental retardation, results from an individually administered intelligence test are generally supplemented with other pertinent information, such as case history, information about school functioning, and results from other cognitive tests and adaptive behavior measures. In addition, at times a multidisciplinary evaluation (e.g., physical, psychological, linguistic, neurological, etc.) may be needed to yield an accurate picture of the person's functioning.

PART III

Testing Applications

11. THE RESPONSIBILITIES OF TEST USERS

Background

Previous chapters have dealt primarily with the responsibilities of those who develop, market, evaluate, or mandate the administration of tests and the rights and obligations of test takers. Many of the standards in these chapters, and in the chapters that follow, refer to the development of tests and their use in specific settings. The present chapter includes standards of a more general nature that apply in almost all measurement contexts. In particular, attention is centered on the responsibilities of those who may be considered the *users* of tests. This group includes psychologists, educators, and other professionals who select the specific instruments or supervise test administration—on their own authority or at the behest of others. It also includes all individuals who actively participate in the interpretation and use of test results, other than the test takers themselves.

It is presumed that a legitimate educational, psychological, or employment purpose justifies the time and expense of test administration. In most settings, the user communicates this purpose to those who have a legitimate interest in the measurement process and subsequently conveys the implications of examinee performance to those entitled to receive the information. Depending on the measurement setting, this group may include individual test takers, parents and guardians, educators, employers, policymakers, the courts, or the general public.

Where administration of tests or use of test data is mandated for a specific population by governmental authorities, educational institutions, licensing boards, or employers, the developer and user of an instrument may be essentially the same. In such settings, there often is no clear separation between the professional responsibilities of those who produce the instrument and those who administer the test and interpret the results. Instruments produced by independent publishers, on the other hand, present a somewhat different picture. Typically, these tests will be used with a variety of populations and for diverse purposes.

The conscientious developer of a standardized test attempts to screen and educate potential users. Furthermore, most publishers and test sponsors work vigorously to prevent the misuse of standardized measures and the misinterpretation of individual scores and group averages. Test manuals often illustrate sound and unsound interpretations and applications. Some identify specific practices that are not appropriate and should be discouraged. Despite the best efforts of test developers, however, appropriate test use and sound interpretation of test scores are likely to remain primarily the responsibility of the test user.

Test takers, parents and guardians, legislators, policymakers, the media, the courts, and the public at large often yearn for unambiguous interpretations of test data. In particular, they often tend to attribute positive or negative results, including group differences, to a single factor or to the conditions that prevail in one social institution—most often, the home or the school. These consumers of test data frequently press for explicit rationales for decisions that are based only in part on test scores. The wise test user helps all interested parties understand that sound decisions regarding test use and score interpretation involve an element of professional judgment. It is not always obvious to the consumers that the choice of various information-gathering procedures often involves experience that is not easily quantified or verbalized. The user can help them appreciate the fact that the weighting of quantitative data, educational and occupational information, behavioral observations, anecdotal reports, and other relevant data often cannot be specified precisely.

Because of the appearance of objectivity and numerical precision, test data are sometimes allowed to totally override other sources of evidence about test takers. There are circumstances in which selection based exclusively on test scores may be appropriate. For example, this may be the case in pre-employment screening. But in educational and psychological settings, test users are well advised, and may be legally required, to consider other relevant sources of information on test takers, not just test scores. In the latter situations, the psychologist or educator familiar with the local setting and with local test takers is best qualified to integrate this diverse information effectively.

As reliance on test results has grown in recent years, greater pressure has been placed on test users to explain to the public the rationale for test-based decisions. More than ever before, test users are called upon to defend their testing practices. They do this by documenting that their test uses and score interpretations are supported by measurement authorities for the given purpose, that the inferences drawn from their instruments are validated for use with a given population, and that the results are being used in conjunction with other information, not in isolation. If these conditions are met, the test user can convincingly defend the decisions made or the administrative actions taken in which tests played a part.

It is not appropriate for these *Standards* to dictate minimal levels of test-criterion correlation, classification accuracy, or reliability for any given purpose. Such levels depend on whether decisions must be made immediately on the strength of the best available evidence, however weak, or whether decisions can be delayed until better evidence becomes available. But it is appropriate to expect the user to ascertain what the alternatives are, what the quality and consequences of these alternatives are, and whether a delay in decision making would be beneficial. Cost-benefit compromises become necessary in test use, as they often are in test development. It should be noted, however, that in some contexts legal requirements may place limits on the extent to which such compromises can be made. As with standards for the various phases of test development, when relevant standards are not met in test use, the reasons should be persuasive. The greater the potential impact on test takers, for good or ill, the greater the need to identify and satisfy the relevant standards.

In selecting a test and interpreting a test score, the test user is expected to have a clear understanding of the purposes of the testing and its probable consequences. The knowledgeable user has definite ideas on how to achieve these purposes and how to avoid bias, unfairness, and undesirable consequences. In subscribing to these *Standards*, test publishers and agencies mandating test use agree to provide information on the strengths and weaknesses of their instruments. They accept the responsibility to warn against likely misinterpretations by unsophisticated interpreters of individual scores or aggregated data. However, the ultimate responsibility for appropriate test use and interpretation lies predominantly with the test user. In assuming this responsibility, the user must become knowledgeable about a test's appropriate uses and the populations for which it is suitable. The user must also become adept, particularly in statewide and community-wide assessment programs, in communicating the implications of test results to those entitled to receive them.

In some instances, users may be obligated to collect additional evidence about a test's technical quality. For example, if performance assessments are locally scored, evidence of the degree of inter-scorer agreement may be required. Users also should be alert to the probable local consequences of test use, particularly in the case of large-scale testing programs. If the same test material is used in successive years, users should actively monitor the program to ensure that reuse has not compromised the integrity of the results.

Some of the standards that follow reiterate ideas contained in other chapters, principally chapter 5 "Test Administration, Scoring, and Reporting," chapter 7 "Fairness in Testing and Test Use," chapter 8 "Rights and Responsibilities of Test Takers," and chapter 13 "Educational Testing and Assessment." This repetition is intentional. It permits an enumeration in one chapter of the major obligations that must be assumed largely by the test administrator and user, though these responsibilities may refer to topics that are covered more fully in other chapters.

Standard 11.1

Prior to the adoption and use of a published test, the test user should study and evaluate the materials provided by the test developer. Of particular importance are those that summarize the test's purposes, specify the procedures for test administration, define the intended populations of test takers, and discuss the score interpretations for which validity and reliability data are available.

Comment: A prerequisite to sound test use is knowledge of the materials accompanying the instrument. As a minimum, these include manuals provided by the test developer. Ideally, the user should be conversant with relevant studies reported in the professional literature. The degree of reliability and validity required for sound score interpretations depends on the test's role in the assessment process and the potential impact of the process on the people involved. The test user should be aware of legal restrictions that may constrain the use of the test. On occasion, professional judgment may lead to the use of instruments for which there is little documentation of validity for the intended purpose. In these situations, the user should interpret scores cautiously and take care not to imply that the decisions or inferences are based on test results that are well-documented with respect to reliability or validity.

Standard 11.2

When a test is to be used for a purpose for which little or no documentation is available, the user is responsible for obtaining evidence of the test's validity and reliability for this purpose.

Comment: The individual who uses test scores for purposes that are not specifically recommended by the test developer is responsible for collecting the necessary validity evidence. Support for such uses may sometimes be found in the professional literature. If previous evidence is not sufficient, then additional data should be collected. The provisions of this standard should not be construed to prohibit the generation of hypotheses from test data. For example, though some clinical tests have limited or contradictory validity evidence for common uses, clinicians generate hypotheses based appropriately on examinee responses to such tests. However, these hypotheses should be clearly labeled as tentative. Interested parties should be made aware of the potential limitations of the test scores in such situations.

Standard 11.3

Responsibility for test use should be assumed by or delegated only to those individuals who have the training, professional credentials, and experience necessary to handle this responsibility. Any special qualifications for test administration or interpretation specified in the test manual should be met.

Comment: Test users should not attempt to interpret the scores of test takers whose special needs or characteristics are outside the range of the user's qualifications. This standard has special significance in areas such as clinical testing, forensic testing, testing in special education, testing people with disabilities or limited exposure to the dominant culture, and in other such situations where potential impact is great. When the situation falls outside the user's experience, assistance should be obtained. A number of professional organizations have codes of ethics that specify the qualifications of those who administer tests and interpret scores.

Standard 11.4

The test user should have a clear rationale for the intended uses of a test or evaluation procedure in terms of its validity and contribution to the assessment and decision-making process.

Comment: Justification for the role of each instrument in selection, diagnosis, classification, and decision making should be arrived

at before test administration, not afterwards. Preferably, the rationale should be available in printed materials prepared by the test publisher or by the user.

Standard 11.5

Those who have a legitimate interest in an assessment should be informed about the purposes of testing, how tests will be administered, the factors considered in scoring examinee responses, how the scores are typically used, how long the records will be retained, and to whom and under what conditions the records may be released.

Comment: This standard has greater relevance and application to educational and clinical testing than to employment testing. In most uses of tests for screening job applicants and applicants to educational programs, for licensing professionals and awarding credentials, or for measuring achievement, the purposes of testing and the uses to be made of the test scores are obvious to the examinee. Nevertheless, it is wise to communicate this information at least briefly even in these settings. In some situations, however, the rationale for the testing may be clear to relatively few test takers. In such settings, a more detailed and explicit discussion may be called for. Retention and release of records, even when such release would clearly benefit the examinee, are often governed by statutes or institutional practices. As relevant, examinees should be informed about these constraints and procedures.

Standard 11.6

Unless the circumstances clearly require that the test results be withheld, the test user is obligated to provide a timely report of the results that is understandable to the test taker and others entitled to receive this information.

Comment: The nature of score reports is often dictated by practical considerations. In some cases only a terse printed report may be feasible. In others, it may be desirable to provide both an oral and a written report. The interpretation should vary according to the level of sophistication of the recipient. When the examinee is a young child, an explanation of the test results is typically provided to parents or guardians. Feedback in the form of a score report or interpretation is not typically provided when tests are administered for personnel selection or promotion.

Standard 11.7

Test users have the responsibility to protect the security of tests, to the extent that developers enjoin users to do so.

Comment: When tests are used for purposes of selection, licensure, or educational accountability, the need for rigorous protection of test security is obvious. On the other hand, when educational tests are not part of a high-stakes program, some publishers consider teacher review of test materials to be a legitimate tool in clarifying teacher perceptions of the skills measured by a test. Consistency and clarity in the definition of acceptable and unacceptable practices is critical in such situations. When tests are involved in litigation, inspection of the instruments should be restricted—to the extent permitted by law—to those who are legally or ethically obligated to safeguard test security.

Standard 11.8

Test users have the responsibility to respect test copyrights.

Comment: Legally and ethically, test users may not reproduce copyrighted materials for routine test use without consent of the copyright holder. These materials—in both paper and electronic form—include test items, ancillary forms such as answer sheets or profile forms, scoring templates, conversion tables of raw scores to derived scores, and tables of norms.

Standard 11.9

Test users should remind test takers and others who have access to test materials that the legal rights of test publishers, including copyrights, and the legal obligations of other participants in the testing process may prohibit the disclosure of test items without specific authorization.

Standard 11.10

Test users should be alert to the possibility of scoring errors; they should arrange for rescoring if individual scores or aggregated data suggest the need for it.

Comment: The costs of scoring error are great, particularly in high-stakes testing programs. In some cases, rescoring may be requested by the test taker. If such a test taker right is recognized in published materials, it should be respected. In educational testing programs, users should not depend entirely on test takers to alert them to the possibility of scoring errors. Monitoring scoring accuracy should be a routine responsibility of testing program administrators wherever feasible.

Standard 11.11

If the integrity of a test taker's scores is challenged, local authorities, the test developer, or the test sponsor should inform the test takers of their relevant rights, including the possibility of appeal and representation by counsel.

Comment: Proctors in entrance or licensure testing programs may report irregularities in the test process that result in challenges. University admissions officers may raise challenges when test scores are grossly inconsistent with other applicant information. Test takers should be apprised of their rights in such situations.

Standard 11.12

Test users or the sponsoring agency should explain to test takers their opportunities, if any, to retake an examination; users should also indicate whether the earlier as well as later scores will be reported to those entitled to receive the score reports.

Comment: Some testing programs permit test takers to retake an examination several times, to cancel scores, or to have scores withheld from potential recipients. If test takers have such privileges, they and score recipients should be so informed.

Standard 11.13

When test-taking strategies that are unrelated to the domain being measured are found to enhance or adversely affect test performance significantly, these strategies and their implications should be explained to all test takers before the test is administered. This may be done either in an information booklet or, if the explanation can be made briefly, along with the test directions.

Comment: Test-taking strategies, such as guessing, skipping time-consuming items, or initially skipping and then returning to difficult items as time allows, can influence test scores positively or negatively. The effects of various strategies depend on the scoring system used and aspects of item and test design such as speededness or the number of response alternatives provided in multiple-choice items. Differential use of such strategies by test takers can affect the validity and reliability of test score interpretations. The goal of test directions should be to convey information on the possible effectiveness of various strategies and, thus, to provide all test takers an equal opportunity to perform optimally. The use of such strategies by all test takers should be encouraged if their effect facilitates performance and discouraged if their effect interferes with performance.

Standard 11.14

Test users are obligated to protect the privacy of examinees and institutions that are involved in a measurement program, unless a disclosure of private information is agreed upon, or is specifically authorized by law.

Comment: Protection of the privacy of individual examinees is a well-established principle in psychological and educational measurement. In some instances, test takers and test administrators may formally agree to a lesser degree of protection than the law appears to require. In other circumstances, test users and testing agencies may adopt more stringent restrictions on the communication and sharing of test results than relevant law dictates. The more rigorous standards sometimes arise through the codes of ethics adopted by relevant professional organizations. In some testing programs the conditions for disclosure are stated to the examinee prior to testing, and taking the test can constitute agreement for the disclosure of test score information as specified. In other programs, the test taker or his/her parents or guardians must formally agree to any disclosure of test information to individuals or agencies other than those specified in the test administrator's published literature. It should be noted that the right of the public and the media to examine the aggregate test results of public school systems is guaranteed in some states.

Standard 11.15

Test users should be alert to potential misinterpretations of test scores and to possible unintended consequences of test use; users should take steps to minimize or avoid foreseeable misinterpretations and unintended negative consequences.

Comment: Well-meaning, but unsophisticated, audiences may adopt simplistic interpretations of test results or may attribute high or low scores or averages to a single causal factor.

Experienced test users can sometimes anticipate such misinterpretations and should try to prevent them. Obviously, not every unintended consequence can be anticipated. What is required is a reasonable effort to prevent negative consequences and to encourage sound interpretations.

Standard 11.16

Test users should verify periodically that their interpretations of test data continue to be appropriate, given any significant changes in their population of test takers, their modes of test administration, and their purposes in testing.

Comment: Over time, a gradual change in the demographic characteristics of an examinee population may significantly affect the inferences drawn from group averages. The accommodations made in test administration in recognition of examinee disabilities or in response to unforeseen circumstances may also affect interpretations.

Standard 11.17

In situations where the public is entitled to receive a summary of test results, test users should formulate a policy regarding timely release of the results and apply that policy consistently over time.

Comment: In school testing programs, districts commonly viewed as a coherent group may avoid controversy by adopting the same policies regarding the release of test results. If one district routinely releases aggregated data in much greater detail than another, groundless suspicions can develop that information is being suppressed in the latter district.

Standard 11.18

When test results are released to the public or to policymakers, those responsible for the release should provide and explain any supplemental information that will minimize possible misinterpretations of the data.

Comment: Preliminary briefings prior to the release of test results can give reporters for the news media an opportunity to assimilate relevant data. Misinterpretation can often be the result of the limited time reporters have to prepare media reports or inadequate presentation of information that bears on test score interpretation. It should be recognized, however, that the interests of the media are not always consistent with the intended purposes of measurement programs.

Standard 11.19

When a test user contemplates an approved change in test format, mode of administration, instructions, or the language used in administering the test, the user should have a sound rationale for concluding that validity, reliability, and appropriateness of norms will not be compromised.

Comment: In some instances, minor changes in format or mode of administration may be reasonably expected, without evidence, to have little or no effect on validity, reliability, and appropriateness of norms. In other instances, however, changes in format or administrative procedures can be assumed a priori to have significant effects. When a given modification becomes widespread, consideration should be given to validation and norming under the modified conditions.

Standard 11.20

In educational, clinical, and counseling settings, a test taker's score should not be interpreted in isolation; collateral information that may lead to alternative explanations for the examinee's test performance should be considered.

Comment: It is neither necessary nor feasible to make an intensive review of every test taker's score. In some settings there may be little or no collateral information of value. In counseling, clinical, and educational settings, however, considerable relevant information is likely to be available. Obvious alternative explanations of low scores include low motivation, limited fluency in the language of the test, unfamiliarity with cultural concepts on which test items are based, and perceptual or motor impairments. In clinical and counseling settings, the test user should not ignore how well the test taker is functioning in daily life.

Standard 11.21

Test users should not rely on computer-generated interpretations of test results unless they have the expertise to consider the appropriateness of these interpretations in individual cases.

Comment: The scoring agency has the responsibility of documenting the basis for the interpretations. The user of a computerized scoring and reporting service has the obligation to be familiar with the principles on which such interpretations were derived. The user should have the ability to evaluate a computer-based score interpretation in the light of other relevant evidence on each test taker. Automated, narrative reports are not a substitute for sound professional judgment.

Standard 11.22

When circumstances require that a test be administered in the same language to all examinees in a linguistically diverse population, the test user should investigate the validity of the score interpretations for test takers believed to have limited proficiency in the language of the test.

Comment: The achievement, abilities, and traits of examinees who do not speak the language of the test as their primary language may be seriously mismeasured by the test.

The scores of test takers with severe linguistic limitations will probably be meaningless. If language proficiency is not relevant to the purposes of testing, the test user should consider excusing these individuals, without prejudice, from taking the test and substituting alternative evaluation methods. However, it is recognized that such actions may be impractical, unnecessary, or legally unacceptable in some settings.

Standard 11.23

If a test is mandated for persons of a given age or all students in a particular grade, users should identify individuals whose disabilities or linguistic background indicates the need for special accommodations in test administration and ensure that these accommodations are employed.

Comment: Appropriate accommodations depend upon the nature of the test and the needs of the test taker. The mandating authority has primary responsibility for defining the acceptable accommodations for various categories of test takers. The user must take responsibility for identifying those test takers who fall within these categories and implement the appropriate accommodations.

Standard 11.24

When a major purpose of testing is to describe the status of a local, regional, or particular examinee population, the program criteria for inclusion or exclusion of individuals should be strictly adhered to.

Comment: In census-type programs, biased results can arise from the exclusion of particular subgroups of students. Financial and other advantages may accrue either from exaggerating or from reducing the proportion of high-achieving or low-achieving students. Clearly, these are unprofessional practices.

12. PSYCHOLOGICAL TESTING AND ASSESSMENT

Background

This chapter addresses issues important to professionals who use psychological tests with their clients. Topics include test selection and administration, test interpretation, collateral information used in psychological testing, types of tests, and purposes of testing. The types of psychological tests reviewed in this chapter include cognitive and neuropsychological; adaptive, social, and problem behavior; family and couples; personality; and vocational. In addition, the chapter includes an overview of four common uses of psychological tests: diagnosis; intervention planning and outcome evaluation; legal and governmental decisions; and personal awareness, growth, and action.

Employment testing is another context in which psychological testing is used. The standards in this chapter are applicable to those employment settings in which individual in-depth assessment is conducted (e.g., an evaluation of a candidate for a senior executive position). Employment settings in which tests are designed to measure specific job-related characteristics across multiple candidates are treated in the text and standards of chapter 14.

For all professionals who use tests, knowledge of cultural background and physical capabilities that influence (a) a test taker's development, (b) the methods for obtaining and conveying information, and (c) the planning and implementation of interventions is critical. Therefore, readers are encouraged to review chapters 7, 8, 9, and 10 that discuss fairness and bias in testing, the rights and responsibilities of test takers, testing individuals of diverse linguistic backgrounds, and testing individuals with disabilities. Readers will find important additional detail on validity; reliability; test development; scaling; test administration, scoring, and reporting; and general responsibilities of test users in chapters 1, 2, 3, 4, 5, and 11, respectively.

The use of tests provides one method of collecting information within the larger framework of a psychological assessment of an individual. Typically, psychological assessments involve an interaction between a professional who is trained and experienced in testing and a client. Clients may include patients, counselees, parents, employees, employers, attorneys, students, and other responsible parties who are test takers or who use the test results contained in psychological reports.

The results from tests and inventories, used within the context of a psychological assessment, may help the professional to understand the client more fully and to develop more informed and accurate hypotheses, inferences, and decisions about a client's situation. A psychological assessment is a comprehensive examination undertaken to answer specific questions about a client's psychological functioning during a particular time interval or to predict a client's psychological functioning in the future. An assessment may include administering and scoring tests, and interpreting test scores, all within the context of the individual's personal history. Inasmuch as test scores characteristically are interpreted in the context of other information about the client, an individual psychological assessment usually also includes interviewing the client; observing client behavior; reviewing educational, psychological, and other relevant records; and integrating these findings with other information that may be provided by third parties. The tasks of a psychological assessment—collecting, evaluating, integrating, and reporting salient information relevant to those aspects of a client's functioning that are under examination—comprise a complex and sophisticated set of professional activities.

The interpretation of tests and inventories can be a valuable part of the intervention process and, if used appropriately, can provide useful information to clients as well as to other users of the test interpretation. For example, the results of tests and inventories may be used to assess the psychological functioning of an individual; to assign diagnostic classifications; to detect neuropsychological impairment; to assess cognitive and personality strengths, vocational interests, and values; to determine developmental stages; and to evaluate treatment outcomes. Test results also may provide information used to make decisions that have a powerful and lasting impact on people's lives (e.g., vocational and educational decision making; diagnosis; treatment planning; selection decisions; intervention and outcome evaluation; parole, sentencing, civil commitment, child custody, and competency to stand trial decisions; and personal injury litigation).

TEST SELECTION AND ADMINISTRATION

Prior to beginning the assessment process, the test taker should understand who will have access to the test results and the written report, how test results will be shared with the test taker, and if and when decisions based on the test results will be shared with the test taker and/or a third party. The assessment process begins by clarifying, as much as is possible, the reasons for which a client is presented for assessment. Guided by these reasons or other relevant concerns, the tests, inventories, and diagnostic procedures to be used are chosen, and other sources of information needed to evaluate the client and the referral issues are identified. The professional reviews more than the name of the test in choosing a test and is guided by the validity and reliability evidence and the applicability of the normative data available in the test's accumulated research literature. In addition to being thoroughly versed in proper administrative procedure, the professional is responsible for being familiar with the validity and reliability evidence for the intended use and purposes of the tests and inventories selected and for being prepared to develop a logical analysis that supports the various facets of the assessment and the inferences made from the assessment.

Validity and reliability considerations are paramount, but the demographic characteristics (e.g., gender, age, income, sociocultural and language background, education and other socioeconomic variables) of the group for which the test was originally constructed and for which initial and subsequent normative data are available also are important test selection issues. Selecting a test with demographically appropriate normative groups relevant for the client being tested is important to the generalizability of the inferences that the professional seeks to make. Sometimes the items or tasks contained in a test are designed for a particular group and are viewed as irrelevant for another group. A test constructed for one group may be applied to other groups with appropriate qualifications that explain the test choice based on the supporting research data and on professional experience.

The selection of psychological tests and inventories, for a particular client, often is individualized. However, in some settings a predetermined battery of tests may be taken by all participants, and group interpretations may be provided. The test taker may be a child, an adolescent, or an adult. The settings in which the tests or inventories are used include (but are not limited to) preschool, elementary, middle, or secondary schools; colleges or universities; pre-employment or employment settings; mental health or outpatient clinics; hospitals; prisons; or professionals' offices.

Professionals who oversee testing and assessment are responsible for ensuring that all persons who administer and score tests have received the appropriate education and training needed to perform these tasks. In addition, they are responsible in group testing situations for ensuring that the individuals who use the test results are trained to interpret the scores properly.

When conducting psychological testing, standardized test administration procedures should be followed. When nonstandard administration procedures are needed, they are to be described and justified. Professionals also are responsible for ensuring that testing conditions are appropriate. For example, the examiner may need to determine if the client is capable of reading at the level required, and if clients with vision, hearing, or neurological disabilities are adequately accommodated. Finally, professionals are responsible for protecting the confidentiality and security of the test results and the testing materials.

One advantage of individually administered measures is the opportunity to observe and adjust testing conditions as needed. In some circumstances, test administration may provide the opportunity for skilled examiners to carefully observe the performance of persons under standardized conditions. For example, their observations may allow them to more accurately record behaviors being assessed, to understand better the manner in which persons arrive at their answers, to identify personal strengths and weaknesses, and to make modifications in the testing process. Thus, the observations of trained professionals can be important to all aspects of test use.

TEST SCORE INTERPRETATION

Test scores ideally are interpreted in light of the available normative data, the psychometric properties of the test, the temporal stability of the constructs being measured, and the effect of moderator variables and demographic characteristics (e.g., gender, age, income, sexual orientation, sociocultural and language background, education, and other socioeconomic variables) on test results. The professional rarely has the resources available to personally conduct the research or to assemble representative norms needed to make accurate inferences about each individual client's current and future functioning. Therefore, the professional may rely on the research and the body of scientific knowledge available for the test that warrants appropriate inferences. Presentation and analyses of validity and reliability evidence often are not needed in a written report, but the professional

strives to understand, and prepares to articulate, such evidence as the need arises.

Tests and inventories that meet high technical standards of quality are a necessary but not a sufficient condition to ensure the responsible use and interpretation of test scores. The level of competence of the professional who interprets the scores and integrates the inferences derived from psychological tests depends upon the educational and experiential qualifications of the professional. With experience, professionals learn that the challenges in psychological test score interpretation increase in magnitude along a continuum of professional judgment with brief screening inventories at one end of the continuum and comprehensive multidimensional assessments at the other. For example, the interpretations of achievement and ability test scores, personality test scores, and batteries of neuropsychological test scores represent points on a continuum that require increasing levels of specialized knowledge, judgment, and skill by an experienced professional regardless of the soundness of the technical characteristics of the tests being used. The education and experience necessary to administer group tests and/or proctor computer-administered tests generally are less stringent than are the qualifications necessary to interpret individually administered tests. The use and interpretation of individually administered tests requires completion of rigorous educational and applied training, a high degree of professional judgment, appropriate credentialing, and adherence to the professional's ethical guidelines.

When making inferences about a client's past, present, and future behaviors and other characteristics from test scores, the professional reviews the literature to develop familiarity with supporting evidence. When there is strong evidence supporting the reliability and validity of a test, including its applicability to the client being assessed, the professional's ability to draw inferences increases. Nevertheless, the professional still corroborates results from testing with additional information from a variety of sources such as interviews and results from other tests. When an inference is based on a single study or based on several studies whose samples are not representative of the client, the professional is more cautious about the inferences. Corroborating data from the assessment's multiple sources of information—including stylistic and test-taking behaviors inferred from observations during the test—will strengthen the confidence placed in the inference. Importantly, data that are not supportive of the inference are acknowledged and either reconciled or noted as limits to the confidence placed in the inference.

An interpretation of a test taker's test scores based upon existing research examines not only the demonstrated relationship between the scores and the criterion or criteria, but also the appropriateness of the latter. The criterion and the chosen predictor test or tests are subjected to a similar examination to understand the degree to which their underlying constructs are congruent with the inferences under consideration.

Threats to the interpretability of obtained scores are minimized by clearly defining how particular psychological tests are used. These threats occur as a result of construct-irrelevant variance (i.e., aspects of the test that are not relevant to the purpose of the test scores) and construct underrepresentation (i.e., important facets relevant to the purpose of the testing, but for which the test does not account). A client's response bias is another example of a construct-irrelevant component that may significantly skew the obtained scores, possibly rendering the scores uninterpretable. In situations where response bias is anticipated, the professional may choose a test that has scales (e.g., faking good, faking bad, social desirability, percent yes, percent no) that clarify the threats to validity from the test taker's response bias. In so doing, the professional may be able to assess the degree to which test takers are acquiescing to the perceived demands of the test administrator or attempting to portray themselves as impaired by "faking bad," or well-functioning by "faking good." In interpreting the test taker's obtained

response bias score(s), the evidence of validity for constructs underlying each response bias scale, each scale's internal consistency, its interrelations with other scales, and evidence of validity are considered.

For some purposes, including career counseling and neuropsychological assessment, test batteries frequently are used. Such batteries often include tests of verbal ability, numerical ability, nonverbal reasoning, mechanical reasoning, clerical speed and accuracy, spatial ability, and language usage. Some batteries also include interest and personality inventories. When psychological test batteries incorporate multiple methods and scores, patterns of test results frequently are interpreted to reflect a construct or even an interaction among constructs underlying test performances. Higher order interactions among the constructs underlying configurations of test outcomes may be postulated on the basis of test score patterns. The literature reporting evidence of reliability and validity that supports the proposed interpretations should be identifiable. If the literature is incomplete, the resulting inferences may be presented with the qualification that they are hypotheses for future verification rather than probabilistic statements that imply some known validity evidence.

COLLATERAL INFORMATION USED IN PSYCHOLOGICAL TESTING AND PSYCHOLOGICAL ASSESSMENT

The quality of psychological testing and psychological assessment is enhanced by obtaining credible collateral information from various third-party sources such as teachers, personal physicians, family members, and school or employment records. Psychological testing also is enhanced by using various methods to acquire information. Structured behavioral observations, checklists and ratings, interviews, and criterion- and norm-referenced measures are but a few of the methods that may be used to acquire information. The use of psychological tests also can be enhanced by acquiring information about multiple traits or attributes to help characterize a person. For example, an evaluation of career goals may be enhanced by obtaining a history of current and prior employment as well as by administering tests to assess academic aptitude and achievement, vocational interests, work values, and personality and temperament characteristics. The availability of information on multiple traits or attributes, when acquired from various sources and through the use of various methods, enables professionals to assess more accurately an individual's psychosocial functioning and facilitates more effective decision making.

Types of Psychological Tests

For purposes of this chapter, the types of psychological tests have been divided into five categories: cognitive and neuropsychological tests; adaptive, social, and problem behavior tests; family and couples tests; personality tests; and vocational tests.

COGNITIVE AND NEUROPSYCHOLOGICAL TESTING

Tests often are used to assess various classes of cognitive and neuropsychological functioning including intelligence; broad ability domains (e.g., verbal, quantitative, and spatial abilities); and more focused domains (e.g., attention, sensorimotor functions, perception, learning, memory, reasoning, executive functions, and language). Overlap may occur in the constructs that are assessed by tests of differing functions or domains. In common with other types of tests, cognitive and neuropsychological tests require a minimally sufficient level of test-taker attentional capacity.

Cognitive Ability. Measures designed to quantify cognitive abilities are among the most widely administered tests. The interpretation of cognitive ability tests is guided by the theoretical constructs used to develop the test.

Many cognitive ability tests consist of multidimensional test batteries that are designed to assess a broad range of abilities and skills. Individually administered test batteries also are required for testing for purposes such as diag-

nosing a cognitive disorder. Test results are used to draw inferences about a person's overall level of intellectual functioning as well as strengths and weaknesses in various cognitive abilities. Because each test in a battery examines a different function, ability, skill, or combination thereof, the test taker's performance can be understood best when scores are not combined or aggregated, but rather when each score is interpreted within the context of all other scores and other assessment data. For example, low scores on timed tests alert the examiner to slowed responding as a problem that may not be apparent if scores on different kinds of tests are combined.

Attention. Attention refers to that class of functioning that encompasses arousal, establishment and deployment of sets, sustained attention, and vigilance as constructs. Tests may measure levels of alertness, orientation, and localization; the ability to focus, shift, and maintain attention and to track one or more stimuli under various conditions; span of attention; information processing speed and choice reaction time; and short-term information storage capacity. Scores for each aspect of attention that has been examined should be reported individually so that the nature of an attention disorder can be clarified.

Motor, Sensorimotor Functions, and Lateral Preferences. Visual, auditory, somatosensory and other sensory sensitivity and discrimination can be measured by simple motor or verbal responses to selective stimulation upon command.

Perception and Perceptual Organization/Integration. This class of functioning involves reasoning and judgment as they relate to the processing and elaboration of complex sensory combinations and inputs. Tests of perception may emphasize immediate perceptual processing but also may require conceptualizations that involve some reasoning and judgmental processes. Some tests have a motor component ranging from a simple motor response to an elaborate construction. Also, some of these tests penalize the test taker for slow performance that may be caused by something other than perceptual dysfunction.

Learning and Memory. This class of functions involves the acquisition and retention of information beyond the attentional requirements of immediate or short-term information processing and storage. These tests may measure acquisition of new information through various sensory channels and by means of assorted test formats (e.g., word lists, prose passages, geometric figures, formboards, digits, and musical melodies). Memory tests also may require retention and recall of old information (e.g., personal data as well as commonly learned facts and skills).

Abstract Reasoning and Categorical Thinking. Tests of reasoning and thinking vary widely. They assess the examinee's ability to infer relationships or to respond to changing environmental circumstances and to act in goal-oriented situations.

Executive Functions. This class of functions is involved in the organized performances that are necessary for the independent, purposive and effective attainment of personal goals in various cognitive processing, problem-solving and social situations. Some tests emphasize reasoned plans of action that anticipate consequences of alternative solutions, motor performance in problem-solving situations that require goal-oriented intentions, and regulation of performance for achieving a desired outcome.

Language. Language assessment typically focuses on phonology, morphology, syntax, semantics, and pragmatics. Receptive and expressive language functions may be assessed, including listening, reading, talking, and written language skills and abilities. Assessment of central language disorders focuses on functional speech and verbal comprehension measured through oral, written, or gestural modes; lexical access and elaboration; repetition of spoken language; and associative verbal fluency.

When assessing persons who are non-native English speakers or who are bilingual or multilingual, language assessment often includes an assessment of language competence and the order of dominance among the different languages. If a multilingual person is assessed for a possible language disorder, one issue for the professional to consider is the degree to which the disorder may be due more directly to language-related qualities (e.g., phonological, morphological, syntactic, semantic, pragmatic delays; mental retardation; peripheral sensory or central neurological impairment; psychological conditions; hearing disorders) than to dominance of a non-English language.

Academic Achievement. Academic achievement tests are measures of academic knowledge and skills that a person has acquired in formal and informal learning opportunities. Two major types of academic achievement tests include general achievement batteries and diagnostic achievement tests. General achievement batteries are designed to assess a person's level of learning in multiple areas (e.g., reading, mathematics, spelling, social studies, science). Diagnostic achievement tests, on the other hand, typically focus on one particular subject area (e.g., reading) and assess important academic skills in greater detail. Test results are used to determine the test taker's strengths as well as specific difficulties and may help identify sources of the difficulties and ways to overcome them. Chapter 13 provides additional detail on academic achievement testing in educational settings.

SOCIAL, ADAPTIVE, AND PROBLEM BEHAVIOR TESTING

Measures of social, adaptive, and problem behaviors assess ability and motivation to care for one's self and to relate to others. Adaptive behaviors include a repertoire of knowledge, skills, and abilities that enable a person to meet the daily demands and expectations of the environment, such as eating, dressing, using transportation, interacting with peers, communicating with others, making purchases, managing money, maintaining a schedule, remaining in school, and maintaining a job.

Problem behaviors include behavioral adjustment difficulties that interfere with a person's effective functioning in daily life situations.

FAMILY AND COUPLES TESTING

Family testing addresses the issues of family dynamics, cohesion, and interpersonal relations among family members including partners, parents, children, and extended family members. Tests developed to assess families and couples are distinguished by measuring the interaction patterns of partial or whole families, requiring simultaneous focus on two or more family members in terms of their transactions. Testing with couples may address personal factors such as issues of intimacy, compatibility, shared interests, trust, and spiritual beliefs.

PERSONALITY TESTING

Broadly considered, the assessment of personality requires a synthesis of aspects of an individual's functioning that contribute to the formulation and expression of thoughts, attitudes, emotions, and behaviors. In the assessment of an individual, cognitive and emotional functioning may be considered separately, but their influences are interrelated. For example, a person whose perceptions are highly accurate, or who is relatively stable emotionally, may be able to control suspiciousness better than can a person whose perceptions are inaccurate or distorted or who is emotionally unstable.

Scores on a personality test may be regarded as reflecting the underlying theoretical constructs or empirically derived scales or factors that guided the test's construction. The stimulus and response formats of personality tests vary widely. Some include a series of questions (e.g., self-report inventories) to which the test taker is required to choose from several well-defined options; others involve being placed in a novel situation in which the test taker's response is not completely structured (e.g., responding to visual stimuli, telling stories, discussing pictures, or responding to other projective stimuli). The responses are scored and combined into either

logically or statistically derived dimensions established by previous research.

Personality tests may be designed to focus on the assessment of normal or abnormal attitudes, feelings, traits, and related characteristics. Tests intended to measure normal personality characteristics are constructed to yield scores reflecting the degree to which a person manifests personality dimensions empirically identified and hypothesized to be present in the behavior of most individuals. A person's configuration of scores on these dimensions is then used to infer how the person behaves presently and how she/he may behave in new situations. Test scores outside of the expected range may be considered extreme expressions of normal traits or indicative of psychopathology. Such scores also may reflect normal functioning of the person within a culture different from that of the normative population sample.

Other personality tests are designed specifically to measure constructs underlying abnormal functioning and psychopathology. Developers of some of these tests use previously diagnosed individuals to construct their scales and base their inferences on the association between the test's scale scores, within a given range, and the behavioral correlates of persons who scored within that range. If inferences made from scores go beyond the theory that guided the test's construction, then the inferences must be validated by collecting and analyzing additional relevant data.

VOCATIONAL TESTING

Vocational testing generally includes the measurement of interests, work needs, and values, as well as consideration and assessment of related elements of career development, maturity, and indecision. The results from inventories that assess these constructs often are used for enhancing personal growth and understanding, career counseling, outplacement counseling, and vocational decision making. These interventions frequently take place in the context of educational settings.

However, interest inventories and measures of work values also may be used in workplace settings as part of training and development programs, for career planning, or for selection, placement, and advancement decisions.

Interest Inventories. The measurement of interests is designed to identify a person's preferences for various activities. Self-report interest inventories are widely used to assess personal preferences including likes and dislikes for various work and leisure activities, school subjects, occupations, or types of people. The resulting scores may provide insight into types and patterns of differential interests in educational curricula (e.g., college majors), in different fields of work (e.g., specific occupations), or in more general or basic areas of interests related to specific activities (e.g., sales, office practices, or mechanical activities).

Work Values Inventories. The measurement of work values identifies a person's preferences for the various reinforcements one may obtain from work activities. Sometimes these values are identified as needs that persons seek to satisfy. Work values or needs may be categorized as intrinsic and important for the pleasure gained from the activity (e.g., independence, ability utilization, achievement) or as extrinsic and important for the rewards they bring (e.g., coworkers, supervisory relations, working conditions). The format of work values tests usually involves a self-rating of the importance of the value associated with qualities described by the items.

Measures of Career Development, Maturity, and Indecision. Additional areas of vocational assessment include measures of career development and maturity and measures of career indecision. Inventories that measure career development and maturity typically elicit client self-descriptions in response to items that inquire about the individual's knowledge of the world of work; self-appraisal of one's decision-making skills; attitudes toward careers and career choices; and the degree to which the individual already has engaged in career planning. Measures of career indecision usually are constructed and standardized to assess both the level of career indecision of a client as well as the reasons for, or antecedents of, indecision. Such career development, maturity, and indecision findings may be used with individuals and groups to guide the design and delivery of career services and to evaluate the effectiveness of career interventions.

Purposes of Psychological Testing

For purposes of this chapter, psychological test uses have been divided into four categories: testing for diagnosis; intervention planning and outcome evaluation; legal and governmental decisions; and personal awareness, growth and action. However, these categories are not always mutually exclusive.

TESTING FOR DIAGNOSIS

Diagnosis refers to a process that includes the collection and integration of test results with prior and current information about a person together with relevant contextual conditions to identify characteristics of healthy psychological functioning as well as psychological disorders. Disorders may manifest themselves in information obtained during the testing of an individual's cognitive, emotional, social, personality, neuropsychological, physical, perceptual, and motor attributes.

Psychodiagnosis. Psychological tests are helpful to professionals involved in the psychological diagnosis of an individual. Testing may be performed to confirm a hypothesized diagnosis or to rule out alternative diagnoses. Psychodiagnosis is complicated by the prevalence of comorbidity between diagnostic categories. For example, a client diagnosed as suffering from schizophrenia simultaneously may be diagnosed as suffering from depression. Or, a child diagnosed as having a learning disability also may be diagnosed as suffering from an attention deficit disorder. The goal of psychodiagnosis is to assist each client in receiving the appropriate interventions for the psychological or behavioral dysfunctions that the client, or a third party, views as impairing the client's expected functioning and/or enjoyment of life. In developing treatment plans, professionals often use non-categorical diagnostic descriptions of client functioning along treatment-relevant dimensions (e.g., degree of anxiety, amount of suspiciousness, openness to interpretations, amount of insight into behaviors, and level of intellectual functioning).

The first step in evaluating a test's suitability to yield scores or information indicative of a particular diagnostic syndrome is to compare the construct that the test is intended to measure with the symptomatology described in the diagnostic criteria. This step is important because different diagnostic systems may use the same diagnostic term to describe different symptoms; even within one diagnostic system the symptoms described by the same term may differ between editions of the manual identifying the diagnostic criteria. Similarly, a test that uses a diagnostic term in its title may differ significantly from another test using a similar title or from a subscale with the same term. For example, some diagnostic systems may define depression by behavioral symptomatology (e.g., psychomotor retardation, disturbance in appetite or sleep) or by affective symptomatology (e.g., dysphoric feeling, emotional flatness) or by cognitive symptomatology (e.g., thoughts of hopelessness, morbidity) or some other symptomatology. Further, rarely are the symptoms of diagnostic categories mutually exclusive. Hence, it can be expected that a given symptom may be shared by several diagnostic categories. More knowledgeable and precisely drawn inferences relating to a diagnosis may be obtained from test scores if appropriate weight is given to the symptoms included in the diagnostic category and to the suitability of each test to assess the symptoms.

Different methods may be used to assess particular diagnostic categories. Some methods rely primarily on structured interviews using a "yes" or "no" format in which the professional is interested in the presence or absence of diagnosis-specific symptomatology. Other methods often rely principally on tests of personality or cognitive functioning and use configurations of obtained scores. These configurations of scores indicate the degree to which a client's responses are similar to those of individuals who have been determined by prior research to belong to a specific diagnostic group.

Diagnoses made with the help of test scores typically are based on empirically demonstrated relationships between the test score and the diagnostic category. Validity studies that demonstrate relationships between test scores and diagnostic categories currently are available for some diagnostic categories. Sometimes tests that do not have supporting validity studies also may be useful to the professional in arriving at a diagnosis. This also may occur, for example, when the symptoms assessed by a test are a subset of the criteria that comprise a particular diagnostic category. While it often is not feasible for individual professionals to personally conduct research into relationships between obtained scores and inferences, their familiarity with the body of the research literature that examines these relationships is important.

The professional often can enhance the diagnostic inferences derived from test scores by integrating the test results with inferences made from other sources of information regarding the client's functioning such as self-reported history or information provided by significant others or systematic observations in the natural environment or in the testing setting. In arriving at a diagnosis, a professional also looks for information that does not corroborate the diagnosis, and in those instances, places appropriate limits on the degree of confidence placed in the diagnosis. When relevant to the referral issue, the professional acknowledges alternative diagnoses that may require consideration. Particular attention is paid to all relevant available data before concluding that a client falls into a diagnostic category. Cultural sensitivity is paramount to avoid misdiagnosing and over pathologizing culturally appropriate behavior, affect or cognition. Tests also are used to assess the appropriateness of continuing the initial diagnostic characterization, especially after a course of treatment or if the client's psychological functioning has changed over time.

Neuropsychodiagnosis. Neuropsychological testing analyzes the current psychological and behavioral status, including manifestations of neurological, neuropathological, and neurochemical changes that may arise during development or from brain injury or illness. The purposes of neuropsychological testing typically include, but are not limited to, the following: differential diagnoses between psychogenic and neurogenic sources of cognitive, perceptual, and personality dysfunction; differential diagnoses between two or more suspected etiologies of cerebral dysfunction; evaluation of impaired functioning secondary to a cerebral, cortical, or subcortical event; establishment of neuropsychological baseline measurements for monitoring progressive cerebral disease or recovery effects; comparison of pre- and post-pharmacologic, surgical, behavioral, or psychological interventions; identification of patterns of higher cortical function and dysfunction for the formulation of rehabilitation strategies and for the design of remedial procedures; and characterizing brain-behavior functions to assist the trier of fact in criminal and civil legal actions.

TESTING FOR INTERVENTION PLANNING AND OUTCOME EVALUATION

Professionals often rely on test results for assistance in planning, executing, and evaluating interventions. Therefore, their awareness of validity information that supports or does not support the relationship between test results, prescribed interventions, and desired outcome is important. Interventions may be intended to prevent the onset of one or more symptoms, to stabilize or overcome them, to ameliorate their effects, to minimize their impact, and to provide for a person's basic physical, psychological, and social needs. Intervention planning typical-

ly occurs following an evaluation of the nature and severity of a disorder and a review of personal and contextual conditions that may impact its resolution. Subsequent evaluations may occur in an effort to diagnose further the nature and severity of the disorder, to review the effects of interventions, to revise them as needed, and to meet ethical and legal standards.

TESTING FOR JUDICIAL AND GOVERNMENTAL DECISIONS

Clients may voluntarily seek psychological testing as part of psychological assessments to assist in matters before a court or other governmental agencies. Conversely, courts or other governmental agencies sometimes require a client to submit involuntarily to a psychological or neuropsychological assessment that may involve a wide range of psychological tests. The goal of these psychological assessments is to provide important information to a third party, client's attorney, opposing attorney, judge, or administrative board about the psychological functioning of the client that has bearing on the legal issues in question. At the outset of evaluations for judicial and government decisions, it is imperative to clarify the purpose of the evaluation, who will have access to the test results and the reports, and any rights that the client may have to refuse to participate in court-ordered evaluations.

The goals of psychological testing in judicial and governmental settings are informed and constrained by the legal issues to be addressed, and a detailed understanding of their salient aspects is essential. Legal issues may arise as part of a civil proceeding (e.g., involuntary commitment, testamentary capacity, competence to stand trial, parole, child custody, personal injury, discrimination issues), a criminal proceeding (e.g., competence to stand trial, not guilty by reason of insanity, mitigating circumstances in sentencing), determination of reasonable accommodations for employees with disabilities, or an administrative proceeding or decision (e.g., license revocation, parole, worker's compensation). Each of these legal issues is defined in law applicable to a particular legislative jurisdiction. The definition of each legal issue may be jurisdiction specific. For example, the criteria by which a person can be involuntarily committed often differ between legislative jurisdictions. Furthermore, tests initially administered for one purpose also may be used for another purpose (e.g., initially used for a civil case but later used in administrative or criminal proceedings).

Legislatures, courts, and other adminstrative bodies often define legal issues in commonly used language, not in diagnostic or other technical psychological terms. The professional is responsible for explaining the diagnostic frame of reference, including test scores and inferences made from them, in terms of the legal criteria by which the jury, judge, or administrative board will decide the legal issue. For example, a diagnosis of schizophrenia or neuropsychological impairment, which does not also include a reference to the legal criteria, neither precludes an examinee from obtaining sole custody of children in a child custody dispute nor does it necessarily acquit a person of criminal responsibility.

In instances involving legal or quasi-legal issues, it is important to assess the examinee's test-taking orientation including response bias to ensure that the legal proceedings have not affected the responses given. For example, a person seeking to obtain the greatest possible monetary award for a personal injury may be motivated to exaggerate cognitive and emotional symptoms, while persons attempting to forestall the loss of a professional license may attempt to portray themselves in the best possible light by minimizing symptoms or deficits. In forming an assessment opinion, it is necessary to interpret the test scores with informed knowledge relating to the available validity and reliability evidence. When forming such opinions, it also is necessary to integrate a client's test scores with all other sources of information that bear on current status including psychological, medical, educational, occupational, legal, and other relevant collateral records.

Some tests are intended to provide information about a client's functioning that helps clarify a given legal issue (e.g., parental functioning in a child custody case or ability to understand charges against a defendant in competency to stand trial matters). The manuals of some tests also provide demographic and actuarial data for normative groups that are representative of persons involved in the legal system. However, many tests measure constructs that are generally relevant to the legal issues even though norms specific to the judicial or governmental context may not be available. Professionals are expected to make every effort to be aware of evidence of validity and reliability that supports or does not support their inferences and to place appropriate limits on the opinions rendered. Test users who practice in judicial and government settings are expected to be aware of conflicts of interest that may lead to bias in the interpretation of test results.

Protecting the confidentiality of a client's test results and of the test instrument itself poses particular challenges for professionals involved with attorneys, judges, jurors, and other legal and quasi-legal decision makers. The test taker does have a right to expect that test results will be communicated only to persons who are legally authorized to receive them and that other information from the testing session that is not relevant to the evaluation will not be reported. It is important for the professional to be apprised of possible threats to confidentiality and test security (e.g., releasing the test questions, the examinee's responses, and raw and scaled scores on tests to another qualified professional) and to seek, if necessary, appropriate legal and professional remedies.

TESTING FOR PERSONAL AWARENESS, GROWTH, AND ACTION

Tests and inventories frequently are used to provide information to help individuals to understand themselves, to identify their own strengths and weaknesses, and to otherwise clarify issues important to their own decision making and development. For example, test results from personality inventories may help clients better understand themselves and also understand their interactions with others. Results from interest inventories and tests of ability may be useful to individuals who are making educational and career decisions. Appropriate cognitive and neuropsychological tests that have been normed and standardized for children may facilitate the monitoring of development and growth during the formative years when relevant interventions may be more efficacious for preventing potentially disabling learning disabilities from being overlooked or misdiagnosed.

Test results may be used for self-exploration, self-growth, and decision making in several ways. First, the results can provide individuals with new information that allows them to compare themselves with others or to evaluate themselves by focusing on self-descriptions and characterizations. Test results also may serve to stimulate discussions between a client and professional, to facilitate client insights, to provide directions for future considerations, to help individuals identify strengths and assets, and to provide the professional with a general framework for organizing and integrating information about an individual. Testing for personal growth may take place in training and development programs, within an educational curriculum, during psychotherapy, in rehabilitation programs as part of an educational or career planning process, or in other situations.

Summary

The application of psychological tests continues to expand in scope and depth on a course that is characterized by an increasingly diverse set of purposes, procedures, and assessment needs and challenges. Therefore, the responsible use of tests in practice requires a commitment by the professional to develop and maintain the necessary knowledge and competence to select, administer, and interpret tests and inventories

as crucial elements of the psychological testing and assessment process. The standards in this chapter provide a framework for guiding the professional toward achieving relevance and effectiveness in the use of psychological tests within the boundaries or limits defined by the professional's educational, experiential and ethical foundations. Earlier chapters and standards that are relevant to psychological testing and assessment describe general aspects of test quality (chapters 1-6, chapter 11), test fairness (chapters 7-10), and test use (chapter 11). Chapter 13 discusses educational applications; chapter 14 discusses test use in the workplace, including credentialing, and the importance of collecting data that provide evidence of a test's accuracy for predicting job performance; and chapter 15 discusses test use in program evaluation and public policy.

Standard 12.1

Those who use psychological tests should confine their testing and related assessment activities to their areas of competence, as demonstrated through education, supervised training, experience, and appropriate credentialing.

Comment: The responsible use and interpretation of test scores require appropriate levels of experience and sound professional judgment. Competency also requires sufficient familiarity with the population from which the test taker comes to allow appropriate interaction, test selection, test administration, and test interpretation. For example, when personality tests and neuropsychological tests are administered as part of a psychological assessment of an individual, the test scores must be understood in the context of the individual's physical and emotional state, as well as the individual's cultural, educational, occupational, and medical background, and must take into account other evidence relevant to the tests used. Test interpretation in this context requires professionally responsible judgment that is exercised within the boundaries of knowledge and skill afforded by the professional's education, training, and supervised experience.

Standard 12.2

Those who select tests and interpret test results should refrain from introducing biases that accommodate individuals or groups with a vested interest in decisions affected by the test interpretation.

Comment: Individuals or groups with a vested interest in the significance or meaning of the findings from psychological testing include many school personnel, attorneys, referring health professionals, employers, professional associates, and managed care organizations. In some settings a professional may have a professional relationship with multiple clients (e.g.,

with both the test taker and the organization requesting assessment). A professional engaged in a professional relationship with multiple clients takes care to ensure that the multiple relationships do not become a conflict of interest that would occur when the professional's judgment toward one client is unduly influenced by his or her relationship with the other client. Test selections and interpretations that favor a special external expectation or perspective by deviating from established principles of sound test interpretation are unprofessional and unethical.

Standard 12.3

Tests selected for use in individual testing should be suitable for the characteristics and background of the test taker.

Comment: Considerations for test selection should include culture, language and/or physical requirements of the test and the availability of norms and evidence of validity for a population representative of the test taker. If no normative or validity studies are available for the population at issue, test interpretations should be qualified and presented as hypotheses rather than conclusions.

Standard 12.4

If a publisher suggests that tests are to be used in combination with one another, the professional should review the evidence on which the procedures for combining tests is based and determine the rationale for the specific combination of tests and the justification of the interpretation based on the combined scores.

Comment: For example, if measures of developed abilities (e.g., achievement or specific or general abilities) or personality are packaged with interest measures to suggest a requisite combination of scores, or a neuropsychological battery is being applied, then supporting validity data for such combinations of scores should be available.

Standard 12.5

The selection of a combination of tests to address a complex diagnosis should be appropriate for the purposes of the assessment as determined by available evidence of validity. The professional's educational training and supervised experience also should be commensurate with the test user qualifications required to administer and interpret the selected tests.

Comment: For example, in a neuropsychological assessment for evidence of an injury to a particular area of the brain, it is necessary to select a combination of tests of known diagnostic sensitivity and specificity to impairments arising from trauma to various regions of the cerebral hemispheres.

Standard 12.6

When differential diagnosis is needed, the professional should choose, if possible, a test for which there is evidence of the test's ability to distinguish between the two or more diagnostic groups of concern rather than merely to distinguish abnormal cases from the general population.

Comment: Professionals will find it particularly helpful if evidence of validity is in a form that enables them to determine how much confidence can be placed in inferences regarding an individual. Differences between group means and their statistical significance provide inadequate information regarding validity for individual diagnostic purposes. Additional information might consist of confidence intervals, effect sizes, or a table showing the degree of overlap of predictor distributions among different criterion groups.

Standard 12.7

When the validity of a diagnosis is appraised by evaluating the level of agreement between test-based inferences and the diagnosis, the diagnostic terms or categories employed should be carefully defined or identified.

Standard 12.8

Professionals should ensure that persons under their supervision, who administer and score tests, are adequately trained in the settings in which the testing occurs and with the populations served.

Standard 12.9

Professionals responsible for supervising group testing programs should ensure that the individuals who interpret the test scores are properly instructed in the appropriate methods for interpreting them.

Comment: If, for example, interest inventories are given to college students for use in academic advising, the professional who supervises the academic advisors is responsible for ensuring that the advisors know how to provide an examinee an appropriate interpretation of the test results.

Standard 12.10

Prior to testing, professionals and test administrators should provide the test taker with appropriate introductory information in language understandable to the test taker. The test taker who inquires also should be advised of opportunities and circumstances, if any, for retesting.

Comment: The client should understand testing time limits, who will have access to the test results, if and when test results will be shared with the test taker, and if and when decisions based on the test results will be shared with the test taker.

Standard 12.11

Professionals and others who have access to test materials and test results should ensure the confidentiality of the test results and testing materials consistent with legal and professional ethics requirements.

Comment: Professionals should be knowledgeable and conform to record-keeping and confidentiality guidelines required by the state or province in which they practice and the professional organizations to which they belong. Confidentiality has different meanings for the test developer, the test user, the test taker, and third parties (e.g., school, court, employer). To the extent possible, the professional who uses tests is responsible for managing the confidentiality of test information across all parties. It is important for the professional to be aware of possible threats to confidentiality and the legal and professional remedies available. Professionals also are responsible for maintaining the security of testing materials and for protecting the copyrights of all tests to the extent permitted by law.

Standard 12.12

The professional examines available norms and follows administration instructions, including calibration of technical equipment, verification of scoring accuracy and replicability, and provision of settings for testing that facilitate optimal performance of test takers. However, in those instances where realistic rather than optimal test settings will best satisfy the assessment purpose, the professional should report the reason for using such a setting and, when possible, also conduct the testing under optimal conditions to provide a comparison.

Comment: Because the normative data against which a client's performance will be evaluated were collected under the reported standard procedures, the professional needs to be aware of and take into account the effect that nonstandard procedures may have on the client's obtained score. When the professional uses

tests that employ an unstructured response format, such as some projective techniques and informal behavioral ratings, the professional should follow objective scoring criteria, where available and appropriate, that are clear and minimize the need for the scorer to rely only on individual judgment. The testing may be conducted in a realistic, less than optimal, setting to determine how a client with an attentional disorder, for example, performs in a noisy or distracting environment rather than in an optimal environment that typically protects the test taker from such external threats to performance efficiency.

Standard 12.13

Those who select tests and draw inferences from test scores should be familiar with the relevant evidence of validity and reliability for tests and inventories used and should be prepared to articulate a logical analysis that supports all facets of the assessment and the inferences made from the assessment.

Comment: A presentation and analysis of validity and reliability evidence generally is not needed in a written report, because it is too cumbersome and of little interest to most report readers. However, in situations in which the selection of tests may be problematic (e.g., verbal subtests with deaf clients), a brief description of the rationale for using or not using particular measures is advisable.

When potential inferences derived from psychological test data are not supported by evidence of validity yet may hold promise for future validation, they may be described by the test developer and professional as hypotheses for further validation in test interpretation. Such interpretive remarks should be qualified to communicate to the source of the referral that such inferences do not as yet have adequately demonstrated evidence of validity and should not be the basis for a diagnostic decision or prognostic formulation.

Standard 12.14

The interpretation of test results in the assessment process should be informed when possible by an analysis of stylistic and other qualitative features of test-taking behavior that are inferred from observations during interviews and testing and from historical information.

Comment: Such features of test-taking behavior include manifestations of fatigue, momentary fluctuations in emotional state, rapport with the examiner, test taker's level of motivation, withholding or distortion of response as seen in instances of deception and malingering or in instances of pseudoneurological conditions, and unusual response or general adaptation to the testing environment.

Standard 12.15

Those who use computer-generated interpretations of test data should evaluate the quality of the interpretations and, when possible, the relevance and appropriateness of the norms upon which the interpretations are based.

Comment: Efforts to reduce a complex set of data into computer-generated interpretations of a given construct may yield grossly misleading or simplified analyses of meanings of test scores, that in turn may lead to faulty diagnostic and prognostic decisions as well as mislead the trier of fact in judicial and government settings.

Standard 12.16

Test interpretations should not imply that empirical evidence exists for a relationship among particular test results, prescribed interventions, and desired outcomes, unless empirical evidence is available for populations similar to those representative of the examinee.

Standard 12.17

Criterion-related evidence of validity should be available when recommendations or decisions are presented by the professional as having an actuarial basis.

Standard 12.18

The interpretation of test or test battery results generally should be based upon multiple sources of convergent test and collateral data and an understanding of the normative, empirical, and theoretical foundations as well as the limitations of such tests.

Comment: A given pattern of test performances represents a cross-sectional view of the individual being assessed within a particular context (i.e., medical, psychosocial, educational, vocational, cultural, ethnic, gender, familial, genetic, and behavioral). The interpretation of findings derived from a complex battery of tests in such contexts requires appropriate education, supervised experience, and an appreciation of procedural, theoretical, and empirical limitations of the tests.

Standard 12.19

The interpretation of test scores or patterns of test battery results should take cognizance of the many factors that may influence a particular testing outcome. Where appropriate, a description and analysis of the alternative hypotheses or explanations that may have contributed to the pattern of results should be included in the report.

Comment: Many factors (e.g., unusual testing conditions, motivation, educational level, employment status, lateral sensorimotor usage preferences, health, or disability status) may influence individual testing results. When such factors are known to introduce construct-irrelevant variance in component test scores, those factors should be considered during test score interpretations.

Standard 12.20

Except for some judicial or governmental referrals, or in some employment testing situations when the client is the employer, professionals should share test results and interpretations with the test taker. Such information should be expressed in language that the test taker, or when appropriate the test taker's legal representative, can understand.

Comment: For example, in rehabilitation settings, where clients typically are required to participate actively in intervention programs, sharing of such information, expressed in terms that can be understood readily by the client and family members, may facilitate the effectiveness of intervention.

13. EDUCATIONAL TESTING AND ASSESSMENT

Background

This chapter concerns testing in formal educational settings from kindergarten through postgraduate training. Results of tests administered to students are used to make judgments, for example, about the status, progress, or accomplishments of individuals or groups. Tests that provide information about individual performance are used to (a) evaluate a student's overall achievement and growth in a content domain, (b) diagnose student strengths and weaknesses in and across content domains, (c) plan educational interventions and to design individualized instructional plans, (d) place students in appropriate educational programs, (e) select applicants into programs with limited enrollment, and (f) certify individual achievement or qualifications. Tests that provide information about the status, progress, or accomplishments of groups such as schools, school districts, or states are used (a) to judge and monitor the quality of educational programs for all or for particular subsets of individuals, and (b) to infer the success of policies and interventions that have been selected for evaluation. These testing purposes are typically mandated by institutions such as schools and colleges and by governing bodies of public and privately administered educational programs.

In this chapter, three broad areas of educational testing are considered that encompass one or more of the above purposes: (a) routine school, district, state, or other system-wide testing programs; (b) testing for selection in higher education; and (c) individualized and special needs testing. While the second and third areas refer to relatively specific purposes of testing, system-wide testing programs can encompass multiple individual and group purposes. For each of these areas, the chapter elaborates on the specific purposes and domains encompassed and raises specific issues of tech-

nical quality and fairness in testing that may not be addressed or emphasized in the preceding chapters. This chapter does not explicitly address issues related to tests constructed and administered by teachers for their own classroom use or provided by publishers of instructional materials. While many aspects of the *Standards*, particularly those in the areas of validity, reliability, test development, and fairness, are relevant to such tests, this document is not intended for tests used by teachers for their own classroom purposes.

Issues in Educational Testing

This chapter first considers some cross-cutting issues: the distinctions among types of tests, the design or use of tests to serve multiple purposes including the measurement of change, and the "stakes" associated with different purposes for testing in education.

DISTINCTIONS AMONG TYPES OF TESTS AND ASSESSMENTS

Tests used in educational settings range from tests consisting of traditional item formats such as multiple-choice items to performance assessments including scorable portfolios. Every test, regardless of its format, measures test-taker performance in a specified domain. Performance assessments, however, attempt to emulate the context or conditions in which the intended knowledge or skills are actually applied. As discussed in chapter 3, they are diverse in nature and can be product-based as well as behavior-based. The execution of the tasks posed in these tests often involves relatively extended time periods, ranging from a few minutes to a class period or more to several hours or days. Examples of such performances might include solving problems using manipulable materials, making complex inferences after collecting information, or explaining orally or in writing the rationale for a particular course of government action under given economic conditions. The performance task may be undertaken by a single individual or a team of students. Performance assessments may require increased testing time to provide sufficient domain sampling for reasonable estimates of individual attainment and for making generalizations to the broader domain. Extended time periods, collaboration, and the use of ancillary materials pose great challenges to the standardization of administration and scoring of some performance assessments. This is particularly true when test takers define their own tasks or when they select their own work products for evaluation. When this is the case, test takers need to be aware of the basis for scoring as well as the nature of the criteria that will be applied. Further, performance assessments often require complex procedures and training to increase the accuracy of judgments made by those evaluating student performance (see chapter 3).

An individual portfolio may be used as another type of performance assessment. Scorable portfolios are systematic collections of educational products typically collected over time and possibly amended over time. The particular purpose of the portfolio determines whether it will include representative products, the best work of the student, or indicators of progress. The purpose also dictates who will be responsible for compiling the contents of the portfolio—the examiner, the student, or both parties working together. The more standardized the contents and procedures of administration, the easier it is to establish comparability of portfolio-based scores. Establishing comparability requires portfolios to be constructed according to test specifications and standards, and the development of objective procedures to judge their quality. The test specifications for portfolios may indicate that students are to make certain decisions about the nature of the work to be included. For example, in constructing an art portfolio, students may select the media that best represent their work. Establishing compa-

rability also requires specifications regarding the kinds of assistance the student may have received during portfolio preparation. It is particularly difficult to compare the performance of students whose portfolios may vary in content. All performance assessments, including scorable portfolios, are judged by the same standards of technical quality as traditional tests of achievement.

Electronic media are often used both to present testing material and to record and score test takers' responses. These tests may be administered in schools, in special laboratory settings, or in external testing centers. Examples include simple enhancements of text by audio-taped instructions to facilitate student understanding, computer-based tests traditionally given in paper-and-pencil format, computer-adaptive tests, and newer, interactive multimedia testing situations where attributes of performance assessments are supported by computer. Some computer-based tests also may have the capacity to capture aspects of students' processes as they solve test items. They may, for example, monitor time spent on items, solutions tried and rejected, or editing sequences for texts. Electronic media also make it possible to provide test administration conditions designed to assist students with particular needs, such as those with different language backgrounds, attention problems, or physical disabilities. Computers can also help identify the contributions of individuals to a group task completed by a team or in geographically remote locations on a network.

Computer-based tests are evaluated by the same technical quality standards as other tests administered through more traditional means. It is especially important that test takers be familiarized with the media of the test so that any unfamiliarity with computers or strategies does not lead to inferences based on construct-irrelevant variance. Furthermore, it is important to describe scoring algorithms, expert models upon which they may be based, and technical data supporting their use in any documentation accompanying the testing system. It is important, however, to assure that the documentation does not jeopardize the security of the items that could adversely affect the validity of score interpretations. Some computer-based tests may also generate recommendations for instructional practices based on test results. Describing the basis for these recommendations assists the user in evaluating their applicability in a given situation.

MULTIPLE PURPOSES AND MEASURING CHANGE

Many tests are designed or used to serve multiple purposes in education. For example, a test may be used to monitor individual student achievement as well as to evaluate the quality of educational programs at the school or district level. As another example, a test may be used to evaluate an individual's performance relative to the performance of one or more reference populations as well as to evaluate the level of the individual's competence in some defined domain (see chapters 3 and 4). The evidence needed for the technical quality of one purpose, however, will differ from the evidence needed for another purpose. Consequently, it is important to evaluate the evidence of technical quality for each purpose of testing.

Test results may be used to infer the growth or progress as well as the status of individuals or groups of students, such as when tests are expected to reveal the effects of instruction, of changes in educational policy, or of other interventions. In such cases, the test's ability to detect change is essential. If differences in scores are reported, the technical quality of the differences needs attention. More generally, whenever inferences about growth or progress are made, it is important to evaluate the validity of those inferences.

STAKES OF TESTING

The importance of the results of testing programs for individuals, institutions, or groups is often referred to as the *stakes* of the testing program. At the individual level, when significant educational paths or choices of an individual are directly affected by test performance, such as

whether a student is promoted or retained at a grade level, graduated, or admitted or placed into a desired program, the test use is said to have high stakes. A low-stakes test, on the other hand, is one administered for informational purposes or for highly tentative judgments such as when test results provide feedback to students, teachers, and parents on student progress during an academic period. Testing programs for institutions can have high stakes when aggregate performance of a sample or of the entire population of test takers is used to infer the quality of service provided, and decisions are made about institutional status, rewards, or sanctions based on test results. For example, the quality of reading curriculum and instruction may be judged on the basis of test results because test scores can indicate the rate of student progress or the levels of attainment reached by groups of students. Even when test results are reported in the aggregate and intended for a low-stakes purpose such as monitoring the educational system, the public release of data can raise the stakes for particular schools or districts. Judgments about program quality, personnel, and educational programs might be made and policy decisions might be affected, even though the tests were not intended or designed for those purposes.

The higher the stakes associated with a given test use, the more important it is that test-based inferences are supported with strong evidence of technical quality. In particular, when the stakes for an individual are high, and important decisions depend substantially on test performance, the test needs to exhibit higher standards of technical quality for its avowed purposes than might be expected of tests used for lower-stakes purposes (see chapters 1, 2, and 7 for a more thorough discussion on validity, reliability, and bias in testing, respectively). Although it is never possible to achieve perfect accuracy in describing an individual's performance, efforts need to be made to minimize errors in estimating individual scores or in classifying individuals in pass/fail or admit/reject categories.

Further, enhancing validity for high-stakes purposes, whether individual or institutional, typically entails collecting sound collateral information both to assist in understanding the factors that contributed to test results and to provide corroborating evidence that supports inferences based on test results. These issues will be addressed more fully as they relate to the three areas of testing described below.

School, District, State, or Other System-Wide Testing Programs

As indicated previously, system-wide testing programs can span multiple purposes. At the individual level, tests are used for low-stakes purposes, such as monitoring and providing feedback on student progress, and for more high-stakes purposes, such as certifying students' acquisition of particular knowledge and skills for promotion, placement into special instructional programs, or graduation. At the school, district, state, or other aggregate level, a common purpose of tests is to evaluate the progress made by groups of students or to monitor the long-term effectiveness of the overall educational system. Educational testing programs may also permit comparisons among the performance of various groups of students in different programs or in diverse settings for the purpose of making an evaluation of those learning environments. Chapter 15 provides a more thorough discussion on program evaluation.

In these contexts, educational tests are designed to measure certain aspects of students' knowledge and skills as reflected in curriculum goals and standards. There may be considerable variation in the breadth and depth of the knowledge and skills that are measured by such tests. Some educational tests focus on the test takers' general ability or knowledge in a particular content area, such as their understanding of mathematics or science. Other tests focus on test takers' specific knowledge of a topic in detail, such as trigonometry.

Still others emphasize specific skills or procedures, such as the ability to write persuasively or to design, conduct, and interpret the results of a scientific experiment. Tests may address other cognitive aspects of test takers' development, such as their ability to work with others to solve problems or their self-reported habits and attitudes, as well as noncognitive aspects, such as students' ability to perform particular physical tasks. In most cases, valid interpretation of the results requires that evidence of the fit between the test domain and the relevant curriculum goals or standards be ascertained.

Testing programs may involve the use of tests designed to represent a set of general educational standards as determined for instance by the state, district, or relevant educational professional organization. Such tests are conceptually similar to criterion-referenced tests, in that a set of content standards is developed that is intended to provide broad specifications for student performance by delimiting the content and general skills to be measured. Subsequently, descriptive or empirical targets or levels of achievement are developed and referred to as performance standards. These performance standards are intended to define further the knowledge and skills required of students for each of the different categories of proficiency.

This type of testing may involve the development of a new test to assess the relevant content and skills or the selection of an existing test that can be referenced to the standards. Whether a test is designed or selected, valid interpretation of the results in light of the standards entails assessment of the degree of fit between the test domain and contents and the descriptive statements of standards or goals. This involves a process of mapping or referencing the content and skills of the test to those of the standards to be sure that gaps or imbalances do not occur. The curriculum goals or standards may be sufficiently broad to encompass many different ways for students to demonstrate their status, accomplishments, or progress. Moreover, some goals or standards may not lend themselves to conventional test formats. These are cases in which the test may result in construct underrepresentation that refers to the extent to which a test fails to capture important aspects of what it is intended to measure. Chapter 1 provides a more thorough discussion of construct underrepresentation. In these cases, interpretation of test results in light of goals or standards is enhanced by an understanding of what is not covered as well as what is covered by the test. Sometimes, additional commercial or locally developed tests are administered within a particular jurisdiction, and attempts are made to link these existing tests to the proficiency levels reported for the new test or to provide other evidence of comparability. It is important to provide logical and empirical validity evidence of any reported links. For example, evidence can be collected to determine the extent to which the existing test can provide information about the proficiency of individual students and groups of students in the particular content areas and skills addressed by the standards. The validity of such links is problematic to the extent that the tests measure different content (see chapter 4 for a discussion on issues in equating and linking tests).

When inferences are to be drawn about the performance of groups of students, practical considerations and the format of the test (e.g., performance assessment) often dictate that different subgroups of students within each unit respond to different sets of tasks or items, a procedure referred to as matrix sampling. This matrix sampling approach allows for a test to better represent the breadth of the target domain without increasing the testing time for each test taker. Group-level results are most useful when testing programs and student populations remain sufficiently stable to provide information about trends over time. When a testing program is designed for group-level reporting and employs matrix sampling, reporting individual scores generally is not appropriate.

When interpreting and using scores about individuals or groups of students, consideration of relevant collateral information can enhance the validity of the interpretation, by providing corroborating evidence or evidence that helps explain student performance. Test results can be influenced by multiple factors, including institutional and individual factors such as the quality of education provided, students' exposure to education (e.g., through regular school attendance), and students' motivation to perform well on the test.

As the stakes of testing increase for individual students, the importance of considering additional evidence to document the validity of score interpretations and the fairness in testing increases accordingly. The validity of individual interpretations can be enhanced by taking into account other relevant information about individual students before making important decisions. It is important to consider the soundness and relevance of any collateral information or evidence used in conjunction with test scores for making educational decisions. Further, fairness in testing can be enhanced through careful consideration of conditions that affect students' opportunities to demonstrate their capabilities. For example, when tests are used for promotion and graduation, the fairness of individual interpretations can be enhanced by (a) providing students with multiple opportunities to demonstrate their capabilities through repeated testing with alternate forms or through other construct-equivalent means, (b) ensuring students have had adequate notice of skills and content to be tested along with other appropriate test preparation material, (c) providing students with curriculum and instruction that affords them the opportunity to learn the content and skills that are tested, and (d) providing students with equal access to any specific preparation for test taking (e.g., test-taking strategies). Chapter 7 provides a more thorough discussion on fairness in testing.

Collateral information can also enhance interpretation and decisions at the institutional level. For instance, changes in test scores from year to year may not only reflect changes in the capabilities of students but also changes in the student population (e.g., successive cohorts of students). Differences in scores across ethnic groups may be confounded with differences in socioeconomic status of the communities in which they live and, hence, the educational resources to which students have access. Differences in scores from school to school may similarly reflect differences in resources and activities such as the qualification of teachers or the number of advanced course offerings. While local empirical evidence of the influence of these factors may not be readily available, consideration of evidence from similar contexts available in published literature can enhance the quality of the interpretation and use of current results.

Because public participation is an integral part of educational governance, policymakers, professional educators, and members of the public are concerned with the nature of educational tests, the domains that the tests are intended to measure, the choices in test design, adoption, and implementation, and the issues associated with valid interpretation and uses of test results. It is important that test results be reported in a way that all stakeholders can understand, that enables sound interpretations, and that decreases the chance of misinterpretations and inappropriate decisions.

Large-scale testing is increasingly viewed as a tool of educational policy. From this perspective, tests used for program evaluation, such as some state tests that are aligned to the state's own curriculum standards, are not used solely as measures of school outcomes (see chapter 15 for a more thorough discussion on the use of tests for program evaluation). They are also viewed as a means to influence curriculum and instruction, to hold teachers and school administrators accountable, to increase student motivation, and to communicate performance expectations to students, to teachers, and to the public. If such goals are set forth as

part of the rationale for a testing program, the validity of the testing program needs to be examined with respect to these goals. Beyond any intended policy goals, it is important to consider potential unintended effects that may result from large-scale testing programs. Concerns have been raised, for instance, about narrowing the curriculum to focus only on the objectives tested, restricting the range of instructional approaches to correspond to the testing format, increasing the number of dropouts among students who do not pass the test, and encouraging other instructional or administrative practices that may raise test scores without affecting the quality of education. It is important for those who mandate tests to consider and monitor their consequences and to identify and minimize the potential of negative consequences.

Selection in Higher Education

It is widely recognized that tests are used in the selection of applicants for admission to particular educational programs, especially admissions to colleges, universities, and professional schools. Selection criteria may vary within an institution by academic specialization. In addition to scores from selection tests, many other sources of evidence are used in making selection decisions, including past academic records, transcripts, and grade-point average or rank in class. Scores on tests used to certify students for high school graduation may be used in the college admissions process. Other measures used by some institutions are samples of previous work by students, lists of academic and service accomplishments, letters of recommendation, and student-composed statements evaluated for the appropriateness of the goals and experience of the student or for writing proficiency.

Two major points may be made about the role of tests in the admissions process. Often, scores are used in combination with other sources of information. Some of these supplemental sources of evidence may not be reliably assessed or may lack comparability from applicant to applicant. For this reason, it is important that studies be conducted examining the relationships among test scores, data from other sources of information, and college performance. Second, the public and policymakers are to be cautious about the widespread use of reports of college admission test scores to infer the effectiveness of middle school and high school as well as to compare schools or states. Admissions tests, whether they are intended to measure achievement or ability, are not directly linked to a particular instructional curriculum and, therefore, are not appropriate for detecting changes in middle school or high school performance. Because of differential motivational factors and other demographic variables found across and within pre-collegiate programs, self-selection precludes general comparisons of test scores across demographic groups. Therefore, self-selection also precludes comparisons of test scores among the full ranges of pre-collegiate programs.

Individualized and Special Needs Testing

Individually administered tests are used by school psychologists and other professionals in schools and other related settings to facilitate the learning and development of students who may have special educational needs (see chapter 12). Some of these services are reserved for those students who have gifted capabilities as well as for those students who may have relatively minor academic difficulties (e.g., such as those requiring remedial reading). Other services are reserved for students who display behavioral, emotional, physical, and/or more severe learning difficulties. Services may be provided to students who are in regular classroom settings as well as to students who need more specialized instruction outside of the regular classroom. The ultimate purpose of these services is to

assure all students are placed into appropriate educational programs.

Individually administered tests can serve a number of purposes, including screening, diagnostic classification, intervention planning, and program evaluation. For screening purposes, tests are administered to identify students who might differ significantly from their peers and might require additional assessment. For example, screening tests may be used to identify young children who show signs of developmental disorders and to signal the need for further evaluation. For diagnostic purposes, tests may be used to clarify the types and extent of an individual's difficulties or problems in light of well-established criteria. Test results provide an important basis for determining whether the student meets eligibility requirements for special education and other related services and, if so, the specific types of services that the student needs. Test results may be used for intervention purposes in establishing behavior and learning goals and objectives for the student, planning instructional strategies that should be used, and specifying the appropriate setting in which the special services are to be delivered (e.g., regular classroom, resource room, full-time special class, etc.). Subsequent to the student's placement in special services, tests may be administered to monitor the progress of the student toward prescribed learning goals and objectives. Test results may be used also to evaluate the effectiveness of instruction to determine whether the special services need to be continued, modified, or discontinued.

Many types of tests are used in individualized and special needs testing. These include tests of cognitive abilities, academic achievement, learning processes, visual and auditory memory, speech and language, vision and hearing, and behavior and personality. These tests are used typically in conjunction with other assessment methods such as interviews, behavioral observation, and review of records. Each of these may provide useful data for making appropriate decisions about a student. In addition, procedures that aim to link assessment closely to intervention may be used, including behavioral assessments, assessments of learning environments, curriculum-based tests, and portfolios. Regardless of the qualities being assessed and types of data collection methods employed, assessment data used in making special education decisions are evaluated in terms of validity, reliability, and relevance to the specific needs of the students. They must also be judged in terms of their usefulness for designing appropriate educational programs for students who have special needs.

The amount and complexity of the assessment data required for making various decisions about a student will vary depending on the purpose of testing, the needs of the student, and other information already available about the student (e.g., current scores on a relevant test may be on file for some students but not for others). In general, testing for screening and program evaluation purposes typically involves the use of one or two tests rather than comprehensive test batteries. For determining eligibility and designing intervention, testing and assessment is more comprehensive and may involve multiple procedures and sources. Moreover, in-depth analyses and interpretation of the data are necessary.

In special education, tests are selected, administered, and interpreted by school psychologists, school counselors, regular and special educators, speech pathologists, and physical therapists, among other professionals. The validity of inferences will be enhanced if test users possess adequate knowledge of the principles of measurement and evaluation. However, this diverse group of test users may differ in their levels of technical expertise in measurement and degree of professional training in assessment procedures. It is important that professional evaluators administer and interpret only those tests with which they

have training and competence, in order to prevent misuse of tests.

State and federal law generally requires that students who are referred for possible special education services be screened for eligibility. The screening or initial assessment may in turn call for a more comprehensive evaluation. But the large numbers of students to be tested, the high cost of special education programs, and the limits of time create pressures on special education assessment practices. Assessment usually must be completed within a specific number of working days after referral, and, in most instances, the school district is responsible for funding special services recommended by the child study team. Occasionally, administrators might be inclined to use less expensive, less time-consuming, or more readily available testing procedures than a professional evaluator believes are warranted. An example would be the inappropriate use of available, but less adequately trained, staff to evaluate students. There also might be pressures to minimize or overlook problems that require expensive services. These conditions are likely to adversely affect the validity of the interpretation of test results. Adherence to professional standards governing test use in conducting special education assessments is important, in the face of pressures to use more expedient procedures. The responsible use of tests by school personnel can improve the opportunities for promoting the development and learning of all children.

Standard 13.1

When educational testing programs are mandated by school, district, state, or other authorities, the ways in which test results are intended to be used should be clearly described. It is the responsibility of those who mandate the use of tests to monitor their impact and to identify and minimize potential negative consequences. Consequences resulting from the uses of the test, both intended and unintended, should also be examined by the test user.

Comment: Mandated testing programs are often justified in terms of their potential benefits for teaching and learning. Concerns have been raised about the potential negative impact of mandated testing programs, particularly when they result directly in important decisions for individuals or institutions. Frequent concerns include narrowing the curriculum to focus only on the objectives tested, increasing the number of dropouts among students who do not pass the test, or encouraging other instructional or administrative practices simply designed to raise test scores rather than to affect the quality of education.

Standard 13.2

In educational settings, when a test is designed or used to serve multiple purposes, evidence of the test's technical quality should be provided for each purpose.

Comment: In educational testing, it has become common practice to use the same test for multiple purposes (e.g., monitoring achievement of individual students, providing information to assist in instructional planning for individuals or groups of students, evaluating schools or districts). No test will serve all purposes equally well. Choices in test development and evaluation that enhance validity for one purpose may

diminish validity for other purposes. Different purposes require somewhat different kinds of technical evidence, and appropriate evidence of technical quality for each purpose should be provided by the test developer. If the test user wishes to use the test for a purpose not supported by the available evidence, it is incumbent on the user to provide the necessary additional evidence (see chapter 1).

Standard 13.3

When a test is used as an indicator of achievement in an instructional domain or with respect to specified curriculum standards, evidence of the extent to which the test samples the range of knowledge and elicits the processes reflected in the target domain should be provided. Both tested and target domains should be described in sufficient detail so their relationship can be evaluated. The analyses should make explicit those aspects of the target domain that the test represents as well as those aspects that it fails to represent.

Comment: Increasingly, tests are being developed to monitor progress of individuals and groups toward local, state, or professional curriculum standards. Rarely can a single test cover the full range of performances reflected in the curriculum standards. To assure appropriate interpretations of test scores as indicators of performance on these standards, it is essential to document and evaluate both the relevance of the test to the standards and the extent to which the test represents the standards. When existing tests are selected by a school, district, or state to represent local curricula, it is incumbent on the user to provide the necessary evidence of the congruency of the curriculum domain and the test content. Further, conducting studies of the cognitive strategies and skills employed by test takers or studies of the relationships between test scores and other performance indicators relevant to the broader domain enables evaluation of the extent to which generalizations to the broader domain are supported. This information should be made available to all those who use the test and interpret the test scores.

Standard 13.4

Local norms should be developed when necessary to support test users' intended interpretations.

Comment: Comparison of examinees' scores to local as well as more broadly representative norm groups can be informative. Thus, sample size permitting, local norms are often useful in conjunction with published norms, especially if the local population differs markedly from the population on which published norms are based. In some cases, local norms may be used exclusively.

Standard 13.5

When test results substantially contribute to making decisions about student promotion or graduation, there should be evidence that the test adequately covers only the specific or generalized content and skills that students have had an opportunity to learn.

Comment: Students, parents, and educational staff should be informed of the domains on which the students will be tested, the nature of the item types, and the standards for mastery. Reasonable efforts should be made to document the provision of instruction on tested content and skills, even though it may not be possible or feasible to determine the specific content of instruction for every student. Chapter 7 provides a more thorough discussion of the difficulties that arise with this conception of fairness in testing.

Standard 13.6

Students who must demonstrate mastery of certain skills or knowledge before being promoted or granted a diploma should have a reasonable number of opportunities to succeed on equivalent forms of the test or be provided with construct-equivalent testing alternatives of equal difficulty to demonstrate the skills or knowledge. In most circumstances, when students are provided with multiple opportunities to demonstrate mastery, the time interval between the opportunities should allow for students to have the opportunity to obtain the relevant instructional experiences.

Comment: The number of opportunities and time between each testing opportunity will vary with the specific circumstances of the setting. Further, some students may benefit from a different testing approach to demonstrate their achievement. Care must be taken that evidence of construct equivalence of alternative approaches is provided as well as the equivalence of cut scores defining passing expectations.

Standard 13.7

In educational settings, a decision or characterization that will have major impact on a student should not be made on the basis of a single test score. Other relevant information should be taken into account if it will enhance the overall validity of the decision.

Comment: As an example, when the purpose of testing is to identify individuals with special needs, including students who would benefit from gifted and talented programs, a screening for eligibility or an initial assessment should be conducted. The screening or initial assessment may in turn call for more comprehensive evaluation. The comprehensive assessment should involve the use of

multiple measures, and data should be collected from multiple sources. Any assessment data used in making decisions are evaluated in terms of validity, reliability, and relevance to the specific needs of the students. It is important that in addition to test scores, other relevant information (e.g., school record, classroom observation, parent report) is taken into account by the professionals making the decision.

Standard 13.8

When an individual student's scores from different tests are compared, any educational decision based on this comparison should take into account the extent of overlap between the two constructs and the reliability or standard error of the difference score.

Comment: When difference scores between two tests are used to aid in making educational decisions, it is important that the two tests are standardized and, if appropriate, normed on the same population at about the same time. In addition, the reliability and standard error of the difference scores between the two tests are affected by the relationship between the constructs measured by the tests as well as the standard errors of measurement of the scores of the two tests. In the case of comparing ability with achievement test scores, the overlapping nature of the two constructs may render the reliability of the difference scores lower than test users normally would assume. If the ability and/or achievement tests involve a significant amount of measurement error, this will also reduce the confidence one may place on the difference scores. All these factors affect the reliability of difference scores between tests and should be considered by professional evaluators in using difference scores as a basis for making important decisions about a student. This standard is also relevant when comparing scores from different components

of the same test such as multiple aptitude test batteries and selection tests.

Standard 13.9

When test scores are intended to be used as part of the process for making decisions for educational placement, promotion, or implementation of prescribed educational plans, empirical evidence documenting the relationship among particular test scores, the instructional programs, and desired student outcomes should be provided. When adequate empirical evidence is not available, users should be cautioned to weigh the test results accordingly in light of other relevant information about the student.

Comment: The validity of test scores for placement or promotion decisions rests, in part, upon evidence about whether students, in fact, benefit from the differential instruction. Similarly, in special education, when test scores are used in the development of specific educational objectives and instructional strategies, evidence is needed to show that the prescribed instruction enhances students' learning. When there is limited evidence about the relationship among test results, instructional plans, and student achievement outcomes, test developers and users should stress the tentative nature of the test-based recommendations and encourage teachers and other decision makers to consider the usefulness of test scores in light of other relevant information about the students.

Standard 13.10

Those responsible for educational testing programs should ensure that the individuals who administer and score the test(s) are proficient in the appropriate test administration procedures and scoring procedures and that they understand the importance of adhering to the directions provided by the test developer.

Standard 13.11

In educational settings, test users should ensure that any test preparation activities and materials provided to students will not adversely affect the validity of test score inferences.

Comment: In most educational testing contexts, the goal is to use a sample of test items to make inferences to a broader domain. When inappropriate test preparation activities occur, such as teaching items that are equivalent to those on the test, the validity of test score inferences is adversely affected. The appropriateness of test preparation activities and materials can be evaluated, for example, by determining the extent to which they reflect the specific test items and the extent to which test scores are artificially raised without actually increasing students' level of achievement.

Standard 13.12

In educational settings, those who supervise others in test selection, administration, and interpretation should have received education and training in testing necessary to ensure familiarity with the evidence for validity and reliability for tests used in the educational setting and to be prepared to articulate or to ensure that others articulate a logical explanation of the relationship among the tests used, the purposes they serve, and the interpretations of the test scores.

Standard 13.13

Those responsible for educational testing programs should ensure that the individuals who interpret the test results to make decisions within the school context are qualified to do so or are assisted by and consult with persons who are so qualified.

Comment: When testing programs are used as a strategy for guiding instruction, teachers expected to make inferences about instructional needs may need assistance in interpreting test results for this purpose. If the tests are normed locally, statewide, or nationally, teachers and administrators need to be proficient in interpreting the norm-referenced test scores.

The interpretation of some test scores is sufficiently complex to require that the user have relevant psychological training and experience or be assisted by and consult with persons who have such training and experience. Examples of such tests include individually administered intelligence tests, personality inventories, projective techniques, and neuropsychological tests.

Standard 13.14

In educational settings, score reports should be accompanied by a clear statement of the degree of measurement error associated with each score or classification level and information on how to interpret the scores.

Comment: This information should be communicated in a way that is accessible to persons receiving the score report. For instance, the degree of uncertainty might be indicated by a likely range of scores or by the probability of misclassification.

Standard 13.15

In educational settings, reports of group differences in test scores should be accompanied by relevant contextual information, where possible, to enable meaningful interpretation of these differences. Where appropriate contextual information is not available, users should be cautioned against misinterpretation.

Comment: Observed differences in test scores between groups (e.g., classified by gender, race/ethnicity, school/district, geographical region) can be influenced, for example, by differences in course-taking patterns, in curriculum, in teacher's qualifications, or in parental educational level. Differences in performance of cohorts of students across time may be influenced by changes in the population of students tested or changes in learning opportunities for students. Users should be advised to consider the appropriate contextual information and cautioned against misinterpretation.

Standard 13.16

In educational settings, whenever a test score is reported, the date of test administration should be reported. This information and the age of any norms used for interpretation should be considered by test users in making inferences.

Comment: When a test score is used for a particular purpose, the date of the test score should be taken into consideration in determining its worth or appropriateness for making inferences about a student. Depending on the particular domain measured, the validity of score inferences may be questionable as time progresses. For instance, a reading score from a test administered 6 months ago to an elementary school-aged student may no longer reflect the student's current reading level. Thus, a test score should not be used if it has been determined that undue time has passed since the time of data collection and that the score no longer can be considered a valid indicator of a student's current level of proficiency.

Standard 13.17

When change or gain scores are used, such scores should be defined and their technical qualities should be reported.

Comment: The use of change or gain scores presumes the same test or equivalent forms of the test were used and that the test has (or the forms have) not been materially altered between administrations. The standard error of the difference between scores on the pretest and posttest, the regression of posttest scores on pretest scores, or relevant data from other reliable methods for examining change, such as those based on structural equation modeling, should be reported.

Standard 13.18

Documentation of design, models, scoring algorithms, and methods for scoring and classifying should be provided for tests administered and scored using multimedia or computers. Construct-irrelevant variance pertinent to computer-based testing and the use of other media in testing, such as the test taker's familiarity with technology and the test format, should be addressed in their design and use.

Comment: It is important to assure that the documentation does not jeopardize the security of the items that could adversely affect the validity of score interpretations. Computer and multimedia testing need to be held to the same requirements of technical quality as are other tests.

Standard 13.19

In educational settings, when average or summary scores for groups of students are reported, they should be supplemented with additional information about the sample size and shape or dispersion of score distributions.

Comment: Score reports should be designed to communicate clearly and effectively to their intended audiences. In most cases, reports that go beyond average score comparisons are helpful in furthering thoughtful use and interpretation of test scores. Depending on the intended purpose and audience of the score report, additional information might take the form of standard deviations or other common measures of score variability, or of selected percentile points for each distribution. Alternatively, benchmark score levels might be established and then, for each group or region, the proportions of test takers attaining each specified level could be reported. Such benchmarks might be defined, for example, as selected percentiles of the pooled distribution for all groups or regions. Other distributional summaries of reporting formats may also be useful. The goal of more detailed reporting must be balanced against goals of clarity and conciseness in communicating test scores.

14. TESTING IN EMPLOYMENT AND CREDENTIALING

Background

Employment testing is carried out by organizations for purposes of employee selection, promotion, or placement. *Selection* generally refers to decisions about which individuals will enter the organization; *placement* refers to decisions as to how to assign individuals to positions within the work force; and *promotion* refers to decisions about which individuals within the organization will advance. What all three have in common is a focus on the prediction of future job behaviors, with the goal of influencing organizational outcomes such as efficiency, growth, productivity, and employee motivation and satisfaction.

Testing used in the processes of licensure and certification, which will here generically be called credentialing, focuses on the applicant's current skill or competency in a specified domain. In many occupations, individuals must be licensed by governmental agencies in order to engage in the particular occupation. In other occupations, professional societies or other organizations assume responsibility for credentialing. Although licensure is typically a credential for entry into an occupation, credentialing programs may exist at varying levels, from novice to expert in a given field. Certification is usually sought voluntarily, although occupations differ in the degree to which obtaining certification influences employability or advancement. Testing is commonly only a part of a credentialing process, which may also include other requirements, such as education or supervised experiences. The *Standards* apply to the use of tests in the broader credentialing process.

Testing is also carried out in work organizations for a variety of purposes other than employment decision making and credentialing. Testing to detect psychopathology can take place, as in the case of an employee exhibiting behavioral problems at work. Testing as a tool for personal growth can be part of training and development programs, in which instruments measuring personality characteristics, interests, values, preferences, and work styles are commonly used with the goal of providing self-insight to employees. Testing can also take place in the context of program evaluation, as in the case of an experimental study of the effectiveness of a training program, where tests may be administered as pre- and post-measures. The focus of this chapter, though, is on the use of testing in employment and credentialing. Many issues relevant to such testing are discussed in other chapters: technical matters in chapters 1-6, fairness issues in chapters 7-10, general issues of test use in chapter 11, and individualized assessment of job candidates in chapter 12.

Employment Testing

THE INFLUENCE OF CONTEXT ON TEST USE

Employment testing involves using test information to aid in personnel decision making. Both the content and the context of employment testing varies widely. Content may cover various domains of knowledge, skills, abilities, traits, dispositions, and values. The context in which tests are used also varies widely. Some contextual features represent choices made by the employing organization; others represent constraints that must be accommodated by the employing organization. Decisions about the design, evaluation, and implementation of a testing system are specific to the context in which the system is to be used. Important contextual features include the following:

Internal vs. external candidate pool. In some instances, such as promotional settings, the candidates to be tested are already employed by the organization. In others, applications are sought from outside the organization. In others, a mix of internal and external candidates is sought.

Untrained vs. specialized jobs. In some instances, untrained individuals are selected either because the job does not require specialized knowledge or skill or because the organization plans to offer training after the point of hire. In other instances, trained or experienced workers are sought with the expectation that they can immediately step into a specialized job. Thus, the same job may require very different selection systems depending on whether trained or untrained individuals will be hired or promoted.

Short-term vs. long-term focus. In some instances, the goal of the selection system is to predict performance immediately upon or shortly after hire. In other instances, the concern is with longer-term performance, as in the case of predictions as to whether candidates will successfully complete a multiyear overseas job assignment. Concerns about changing job tasks and job requirements also can lead to a focus on characteristics projected to be necessary for performance on the target job in the future, even if not a part of the job as currently constituted.

Screen in vs. screen out. In some instances, the goal of the selection system is to screen in individuals who will perform well on one set of behavioral or outcome criteria of interest to the organization. In others, the goal is to screen out individuals for whom the risk of pathological, deviant, or criminal behavior on the job is deemed too high. A testing system well suited to one objective may be completely inappropriate for another. That an individual is evaluated as a low risk for engaging in pathological behavior does not imply a prediction that the individual will exhibit high levels of job performance. That a test is predictive of one criterion does not support the inference of linkages to other criteria of interest as well.

Mechanical vs. judgmental decision making. In some instances, test information

is used in a mechanical, standardized fashion. This is the case when scores on a test battery are combined by formula and candidates are selected in strict top-down rank order, or when only candidates above specific cut scores are eligible to continue to subsequent stages of a selection system. In other instances, information from a test is judgmentally integrated with information from other tests and with nontest information to form an overall assessment of the candidate.

Ongoing vs. one-time use of a test. In some instances, a test may be used for an extended period of time in an organization, permitting the accumulation of data and experience about the test in that context. In other instances, concerns about test security are such that repeated use is infeasible, and a new test is required for each test administration. For example, a work-sample test for lifeguards, requiring retrieving a mannequin from the bottom of a pool, is not compromised if candidates possess detailed knowledge of the test in advance. In contrast, a written job knowledge test may be severely compromised if some candidates have access to the test in advance. The key question is whether advance knowledge of test content changes the constructs measured by the test.

Fixed applicant pool vs. continuous flow. In some instances, an applicant pool can be assembled prior to beginning the selection process, as in the case of a policy that all candidates applying before a specific date will be considered. In other cases, there is a continuous flow of applicants about whom employment decisions need to be made on an ongoing basis. A ranking of candidates is possible in the case of the fixed pool; in the case of a continuous flow, a decision may need to be made about each candidate independent of information about other candidates.

Small vs. large sample size. Large sample sizes are sometimes available for jobs with many incumbents, in situations in which multiple similar jobs can be pooled, or in situations in which organizations with similar jobs collaborate in selection system development. In other situations, sample sizes are small; at the extreme is the case of the single-incumbent job. Sample size affects the degree to which different lines of evidence can be drawn on in examining validity for the intended inference to be drawn from the test. For example, relying on the local setting for empirical linkages between test and criterion scores is not technically feasible with small sample sizes.

Size of applicant pool, relative to the number of job openings. The size of an applicant pool can constrain the type of testing system that is feasible. For desirable jobs, very large numbers of candidates may vie for a small number of jobs. Under such scenarios, short screening tests may be used to reduce the pool to a size for which the administration of more time-consuming and expensive tests is practicable. Large applicant pools may also pose test security concerns, limiting the organization to testing methods that permit simultaneous test administration to all candidates.

Thus, test use by employers is conditioned by contextual features such as those in the foregoing list. Knowledge of these features plays an important part in the professional judgment that will influence both the type of testing system that will be developed and the strategy that will be used to evaluate critically the validity of the inference(s) drawn using the testing system.

THE VALIDATION PROCESS IN EMPLOYMENT TESTING

The fundamental inference to be drawn from test scores in most applications of testing in employment settings is one of prediction: the test user wishes to make an inference from test results to some future job behavior or job outcome. Even when the validation strategy used does not involve empirical predictor-criterion linkages, as in the case of reliance on validity evidence based on test content, there is an implied criterion. Thus, while different strategies of gathering evidence may be used, the inference to be supported is that scores on

the test can be used to predict subsequent job behavior. The validation process in employment settings involves the gathering and evaluation of evidence relevant to sustaining or challenging this inference. As detailed below, a variety of validation strategies can be used to support this inference.

It thus follows that establishing this predictive inference requires that attention be paid to two domains: that of the test (the predictor) and that of the job behavior or outcome of interest (the criterion). Evaluating the use of a test for an employment decision can be viewed as testing the hypothesis of a linkage between these domains. Operationally, there are many ways of testing this hypothesis. This is illustrated by the following diagram:

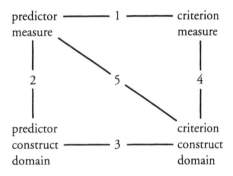

The diagram differentiates between a predictor construct domain and a predictor measure and between a criterion construct domain and a criterion measure. A *predictor construct domain* is defined by specifying the set of behaviors that will be included under a particular construct label (e.g., verbal reasoning, typing speed, conscientiousness). Similarly, a *criterion construct domain* specifies the set of job behaviors or job outcomes that will be included under a particular construct label (e.g., performance of core job tasks, teamwork, attendance, sales volume, overall job performance). Predictor and criterion measures are attempts at operationalizing these domains.

The diagram enumerates a number of inferences commonly of interest. The first is the inference that scores on a predictor measure are related to scores on a criterion measure. This inference is tested through empirical examination of relationships between the two measures. The second and fourth are conceptually similar: both examine the inference that an *operational* measure can be interpreted as representing an individual's standing on the construct domain of interest. Logical analysis, expert judgment, and convergence with or divergence from conceptually similar or different measures are among the forms of evidence that can be examined in testing these linkages. The third is the inference of a relationship between the predictor construct domain and the criterion construct domain. This linkage is established on the basis of theoretical and logical analysis. It commonly draws on systematic evaluation of job content and expert judgment as to the individual characteristics linked to successful job performance. The fifth represents the linkage between the predictor measure and the criterion construct domain.

Some predictor measures are designed explicitly as samples of the criterion construct domain of interest, and, thus, isomorphism between the measure and the construct domain constitutes direct evidence for linkage 5. Establishing linkage 5 in this fashion is the hallmark of approaches that rely heavily on what these *Standards* refer to as "validity evidence based on test content," referred to as content validity in prior conceptualizations of the validation process. Tests in which candidates for lifeguard positions perform rescue operations or in which candidates for word processor positions type and edit text exemplify this approach.

A prerequisite to the use of a predictor measure for personnel selection is that the linkage between the predictor measure and the criterion construct domain be established. As the diagram illustrates, there are multiple strategies for establishing this crucial linkage. One strategy is direct, via linkage 5; a second

involves pairing linkage 1 and linkage 4; and a third involves pairing linkage 2 and linkage 3.

When the test is designed as a sample of the criterion construct domain, this linkage can be established directly via linkage 5. Another strategy for linking a predictor measure and the criterion construct domain focuses on linkages 1 and 4: pairing an empirical link between the predictor and criterion measures with evidence of the adequacy with which the criterion measure represents the criterion construct domain. The empirical link between the predictor measure and the criterion measure is part of what these *Standards* refer to as "validity evidence based on relationships to other variables," referred to as criterion-related validity in prior conceptualizations of the validation process. The empirical link of the test and the criterion measure must be supplemented by evidence of the relevance of the criterion measure to the criterion construct domain to complete the linkage between the test and the criterion construct domain. Evidence of the relevance of the criterion measure to the criterion construct domain is commonly based on job analysis, though in some cases the link between the domain and the measure is so direct that relevance is apparent without job analysis (e.g., when the criterion construct of interest is absenteeism or turnover). Note that this strategy does not necessarily rely on a well-developed predictor construct domain. Predictor measures such as empirically keyed biodata measures are constructed on the basis of empirical links between test item responses and the criterion measure of interest. Such measures may, in some instances, be developed without a fully established a priori conception of the predictor construct domain; the basis for their use is the direct empirical link between test responses and a relevant criterion measure.

Yet another strategy for linking predictor scores and the criterion construct domain focuses on pairing evidence of the adequacy with which the predictor measure represents the predictor construct domain (linkage 2) with evidence of the linkage between the predictor construct domain and the criterion construct domain (linkage 3). As noted above, there is no single direct route to establishing these linkages. They involve lines of evidence subsumed under "construct validity" in prior conceptualizations of the validation process. A combination of lines of evidence, such as expert judgment of the characteristics predictive of job success, inferences drawn from an analysis of critical incidents of effective and ineffective job performance, and interview and observation methods, may support inferences about the predictor constructs linked to the criterion construct domain. Measures of these predictor constructs may then be selected or developed, and the linkage between the predictor measure and the predictor construct domain can be established with various lines of evidence for linkage 2 discussed above.

Thus multiple sources of data and multiple lines of evidence can be drawn on to evaluate the linkage between a predictor measure and the criterion construct domain of interest. There is not a single correct or even a preferred method of inquiry for establishing this linkage. Rather, the test user must consider the specifics of the testing situation and apply professional judgment in developing a strategy for testing the hypothesis of a linkage between the predictor measure and the criterion domain.

For many testing applications, there is a considerable cumulative body of research that speaks to some, if not all, of the inferences discussed above. A meta-analytic integration of this research can form an integral part of the strategy for linking test information to the construct domain of interest. The value of collecting local validation data varies with the magnitude, relevance, and consistency of research findings using similar predictor measures and similar criterion construct domains for similar jobs. In some cases, a small and inconsistent cumulative research record may lead to a validation strategy that relies heavily on local data; in others, a large, consistent research base may make investing resources in additional local data collection unnecessary.

BASES FOR EVALUATING TEST USE

While a primary goal of employment testing is the accurate prediction of subsequent job behaviors or job outcomes, it is important to recognize that there are limits to the degree to which such criteria can be predicted. Perfect prediction is an unattainable goal. First, behavior in work settings is also influenced by a wide variety of organizational and extra-organizational factors, including supervisor and peer coaching, formal and informal training, changes in job design, changes in organizational structures and systems, and changing family responsibilities, among others. Second, behavior in work settings is influenced by a wide variety of individual characteristics, including knowledge, skills, abilities, personality, and work attitudes, among others. Thus any single characteristic will be only an imperfect predictor, and even complex selection systems focus on the set of constructs deemed most critical for the job, rather than on all characteristics that can influence job behavior. Third, some measurement error always occurs even in well-developed test and criterion measures.

Thus, testing systems cannot be judged against a standard of perfect prediction but rather in terms of comparisons with available alternative selection methods. Professional judgment, informed by knowledge of the research literature about the degree of predictive accuracy relative to available alternatives, influences decisions about test use.

Decisions about test use are often influenced by additional considerations including utility (i.e., cost-benefit) evaluation, value judgments about the relative importance of selecting for one criterion domain vs. others, concerns about applicant reactions to test content and process, the availability and appropriateness of alternative selection methods, statutory or regulatory requirements governing test use, and social issues such as workforce diversity. Organizational values necessarily come into play in making decisions about test use; organizations with comparable evidence supporting an intended inference drawn from test scores may thus reach different conclusions about whether to use any particular test.

Testing in Professional and Occupational Credentialing

Tests are widely used in the credentialing of persons for many occupations and professions. Licensing requirements are imposed by state and local governments to ensure that those licensed possess knowledge and skills in sufficient degree to perform important occupational activities safely and effectively. Certification plays a similar role in many occupations not regulated by governments and is often a necessary precursor to advancement in many occupations. Certification has also become widely used to indicate that a person has certain specific skills (e.g., operation of specialized auto repair equipment) or knowledge (e.g., estate planning), which may be only a part of their occupational duties. Licensure and certification, as well as registry and other warrants of expertise, will here generically be called credentialing.

Tests used in credentialing are intended to provide the public, including employers and government agencies, with a dependable mechanism for identifying practitioners who have met particular standards. The standards are strict, but not so stringent as to unduly restrain the right of qualified individuals to offer their services to the public. Credentialing also serves to protect the profession by excluding persons who are deemed to be not qualified to do the work of the occupation. Qualifications for credentials typically include educational requirements, some amount of supervised experience, and other specific criteria, as well as attainment of a passing score on one or more examinations. Tests are used in credentialing in a broad spectrum of profes-

sions and occupations, including medicine, law, psychology, teaching, architecture, real estate, and cosmetology. In some of these, such as actuarial science, clinical neuropsychology, and medical specialties, tests are also used to certify advanced levels of expertise. Relicensure or recertification is also required in some occupations and professions.

Tests used in credentialing are designed to determine whether the essential knowledge and skills of a specified domain have been mastered by the candidate. The focus of performance standards is on levels of knowledge and performance necessary for safe and appropriate practice. Test design generally starts with an adequate definition of the occupation or specialty, so that persons can be clearly identified as engaging in the activity. Then, the nature and requirements of the occupation, in its current form, are delineated. Often, a thorough analysis is conducted of the work performed by people in the profession or occupation to document the tasks and abilities that are essential to practice. A wide variety of empirical approaches is used, including delineation, critical incidence techniques, job analysis, training needs assessments, or practice studies and surveys of practicing professionals. Panels of respected experts in the field often work in collaboration with qualified specialists in testing to define test specifications, including the knowledge and skills needed for safe, effective performance, and an appropriate way of assessing that performance. Forms of testing may include traditional multiple-choice tests, written essays, and oral examinations. More elaborate performance tasks, sometimes using computer-based simulation, are also used in assessing such practice components as, for example, patient diagnosis or treatment planning. Hands-on performance tasks may also be used (e.g., operating a boom crane or filling a tooth) while being observed by one or more examiners.

Credentialing tests may cover a number of related but distinct areas. Designing the testing program includes deciding what areas are to be covered, whether one or a series of tests is to be used, and how multiple test scores are to be combined to reach an overall decision. In some cases high scores on some tests are permitted to offset low scores on other tests, so that additive combination is appropriate. In other cases, an acceptable performance level is required on each test in an examination series.

Validation of credentialing tests depends mainly on content-related evidence, often in the form of judgments that the test adequately represents the content domain of the occupation or specialty being considered. Such evidence may be supplemented with other forms of evidence external to the test. Criterion-related evidence is of limited applicability in licensure settings because criterion measures are generally not available for those who are not granted a license.

Defining the minimum level of knowledge and skill required for licensure or certification is one of the most important and difficult tasks facing those responsible for credentialing. Verifying the appropriateness of the cut score or scores on the tests is a critical element in validity. The validity of the inference drawn from the test depends on whether the standard for passing makes a valid distinction between adequate and inadequate performance. Often, panels of experts are used to specify the level of performance that should be required. Standards must be high enough to protect the public, as well as the practitioner, but not so high as to be unreasonably limiting. Verifying the appropriateness of the cut score or scores on a test used for licensure or certification is a critical element of the validity of test results.

Legislative bodies sometimes attempt to legislate a cut score, such as a score of 70%. Arbitrary numerical specifications of cut scores are unhelpful for two reasons. First, without detailed information about the test, job requirements, and their relationship, sound standard setting is impossible. Second, without detailed information about the format of the test and the difficulty of items, such numerical specifications have little meaning.

Tests for credentialing need to be precise in the vicinity of the passing, or cut, score. They may not need to be precise for those who clearly pass or clearly fail. Sometimes a test used in credentialing is designed to be precise only in the vicinity of the cut score. Computer-based mastery tests may include a procedure to end the testing when a decision about the candidate's performance can be clearly made or when a maximum time limit is reached. This may result in a shorter test for candidates whose performance clearly exceeds or falls far below the minimum performance required for a passing score. The test taker may be told only whether the decision was pass or fail. Because such mastery tests are not designed to indicate how badly the candidate failed, or how well the candidate passed, providing scores that are much higher or lower than the cut score could be misleading. Nevertheless, candidates who fail are likely to profit from information about the areas in which their performance was especially weak. When feedback to candidates about how well or how poorly they performed is intended, precision throughout the score range is needed.

Practice in professions and occupations often changes over time. Evolving legal restrictions, progress in scientific fields, and refinements in techniques can result in a need for changes in test content. When change is substantial, it becomes necessary to revise the definition of the job, and the test content, to reflect changing circumstances. When major revisions are made in the test, the cut score that identifies required test performance is also reestablished.

Because credentialing is an ongoing process, with tests given on a regular schedule, new versions of the test are often needed. From a technical perspective, all versions of a test should be prepared to the same specifications and represent the same content.

Alternate test forms should have comparable score scales so that scores can retain their meaning. Various methods of jointly calibrating alternate forms can be used to assure that the standard for passing represents the same level of performance on all forms. It may be noted that release of past test forms may compromise the quality of test form comparability.

Some credentialing groups consider it necessary, as a practical matter, to adjust their criteria yearly in order to regulate the number of accredited candidates entering the profession. This questionable procedure raises serious problems for the technical quality of the test scores. Adjusting the cut score annually implies higher standards in some years than in others, which, although open and straightforward, is difficult to justify on the grounds of quality of performance. Adjusting the score scale so that a certain number or proportion reach the passing score, while less obvious to the candidates, is technically inappropriate because it changes the meaning of the scores from year to year. Passing a credentialing examination should signify that the candidate meets the knowledge and skill standards set by the credentialing body, independent of the availability of work.

Issues of cheating and test security are of special importance for testing practices in credentialing. Issues of test security are covered in chapters 5 and 11. Issues of cheating by test takers are covered in chapter 8. Issues concerning the technical quality of tests are found in chapters 1-6, and issues of fairness in chapters 7-10.

Standard 14.1

Prior to development and implementation of an employment test, a clear statement of the objective of testing should be made. The subsequent validation effort should be designed to determine how well the objective has been achieved.

Comment: The objectives of employment tests can vary considerably. Some aim to screen out those least suited for the job in question, while others are designed to identify those best suited for the job. Tests also vary in the aspects of job behavior they are intended to predict, which may include quantity or quality of work output, tenure, counterproductive behavior, and teamwork, among others.

Standard 14.2

When a test is used to predict a criterion, the decision to conduct local empirical studies of predictor-criterion relationships and interpretation of the results of local studies of predictor-criterion relationships should be grounded in knowledge of relevant research.

Comment: The cumulative literature on the relationship between a particular type of predictor and type of criterion may be sufficiently large and consistent to support the predictor-criterion relationship without additional research. In some settings, the cumulative research literature may be so substantial and so consistent that a dissimilar finding in a local study should be viewed with caution unless the local study is exceptionally sound. Local studies are of greatest value in settings where the cumulative research literature is sparse (e.g., due to the novelty of the predictor and/or criterion used), where the cumulative record is inconsistent, or where the cumulative literature does not include studies similar to the local setting (e.g., a test with a

large cumulative literature dealing exclusively with production jobs, and a local setting involving managerial jobs).

Standard 14.3

Reliance on local evidence of empirically determined predictor-criterion relationships as a validation strategy is contingent on a determination of technical feasibility.

Comment: Meaningful evidence of predictor-criterion relationships is conditional on a number of features, including (a) the job being relatively stable, rather than in a period of rapid evolution; (b) the availability of a relevant and reliable criterion measure; (c) the availability of a sample reasonably representative of the population of interest; and (d) an adequate sample size for estimating the strength of the predictor-criterion relationship.

Standard 14.4

When empirical evidence of predictor-criterion relationships is part of the pattern of evidence used to support test use, the criterion measure(s) used should reflect the criterion construct domain of interest to the organization. All criteria used should represent important work behaviors or work outputs, on the job or in job-relevant training, as indicated by an appropriate review of information about the job.

Comment: When criteria are constructed to represent job activities or behaviors (e.g., supervisory ratings of subordinates on important job dimensions), systematic collection of information about the job informs the development of the criterion measures, though there is no clear choice among the many available job analysis methods. There is not a clear need for job analysis to support criterion use when measures such as absenteeism or turnover are the criteria of interest.

Standard 14.5

Individuals conducting and interpreting empirical studies of predictor-criterion relationships should identify contaminants and artifacts that may have influenced study findings, such as error of measurement, range restriction, and the effects of missing data. Evidence of the presence or absence of such features, and of actions taken to remove or control their influence, should be retained and made available as needed.

Comment: Error of measurement in the criterion and restriction in the variability of predictor or criterion scores systematically reduce estimates of the relationship between predictor measures and the criterion construct domain, and procedures for correction for the effects of these artifacts are available. When these procedures are applied, both corrected and uncorrected values should be presented, along with the rationale for the correction procedures chosen. Statistical significance tests for uncorrected correlations should not be used with corrected correlations. Other features to be considered include issues such as missing data for some variables for some individuals, decisions about the retention or removal of extreme data points, the effects of capitalization on chance in selecting predictors from a larger set on the basis of strength of predictor-criterion relationships, and the possibility of spurious predictor-criterion relationships, as in the case of collecting criterion ratings from supervisors who know selection test scores.

Standard 14.6

Evidence of predictor-criterion relationships in a current local situation should not be inferred from a single previous validation study unless the previous study of the predictor-criterion relationship was done under favorable conditions (i.e., with a large sample size and a relevant criterion) and if the current situation corresponds closely to the previous situation.

Comment: Close correspondence means that the job requirements or underlying psychological constructs are substantially the same (as is determined by a job analysis), and that the predictor is substantially the same.

Standard 14.7

If tests are to be used to make job classification decisions (e.g., the pattern of predictor scores will be used to make differential job assignments), evidence that scores are linked to different levels or likelihoods of success among jobs or job groups is needed.

Standard 14.8

Evidence of validity based on test content requires a thorough and explicit definition of the content domain of interest. For selection, classification, and promotion, the characterization of the domain should be based on job analysis.

Comment: In general, the job content domain should be described in terms of job tasks or worker knowledge, skills, abilities, and other personal characteristics that are clearly operationally defined so that they can be linked to test content, and for which job demands are not expected to change substantially over a specified period of time. Knowledge, skills, and abilities included in the content domain should be those the applicant should already possess when being considered for the job in question.

Standard 14.9

When evidence of validity based on test content is a primary source of validity evidence in support of the use of a test in selection or promotion, a close link between test content and job content should be demonstrated.

Comment: For example, if the test content samples job tasks with considerable fidelity

(e.g., actual job samples such as machine operation) or, in the judgment of experts, correctly simulates job task content (e.g., certain assessment center exercises), or samples specific job knowledge required for successful job performance (e.g., information necessary to exhibit certain skills), then content-related evidence can be offered as the principal form of evidence of validity. If the link between the test content and the job content is not clear and direct, other lines of validity evidence take on greater importance.

Standard 14.10

When evidence of validity based on test content is presented, the rationale for defining and describing a specific job content domain in a particular way (e.g., in terms of tasks to be performed or knowledge, skills, abilities, or other personal characteristics) should be stated clearly.

Comment: When evidence of validity based on test content is presented for a job or class of jobs, the evidence should include a description of the major job characteristics that a test is meant to sample, including the relative frequency, importance, or criticality of the elements.

Standard 14.11

If evidence based on test content is a primary source of validity evidence supporting the use of a test for selection into a particular job, a similar inference should be made about the test in a new situation only if the critical job content factors are substantially the same (as is determined by a job analysis), the reading level of the test material does not exceed that appropriate for the new job, and there are no discernible features of the new situation that would substantially change the original meaning of the test material.

Standard 14.12

When the use of a given test for personnel selection relies on relationships between a predictor construct domain that the test represents and a criterion construct domain, two links need to be established. First, there should be evidence for the relationship between the test and the predictor construct domain, and second, there should be evidence for the relationship between the predictor construct domain and major factors of the criterion construct domain.

Comment: There should be a clear conceptual rationale for these linkages. Both the predictor construct domain and the criterion construct domain to which it is to be linked should be defined carefully. There is no single route to establishing these linkages. Evidence in support of linkages between the two construct domains can include patterns of findings in the research literature and systematic evaluation of job content to identify predictor constructs linked to the criterion domain. The bases for judgments linking the predictor and criterion construct domains should be articulated.

Standard 14.13

When decision makers integrate information from multiple tests or integrate test and nontest information, the role played by each test in the decision process should be clearly explicated, and the use of each test or test composite should be supported by validity evidence.

Comment: A decision maker may integrate test scores with interview data, reference checks, and many other sources of information in making employment decisions. The inferences drawn from test scores should be limited to those for which validity evidence is available. For example, viewing a high test score as indicating overall job suitability, and thus precluding the need for reference checks, would be an inappropriate inference from a test measuring a single narrow, albeit relevant, domain, such as job knowledge. In other circumstances, decision makers integrate scores across multiple tests, or across multiple scales within a given test.

Standard 14.14

The content domain to be covered by a credentialing test should be defined clearly and justified in terms of the importance of the content for credential-worthy performance in an occupation or profession. A rationale should be provided to support a claim that the knowledge or skills being assessed are required for credential-worthy performance in an occupation and are consistent with the purpose for which the licensing or certification program was instituted.

Comment: Some form of job or practice analysis provides the primary basis for defining the content domain. If the same examination is used in the licensure or certification of people employed in a variety of settings and specialties, a number of different job settings may need to be analyzed. Although the job analysis techniques may be similar to those used in employment testing, the emphasis for licensure is limited appropriately to knowledge and skills necessary for effective practice. The knowledge and skills contained in a core curriculum designed to train people for the job or occupation may be relevant, especially if the curriculum has been designed to be consistent with empirical job or practice analyses. In tests used for licensure, skills that may be important to success but are not directly related to the purpose of licensure (e.g., protecting the public) should not be included. For example, in real estate, marketing skills may be important for success as a broker, and assessment of these skills might have utility for agencies selecting brokers for employment. However, lack of these skills may not present a threat to the public and would appropriately be excluded from consideration for a licensing examination. The fact that successful practitioners possess certain knowledge or skills is relevant but not persuasive. Such information needs to be coupled with an analysis of the purpose of a licensing program and the reasons that the knowledge or skill is required in an occupation or profession.

Standard 14.15

Estimates of the reliability of test-based credentialing decisions should be provided.

Comment: The standards for decision reliability described in chapter 2 are applicable to tests used for licensure and certification. Other types of reliability estimates and associated standard errors of measurement may also be useful, but the reliability of the decision of whether or not to certify is of primary importance.

Standard 14.16

Rules and procedures used to combine scores on multiple assessments to determine the overall outcome of a credentialing test should be reported to test takers, preferably before the test is administered.

Comment: In some cases, candidates may be required to score above a specified minimum on each of several tests. In other cases, the pass-fail decision may be based solely on a total composite score. While candidates may be told that tests will be combined into a composite, the specific weights given to various components may not be known in advance (e.g., to achieve equal effective weights, nominal weights will depend on the variance of the components).

Standard 14.17

The level of performance required for passing a credentialing test should depend on the knowledge and skills necessary for acceptable performance in the occupation or profession and should not be adjusted to regulate the number or proportion of persons passing the test.

Comment: The number or proportion of persons granted credentials should be adjusted, if necessary, on some basis other than modifications to either the passing score or the passing level. The cut score should be determined by a careful analysis and judgment of acceptable performance. When there are alternate forms of the test, the cut score should be carefully equated so that it has the same meaning for all forms.

15. TESTING IN PROGRAM EVALUATION AND PUBLIC POLICY

Background

Tests are widely used in program evaluation and in public policy decision making. Program evaluation is the set of procedures used to make judgments about the client's need for a program, the way it is implemented, its effectiveness, and its value. Policy studies are somewhat broader than program evaluations and refer to studies that contribute to judgments about plans, principles, or procedures enacted to achieve broad public goals. There is no sharp distinction between policy studies and program evaluations, and in many instances there is substantial overlap between the two types of investigations. Test results are often one important source of evidence for the initiation, continuation, modification, termination, or expansion of various programs and policies.

Interpretation of test scores in program evaluation and policy studies usually entails the complex analysis of a number of variables. For example, some programs are mandated for a broad population; others target only certain subgroups. Some are designed to affect attitudes, while others are intended to have a more direct impact on behavior. It is important that the participants included in any study at least meet the specified criteria for the program or policy under review so that appropriate interpretation of test results will be possible. Test results will reflect not only the effects of rules for participant selection and the impact of participation in different programs or treatments, but also the characteristics of those tested. Relevant background information about clients or students may be obtained in order to strengthen the inferences derived from the test results. Valid interpretations may depend upon additional considerations that have nothing to do with the appropriateness of the test or its technical quality, including study design, administrative feasibility, and the quality of

other available data. It is not the intent of this chapter to deal with these varied considerations in any substantial way. In order to develop defensible conclusions, however, investigators conducting program evaluations and policy studies are encouraged to supplement test results with data from other sources. These include information about program characteristics, delivery, costs, client backgrounds, degree of participation, and evidence of side effects. Because test results lend important weight to evaluation and policy studies, it is critical that any tests used in these investigations be sensitive to the questions of the study and appropriate for the test takers.

It is important to evaluate any proposed test in terms of its relevance to the goals of the program or policy and/or to the particular question its use will address. It is relatively rare for a test to be designed specifically for program evaluation or policy study purposes. Typically, the instruments used in such studies were originally developed for purposes other than program or policy evaluation. In addition, because of cost or convenience, certain tests may be adopted for use in a program evaluation or policy study even though they may have been developed for a somewhat different population of respondents. Some tests may be selected for use in program evaluation or policy studies because the tests are well known and thought to be especially credible to the clients or the public consumer. Even though certain tests may be more familiar to the public or may be less time-consuming or less expensive to use than an instrument developed specifically for the evaluation, they may be nonetheless inappropriate for use as criterion measures to determine the need for or to evaluate the effects of particular interventions.

As government agencies and other institutions move to improve their own routine data collection capability, fewer special studies are conducted to evaluate programs and policies. Instead, evaluations and policy studies may depend upon a special analysis of data previously collected for other purposes. In these cases, the investigators may reanalyze test data already obtained and analyzed for another purpose in order to make inferences about program or policy effectiveness. This procedure is called *secondary data analysis*. In some circumstances, it may be difficult to assure a good match between the existing test and the intervention or the policy under examination. Moreover, it may be difficult to reconstruct in detail the conditions under which the data were originally collected. Secondary data analysis also requires consideration of whether adequate informed consent was obtained from subjects in the original data collection to allow secondary analysis to occur without obtaining additional consent. In selecting (or developing) a test or in deciding to use existing data in evaluation and policy studies, careful investigators attempt to balance the purpose of the test, its likelihood to be sensitive to the intervention under study, the credibility of the test to interested parties, and the costs of its administration. Otherwise, test results may lead to inappropriate interpretations about the progress, impact, and overall value of programs and policies under review.

Program Evaluation

Tests may be used in program evaluations to provide information on the status of clients or students before, during, or following an intervention, as well as to provide information on appropriate comparison groups. Whereas understanding the performance of an individual student or client is often the goal of many testing activities, program evaluation targets the performance of, or impact on, groups. Tests are used in program evaluations in a variety of fields, such as social services, education, health services, and military and employment training. The term *program*, broadly interpret-

ed, describes interventions that range from large-scale state or national programs with provisions for local flexibility to small-scale, more experimental projects. In many cases, evaluation is mandated by the agency or funding source for the program, and the intervention is evaluated by judging its effectiveness in meeting stated goals. Some examples of programs that might use test results as part of their evaluation data include psychotherapeutic services, military training programs and job placement programs, school curricula, or services for individuals with special needs.

Test results, along with other information, may be used to compare competing interventions, such as alternative reading curricula or different psychotherapeutic interventions, or to describe the long-term pattern of effects for one or more groups. It is often important to assess a program for its differential effectiveness in meeting the needs of subgroups (such as different ethnic or gender groups within the target population). Even though the performance of groups is of primary interest in program evaluation, the analysis of individuals' histories and test performances may provide additional useful information to aid in the interpretation of test results.

Because of administrative realities, such as cost constraints and response burden, methodological refinements may be adopted to increase the efficiency of testing. One strategy is to obtain a sample of participants to be evaluated from the larger set of those exposed to a program or policy. When there is a sufficient number of clients affected by the program or policy to be evaluated, and when there is a desire to limit the time spent on testing, evaluators can create multiple forms of shorter tests from a larger pool of items. By constructing a number of different test forms consisting of relatively few items and assigning these test forms to different subsamples of test takers (a procedure known as matrix sampling), a larger number of items can be included in the study than could reasonably be administered to any single test taker. When it is desirable to represent a domain with a large number of test items, this approach is often used. However, individual scores are not usually created or interpreted when matrix sampling is employed. Because procedures for sampling individuals or test items may vary in a number of ways, adequate analysis and interpretation of test results for any study depend upon a clear description of how samples were formed and the manner in which test results were aggregated.

Policy Uses of Tests

As noted previously, tests are also used in policy analyses, and the distinction between program evaluation and policy uses of tests is often a matter of degree. Programs are expected to share particular goals, procedures, and resources. Policy is a broader term, applying to plans, principles, procedures, or programs enacted to achieve particular goals in different settings. Programs provide direct services or interventions. Policies may be constructed to achieve their goals by direct or indirect means. Indeed, one direct approach used to achieve a policy goal might include the funding of specific programs. Other examples of direct policy approaches might involve the provision of training resources to improve performance in particular health-service occupations, or the enactment of new recertification requirements for accountants. Studies of the need for or impact of both of these policies could in part depend upon the analyses of test results. To illustrate in more depth, to meet the general policy objective of containing the costs of health care, direct policies might include giving incentives to clients to participate in fitness programs and the development of patient education programs. Tests could measure the understandings and attitudes of participants about the relationship of fitness to the prevention of illness. Another policy example, using a more indirect approach, is to encourage educators to create more effective programs for

children from low-income families. As an approach, a state's educational authorities might require the separate reporting of test scores for children in high-poverty areas. Large differences in group performance would be expected to attract the attention of the public and to place greater pressure on the schools to improve the performance of particular groups of children.

In decentralized governments, policy implementation may be left to local authorities and may be interpreted in a number of different ways. As a result, it may be difficult to select or develop a single test or outcome measure that will be sensitive to the range of different activities or tactics used to implement a given policy. For that reason, policy studies may often use more than one test or outcome measure to provide a more adequate picture of the range of effects.

Issues in Program and Policy Evaluation

Test results are sometimes used as one way to inspire program administrators as well as to infer institutional effectiveness. This use of tests, including the public reporting of results, is thought to encourage an institution to improve its services for its clients. For example, consistently poor achievement test results may trigger special management attention for public schools in some locales. The interpretation of test results is especially complex when tests are used both as an institutional policy mechanism and as a measure of effectiveness. For example, a policy or program may be based on the assumption that providing clear goals and general specifications of test content (such as the type of topics, constructs and cognitive domains, and responses included in the test) may be a reasonable strategy to communicate new expectations to educators. Yet, the desire to influence test or evaluation results to show acceptable institutional performance could lead to inappropriate testing practices, such as teaching the test items in advance, modifying test administration procedures, discouraging certain students or clients from participating in the testing sessions, or focusing exclusively on test-taking procedures. These practices might occur instead of those aimed at helping the test taker learn the domains measured by the test. Because results derived from such practices might lead to spuriously high estimates of impact and might reflect the negative side effects of this particular policy, diligent investigators may estimate the impact of such consequences in order to interpret the test results appropriately. Looking at possible inappropriate consequences of tests as well as their benefits will better assess policy claims that particular types of testing programs lead to improved performance.

On the other hand, policy studies and program evaluations often do not make available reports of results to the test takers and may give no clear reasons to the test taker for participating in the testing procedure. For example, when matrix sampling is used for program evaluation, it may not be feasible to provide such reports. If little effort is made to motivate the test taker to regard the test seriously (for instance, if the purpose of the test is not explained to the test taker), it is possible that test takers might have little reason to try to perform well on the test. Obtained test results then might well underrepresent the impact of the program, institution, or policy because of poor motivation on the part of the test taker. When there is a suspicion that the test might not have been taken seriously, motivation of test takers may be explored by collecting additional information, using observation or interview methods. The issues of inappropriate preparation or unmotivated performance are examples that raise basic questions about the validity of interpretations of test results. In every case, it is important to consider the potential impact of the testing process itself, including test administration and reporting practices, on the test taker.

Public policy decisions are rarely based solely on the results of empirical studies, even when the studies have been well done. The more expansive and indirect the policy, the more likely will it be that other considerations will come into play, such as the political and economic impact of abandoning, changing, or retaining the policy, or the reaction to offering rewards or sanctions to institutions. In a political climate, tests used in policy settings may be subjected to intense and detailed scrutiny. When results do not support a favored position, attempts may be made to discount the appropriateness of the testing procedure, construct, or interpretation.

It is important that all tests used in public evaluation or policy contexts meet the standards described in earlier chapters. As described in chapter 8, tests are to be administered by trained personnel. It is also essential that assistance be provided to those responsible for interpreting study results to practitioners, to the lay public, and to the media. Careful communication of the study's goals, procedures, findings, and limitations increases the chances that the public's interpretations will be accurate and useful.

Additional Considerations

This chapter and its associated standards are directed to users of tests in program evaluation and policy studies and to the conditions under which those studies are usually conducted. Other standards documents that are relevant to this chapter include *The Program Evaluation Standards: How to Assess Evaluations of Educational Programs,* prepared by the Joint Committee on Standards for Educational Evaluation (2nd ed., Thousand Oaks, CA: Sage Publications, 1994), and the *Code of Fair Testing Practices in Education,* prepared by the Joint Committee on Testing Practices (Washington, DC: Joint Committee on Testing Practices, 1988).

Standard 15.1

When the same test is designed or used to serve multiple purposes, evidence of technical quality for each purpose should be provided.

Comment: In educational testing, for example, it has become common practice to use the same test for multiple purposes (e.g., monitoring achievement of individual students, providing information to assist in instructional planning for individuals or groups of students, evaluating schools or districts). No test will serve all purposes equally well. Choices in test development and evaluation that enhance validity for one purpose may diminish validity for other purposes. Different purposes require somewhat different kinds of technical evidence, and appropriate evidence of technical quality for each purpose should be provided by the test developer. If the test user wishes to use the test for a purpose not supported by the available evidence, it is incumbent on the user to provide the necessary additional evidence.

Standard 15.2

Evidence should be provided of the suitability of a test for use in evaluation or policy studies, including the relevance of the test to the goals of the program or policy under study and the suitability of the test for the populations involved.

Comment: Faulty inferences may be made when test scores are not sensitive to the features of a particular intervention. For instance, a test designed for selection may be ineffective as a measure of the effects of an intervention. It is also important to employ tests that are appropriate for the age and background of test takers.

Standard 15.3

When change or gain scores are used, the definition of such scores should be made explicit, and their technical qualities should be reported.

Comment: The use of change or gain scores presumes that the same test or equivalent forms of the test were used and that the test (or forms) have not been materially altered between administrations. The standard error of the difference between scores on pretests and posttests, the regression of posttest scores on pretest scores, or relevant data from other reliable methods for examining change, such as those based on structural equation modeling, should be reported.

Standard 15.4

In program evaluation or policy studies, investigators should complement test results with information from other sources to generate defensible conclusions based on the interpretation of test results.

Comment: Descriptions or analyses of such variables as client selection criteria, services, clients, setting, and resources are often needed to provide a comprehensive picture of the program or policy under review and to aid in the interpretation of test results. Performance on indicators other than tests is almost always useful and in many cases is essential. Examples of other information include attrition rates or patterns of participation. Another source of information might be to determine the degree of motivation of the test takers. When individual scores are not reported to test takers, it is important to determine whether the examinees took the test experience seriously.

Standard 15.5

Agencies using tests to conduct program evaluations or policy studies, or to monitor outcomes, should clearly describe the population the program or policy is intended to serve and should document the extent to which the sample of test takers is representative of that population.

Comment: For example, a clinic with a diverse client population using testing to assess the outcome of a particular treatment may routinely report the extent of participation by subgroups of clients, for instance, those of diverse ethnic backgrounds or for whom English is a second language.

Standard 15.6

When matrix sampling procedures are used for program evaluation or population descriptions, rules for sampling items and test takers should be provided, and reliability analyses must take the sampling scheme into account.

Standard 15.7

When educational testing programs are mandated by school, district, state, or other authorities, the ways in which test results are intended to be used should be clearly described. It is the responsibility of those who mandate the use of tests to identify and monitor their impact and to minimize potential negative consequences. Consequences resulting from the uses of the test, both intended and unintended, should also be examined by the test user.

Comment: Mandated testing programs are often justified in terms of their potential benefits for teaching and learning. Concerns have been raised about the potential negative impact of mandated testing programs, particularly when they affect important deci-

sions for individuals or institutions. To the extent possible, students, parents, and staff should be informed of the domains on which the students will be tested, the nature of the item types, and the standards for mastery. Effort should be made to document the provision of instruction in tested content and skills, even though it may not be possible or feasible to determine the specific content of instruction for every student. An example of negative impact is the use of strategies to raise performance artificially.

Standard 15.8

When it is clearly stated or implied that a recommended test use will result in a specific outcome, the basis for expecting that outcome should be presented, together with relevant evidence.

Comment: A given claim for the benefits of test use, such as improving students' achievement, may be supported by logical or theoretical argument as well as empirical data. Due weight should be given to findings in the scientific literature that may be inconsistent with the stated claim.

Standard 15.9

The integrity of test results should be maintained by eliminating practices designed to raise test scores without improving performance on the construct or domain measured by the test.

Comment: Such practices may include teaching test items in advance, modifying test administration procedures, and discouraging or excluding certain test takers from taking the test. These practices can lead to spuriously high scores that do not reflect performance on the underlying construct or domain of interest.

Standard 15.10

Those who have a legitimate interest in an assessment should be informed about the purposes of testing, how tests will be administered and scored, how long records will be retained, and to whom and under what conditions the records may be released.

Comment: Those with a legitimate interest may include the test takers, their parents or guardians, or personnel who may be affected by results (teachers, program staff).

Standard 15.11

When test results are released to the public or to policymakers, those responsible for the release should provide and explain any supplemental information that will minimize possible misinterpretations of the data.

Comment: The context and limitations of the study should be described, with particular attention given to methods of causal inferences.

Standard 15.12

Reports of group differences in average test scores should be accompanied by relevant contextual information, where possible, to enable meaningful interpretation of these differences. Where appropriate contextual information is not available, users should be cautioned against misinterpretation.

Comment: Observed differences in average test scores between groups (e.g., classified by gender, race/ethnicity, or geographical region) can be influenced, for example, by differences in life experiences, training experience, effort, instructor quality, or level and type of parental support. In education, differences in group performance across time may be influenced by changes in the population of those tested or changes in their experiences. Users

should be advised to consider the appropriate contextual information and be cautioned against misinterpretation.

Standard 15.13

Those who mandate testing programs should ensure that the individuals who interpret the test results to make decisions within the school or program context are qualified to assume this responsibility and proficient in the appropriate methods for interpreting test results.

Comment: When testing programs are used as a strategy for guiding interventions or instruction, professionals expected to make inferences leading to program improvement may need assistance in interpreting test results for this purpose.

The interpretation of some test scores is sufficiently complex to require that the user have relevant psychological training and experience. Examples of such tests include individually administered intelligence tests, personality inventories, projective techniques, and neuropsychological tests.

GLOSSARY

This glossary provides definitions of terms as used in this text. For many of the terms, multiple definitions can be found in the literature; also, technical usage may differ from common usage.

ability/trait parameter In item response theory (IRT), a theoretical value indicating the level of a test taker on the ability or trait measured by the test; analogous to the concept of true score in classical test theory.

ability testing The use of standardized tests to evaluate the current performance of a person in some defined domain of cognitive, psychomotor, or physical functioning.

absolute score interpretation The meaning of a test score for an individual or an average score for a defined group, indicating an individual's or group's level of performance in some defined criterion domain. By contrast, see *relative score interpretation*.

accommodation See *test modification*.

acculturation The process whereby individuals from one culture adopt the characteristics and values of another culture with which they have come in contact.

achievement levels/proficiency levels Descriptions of a test taker's competency in a particular area of knowledge or skill, usually defined as ordered categories on a continuum, often labeled from "basic" to "advanced," or "novice" to "expert," that constitute broad ranges for classifying performance. See *cut score*.

achievement testing A test to evaluate the extent of knowledge or skill attained by a test taker in a content domain in which the test taker had received instruction.

adaptive testing A sequential form of individual testing in which successive items, or sets of items, in the test are chosen based primarily on their psychometric properties and content, in relation to the test taker's responses to previous items.

adjusted validity/reliability coefficient A validity or reliability coefficient—most often, a product-moment correlation—that has been adjusted to offset the effects of differences in score variability, criterion variability, or the unreliability of test and/or criterion. See *restriction of range or variability*.

age equivalent The chronological age in a defined population for which a given score is the median (middle) score. Thus, if children 10 years and 6 months of age have a median score of 17 on a test, the score 17 is said to have an age equivalent of 10-6 for that population. See *grade equivalent*.

alternate forms Two or more versions of a test that are considered interchangeable, in that they measure the same constructs in the same ways, are intended for the same purposes, and are administered using the same directions. *Alternate forms* is a generic term used to refer to any of three categories. *Parallel forms* have equal raw score means, equal standard deviations, equal error structures, and equal correlations with other measures for any given population. *Equivalent forms* do not have the statistical similarity of parallel forms, but the dissimilarities in raw score statistics are compensated for in the conversions to derived scores or in form-specific norm tables. *Comparable forms* are highly similar in content, but the degree of statistical similarity has not been demonstrated. See *linkage*.

analytic scoring A method of scoring in which each critical dimension of performance is judged and scored separately, and the resultant values are combined for an overall score. In some instances, scores on the separate dimensions may also be used in interpreting performance. See *holistic scoring.*

anchor test A common set of items administered with each of two or more different forms of a test for the purpose of equating the scores obtained on these forms.

assessment Any systematic method of obtaining information from tests and other sources, used to draw inferences about characteristics of people, objects, or programs.

attention assessment The process of collecting data and making an appraisal of a person's ability to focus on the relevant stimuli in a situation. The assessment may be directed at mechanisms involved in arousal, sustained attention, selective attention and vigilance, or limitation in the capacity to attend to incoming information.

automated narrative report See *computer-prepared test interpretation.*

back translation A translation of a test, which is itself a translation from an original test, back into the language of the original test. The degree to which a back translation matches the original test indicates the accuracy of the original translation.

battery A set of tests usually administered as a unit. The scores on the several tests usually are scaled so that they can readily be compared or used in combination for decision making.

bias In a statistical context, a systematic error in a test score. In discussing test fairness, bias may refer to construct underrepresentation or construct-irrelevant components of test scores that differentially affect the performance of different groups of test takers.

See *predictive bias, construct underrepresentation, construct irrelevance.*

bilingual The characteristic of being relatively proficient in two languages.

calibration **1**. In linking test score scales, the process of setting the test score scale, including mean, standard deviation, and possibly shape of score distribution, so that scores on a scale have the same relative meaning as scores on a related scale. **2**. In item response theory, the process of determining the parameters of the response function for an item.

certification A voluntary process, often national in scope, by which individuals who have been certified have demonstrated some level of knowledge and skill in an occupation. See *licensing, credentialing.*

classical test theory A psychometric theory based on the view that an individual's observed score on a test is the sum of a true score component for the test taker, plus an independent measurement error component.

classification accuracy The degree to which neither false positive nor false negative categorizations and diagnoses occur when a test is used to classify an individual or event. See *sensitivity* and *specificity.*

coaching Planned short-term instructional activities in which prospective test takers participate prior to the test administration for the primary purpose of improving their test scores. Coaching typically includes simple practice, instruction on test-taking strategies, and related activities. Activities that approximate the instruction provided by regular school curricula or training programs are not typically referred to as coaching.

coefficient alpha An internal consistency reliability coefficient based on the number of parts into which the test is partitioned (e.g., items, subtests, or raters), the interrelationships of the parts, and the total test score variance. Also called *Cronbach's alpha* and, for dichotomous items, *KR 20*.

cognitive assessment The process of systematically gathering test scores and related data in order to make judgments about an individual's ability to perform various mental activities involved in the processing, acquisition, retention, conceptualization, and organization of sensory, perceptual, verbal, spatial, and psychomotor information.

composite score A score that combines several scores according to a specified formula.

computer-administered test A test administered by a computer. Questions appear on a computer-produced display, and the test taker answers by using a keyboard, "mouse" or other similar response device.

computer-based mastery test An adaptive test administered by computer that indicates whether or not the test taker has mastered a certain domain. The test is not designed to provide scores indicating degree of mastery, but only whether the test performance was above or below some specified level. Thus a *computer-based mastery test* is not simply a *mastery test* given by computer. See *mastery test*.

computer-based test See *computer-administered test*.

computer-generated test interpretation See *computer-prepared test interpretation*.

computer-prepared test interpretation A programmed, computer-prepared interpretation of an examinee's test results, based on empirical data and/or expert judgment.

computerized adaptive test An adaptive test administered by computer. See *adaptive testing*.

conditional measurement error variance The variance of measurement errors that affect the scores of examinees at a specified test score level; the square of the conditional standard error of measurement.

conditional standard error of measurement The standard deviation of measurement errors that affect the scores of examinees at a specified test score level.

confidence interval An interval between two values on a score scale within which, with specified probability, a score or parameter of interest lies. The term is also used in these standards to designate Bayesian credibility intervals that define the probability that the unknown parameter falls in the specified interval.

configural scoring rule A rule for scoring a set of two or more elements (such as items or subtests) in which the score depends on a particular pattern of responses to the elements.

construct The concept or the characteristic that a test is designed to measure.

construct domain The set of interrelated attributes (e.g., behaviors, attitudes, values) that are included under a construct's label. A test typically samples from this construct domain.

construct equivalence 1. The extent to which the construct measured by one test is essentially the same as the construct measured by another test. **2.** The degree to which a construct measured by a test in one cultural or linguistic group is comparable to the construct measured by the same test in a different cultural or linguistic group.

construct irrelevance The extent to which test scores are influenced by factors that are irrelevant to the construct that the test is intended to measure. Such extraneous factors distort the meaning of test scores from what is implied in the proposed interpretation.

construct underrepresentation The extent to which a test fails to capture important aspects of the construct that the test is intended to measure. In this situation, the meaning of test scores is narrower than the proposed interpretation implies.

construct validity A term used to indicate that the test scores are to be interpreted as indicating the test taker's standing on the psychological construct measured by the test. A construct is a theoretical variable inferred from multiple types of evidence, which might include the interrelations of the test scores with other variables, internal test structure, observations of response processes, as well as the content of the test. In the current standards, all test scores are viewed as measures of some construct, so the phrase is redundant with validity. The validity argument establishes the construct validity of a test. See *construct, validity argument.*

constructed response item An exercise for which examinees must create their own responses or products rather than choose a response from an enumerated set. Short-answer items require a few words or a number as an answer, whereas extended-response items require at least a few sentences.

content domain The set of behaviors, knowledge, skills, abilities, attitudes or other characteristics to be measured by a test, represented in a detailed specification, and often organized into categories by which items are classified.

content standard A statement of a broad goal describing expectations for students in a subject matter at a particular grade or at the completion of a level of schooling.

content validity A term used in the 1974 *Standards* to refer to a *kind* or *aspect* of validity that was "required when the test user wishes to estimate how an individual performs in the universe of situations the test is intended to represent" (p. 28). In the 1985 *Standards*, the term was changed to *content-related evidence* emphasizing that it referred to one type of evidence within a unitary conception of validity. In the current *Standards*, this type of evidence is characterized as "evidence based on test content."

convergent evidence Evidence based on the relationship between test scores and other measures of the same construct.

credentialing Granting to a person, by some authority, a credential, such as a certificate, license, or diploma, that signifies an acceptable level of performance in some domain of knowledge or activity.

criterion domain The construct domain of a variable used as a criterion. See *construct domain.*

criterion-referenced score interpretation See *criterion-referenced test.*

criterion-referenced test A test that allows its users to make score interpretations in relation to a functional performance level, as distinguished from those interpretations that are made in relation to the performance of others. Examples of criterion-referenced interpretations include comparison to cut scores, interpretations based on expectancy tables, and domain-referenced score interpretations.

cross-validation A procedure in which a scoring system or set of weights for predicting performance, derived from one sample, is applied to a second sample in order to investigate the stability of prediction of the scoring system or weights.

cut score A specified point on a score scale, such that scores at or above that point are interpreted or acted upon differently from scores below that point. See *performance standard*.

derived score A score to which raw scores are converted by numerical transformation (e.g., conversion of raw scores to percentile ranks or standard scores).

diagnostic and intervention decisions Decisions based upon inferences derived from psychological test scores as part of an assessment of an individual that lead to placing the individual in one or more categories. See also *intervention planning*.

differential item functioning A statistical property of a test item in which different groups of test takers who have the same total test score have different average item scores or, in some cases, different rates of choosing various item options. Also known as DIF.

discriminant evidence Evidence based on the relationship between test scores and measures of different constructs.

documentation The body of literature (e.g., test manuals, manual supplements, research reports, publications, user's guides, etc.) made available by publishers and test authors to support test use.

domain sampling The process of selecting test items to represent a specified universe of performance.

empirical evidence Evidence based on some form of data, as opposed to that based on logic or theory. As used here, the term does not specify the type of evidence; this is in contrast to some settings where the term is equated with criterion-related evidence of validity.

equated forms Two or more test forms constructed to cover the same explicit content, to conform to the same statistical specifications, and to be administered under identical procedures (*alternate forms*); through statistical adjustments, the scores on the alternate forms share a common scale.

equating Putting two or more essentially parallel tests on a common scale. See *alternate forms*.

equivalent forms See *alternate forms*.

error of measurement The difference between an observed score and the corresponding true score or proficiency. See *standard error of measurement* and *true score*.

factor 1. Any variable, real or hypothetical, that is an aspect of a concept or construct. 2. In measurement theory, a statistical dimension defined by a factor analysis. See *factor analysis*.

factor analysis Any of several statistical methods of describing the interrelationships of a set of variables by statistically deriving new variables, called factors, that are fewer in number than the original set of variables.

factorial structure 1. The set of factors obtained in a factor analysis. 2. Technically, the correlation of each factor with each of the original variables from which the factors are derived.

fairness In testing, the principle that every test taker should be assessed in an equitable way. See chapter 7.

false negative In classification, diagnosis, or selection, an error in which an individual is assessed or predicted not to meet the criteria for inclusion in a particular group but in truth does (or would) meet these criteria. See *sensitivity* and *specificity*.

false positive In classification, diagnosis, or selection, an error in which an individual is assessed or predicted to meet the criteria for inclusion in a particular group but in truth does not (or would not) meet these criteria. See *sensitivity* and *specificity*.

field test A test administration used to check the adequacy of testing procedures, generally including test administration, test responding, test scoring, and test reporting. A field test is generally more extensive than a pilot test. See *pilot test*.

flag An indicator attached to a test score, a test item, or other entity to indicate a special status. A flagged test score generally signifies a score obtained in a modified, nonstandard test administration. A flagged test item generally signifies an item with undesirable characteristics, such as excessive differential item functioning.

functional equivalence In evaluating test translations, the degree to which similar activities or behaviors have the same functions in different cultural or linguistic groups.

gain score In testing, the difference between two scores obtained by a test taker on the same test or two equated tests taken on different occasions, often before and after some treatment.

generalizability coefficient A reliability index encompassing one or more independent sources of error. It is formed as the ratio of (a) the sum of variances that are considered components of test score variance in the setting under study to (b) the foregoing sum plus the weighted sum of variances attributable to various error sources in this setting. Such indices, which arise from the application of generalizability theory, are typically interpreted in the same manner as reliability coefficients. See *generalizability theory*.

generalizability theory An extension of classical reliability theory and methodology in which the magnitudes of errors from specified sources are estimated through the use of one or another experimental design, and the application of the statistical techniques of the analysis of variance. The analysis indicates the generalizability of scores beyond the specific sample of items, persons, and observational conditions that were studied.

grade equivalent The school grade level for a given population for which a given score is the median score in that population. See *age equivalent*.

high-stakes test A test used to provide results that have important, direct consequences for examinees, programs, or institutions involved in the testing.

holistic scoring A method of obtaining a score on a test, or a test item, based on a judgment of overall performance using specified criteria. See *analytic scoring*.

informed consent The agreement of a person, or that person's legal representative, for some procedure to be performed on or by the individual, such as taking a test or completing a questionnaire. The agreement, which is usually written, is made after the nature, possible effects, and use of the procedure has been explained.

intelligence test A psychological or educational test designed to measure an individual's level of cognitive functioning in accord with some recognized theory of intelligence.

internal consistency coefficient An index of the reliability of test scores derived from the statistical interrelationships of responses among item responses or scores on separate parts of a test.

internal structure In test analysis, the factorial structure of item responses or subscales of a test. See *factorial structure*.

inter-rater agreement The consistency with which two or more judges rate the work or performance of test takers; sometimes referred to as *inter-rater reliability*.

intervention planning The activity of a practitioner that involves the development of a treatment protocol.

inventory A questionnaire or checklist, usually in the form of a self-report, that elicits information about an individual's personal opinions, interests, attitudes, preferences, personality characteristics, motivations, and typical reactions to situations and problems.

item A statement, question, exercise, or task on a test for which the test taker is to select or construct a response, or perform a task. See *item prompt*.

item characteristic curve A mathematical function relating the probability of a certain item response, usually a correct response, to the level of the attribute measured by the item. Also called *item response curve*, or *item response function*, or *icc*.

item pool The aggregate of items from which a test or test scale's items are selected during test development, or the total set of items from which a particular test is selected for a test taker during adaptive testing.

item prompt The question, stimulus, or instructions that direct the efforts of examinees in formulating their responses to a constructed-response exercise.

item response theory (IRT) A mathematical model of the relationship between performance on a test item and the test taker's level of performance on a scale of the ability, trait, or proficiency being measured, usually denoted as θ. In the case of items scored 0 / 1 (incorrect/correct response) the model describes the relationship between θ and the item mean score (P) for test takers at level θ, over the range of permissible values of θ. In most applications, the mathematical function relating P to θ is assumed to be a logistic function that closely resembles the cumulative normal distribution.

job analysis A general term referring to the investigation of positions or job classes to obtain descriptive information about job duties and tasks, responsibilities, necessary worker characteristics (e.g. knowledge, skills, and abilities), working conditions, and/or other aspects of the work.

job performance measurement The measurement of an incumbent's performance of a job. This may include a job sample test, an assessment of job knowledge, and possibly ratings of the incumbent's actual performance on the job.

job sample test A test of the ability of an individual to perform the tasks of which the job is comprised.

licensing The granting, usually by a government agency, of an authorization or legal permission to practice an occupation or profession. See also *certification, credentialing*.

linkage The result of placing two or more tests on the same scale, so that scores can be used interchangeably. Several linking methods are used: See *equating, calibration, moderation,* and *projection,* and *alternate forms*.

literature In this document, a term denoting accessible reports of research, such as books, articles published in professional journals, technical reports, and accessible versions of papers presented at professional meetings.

local evidence Evidence (usually related to reliability or validity) collected for a specific set of test takers in a single institution or at a specific location.

local norms Norms by which test scores are referred to a specific, limited *reference population* of particular interest to the test user (e.g., locale, organization, or institution); local norms are not intended as representative of populations beyond that setting.

local setting The organization or institution where a test is used.

low-stakes test A test used to provide results that have only minor or indirect consequences for examinees, programs, or institutions involved in the testing.

mandated tests Tests that are administered because of a mandate from an external authority.

mastery test 1. A criterion-referenced test designed to indicate the extent to which the test taker has mastered some domain of knowledge or skill. Mastery is generally indicated by attaining a passing score or cut score. 2. In some technical use, a test designed to indicate whether a test taker has or has not attained a prescribed level of mastery of a domain. See *cut score, computer-based mastery test.*

matrix sampling A measurement format in which a large set of test items is organized into a number of relatively short item sets, each of which is randomly assigned to a sub-sample of test takers, thereby avoiding the need to administer all items to all examinees in a program evaluation.

meta-analysis A statistical method of research in which the results from several independent, comparable studies are combined to determine the size of an overall effect or the degree of relationship between two variables.

moderation In test linking, the term moderation, used without a modifier, usually signifies statistical moderation, which is the adjustment of the score scale of one test, usually by setting the mean and standard deviation of one set of test scores to be equal to the mean and standard deviation of another distribution of test scores.

moderator variable In regression analysis, a variable that serves to explain, at least in part, the correlation of two other variables.

modification See *test modification.*

neuropsychodiagnosis Classification or description of inferred central nervous system status on the basis of neuropsychological assessment.

neuropsychological assessment A specialized type of psychological assessment of normal or pathological processes affecting the central nervous system and the resulting psychological and behavioral functions or dysfunctions.

norm-referenced test interpretation A score interpretation based on a comparison of a test taker's performance to the performance of other people in a specified *reference population.* See *criterion-referenced test.*

normalized standard score A derived test score in which a numerical transformation has been chosen so that the score distribution closely approximates a normal distribution, for some specific population.

norms Statistics or tabular data that summarize the distribution of test performance for one or more specified groups, such as test takers of various ages or grades. Norms are usually designed to represent some larger population, such as test takers throughout the country. The group of examinees represented by the norms is referred to as the *reference population.*

operational use The actual use of a test, after initial test development has been completed, to inform an interpretation, decision, or action based, in part, upon test scores.

outcome evaluation An evaluation of the efficacy of an intervention.

parallel forms See *alternate forms*.

percentile The score on a test below which a given percentage of scores fall.

percentile rank Most commonly, the percentage of scores in a specified distribution that fall below the point at which a given score lies. Sometimes the percentage is defined to include scores that fall at the point; sometimes the percentage is defined to include half of the scores at the point.

performance assessments Product- and behavior-based measurements based on settings designed to emulate real-life contexts or conditions in which specific knowledge or skills are actually applied.

performance standard 1. An objective definition of a certain level of performance in some domain in terms of a cut score or a range of scores on the score scale of a test measuring proficiency in that domain. 2. A statement or description of a set of operational tasks exemplifying a level of performance associated with a more general content standard; the statement may be used to guide judgments about the location of a cut score on a score scale. The term often implies a desired level of performance. See *cut score*.

personality inventory An inventory that measures one or more characteristics that are regarded generally as psychological attributes or interpersonal proclivities or skills.

pilot test A test administered to a sample of test takers to try out some aspects of the test or test items, such as instructions, time limits, item response formats, or item response options. See *field test*.

policy The principles, plan, or procedures established by an agency, institution, organization, or government, generally with the intent of reaching a long-term goal.

portfolio In assessment, a systematic collection of educational or work products that have been compiled or accumulated over time, according to a specific set of principles.

precision of measurement A general term that refers to a measure's sensitivity to measurement error. See *standard error of measurement, error of measurement*.

practice analysis A general term referring to the investigation of a certain work position, or profession, to obtain descriptive information about the activities and responsibilities of the position and about the knowledge, skills, and abilities needed to engage in the work of the position. The concept is essentially the same as a job analysis but is generally preferred for professional occupations involving a great deal of individual decision making. See *job analysis*.

predictive bias The systematic under- or over-prediction of criterion performance for people belonging to groups differentiated by characteristics not relevant to criterion performance.

predictive validity A term used in the 1974 *Standards* to refer to a type of "criterion-related validity" that applies "when one wishes to infer from a test score an individual's most probable standing on some other variable called a criterion" (p. 26). In the 1985 *Standards*, the term *criterion-related validity* was changed to *criterion-related evidence*, emphasizing that it referred to one type of evidence within a unitary conception of validity. The current document refers to "evidence based on relations to other variables" that include "test-criterion relationships." Predictive evidence indicates how accurately test data can predict criterion scores that are obtained at a later time.

program evaluation The collection and synthesis of systematic evidence about the use, operation, and effects of some planned set of procedures.

program norms See *user norms*.

projection In test scaling, a method of linking in which scores on one test (X) are used to predict scores on another test (Y). The projected Y score is the average Y score for all persons with a given X score. Like regression, the projection of test Y onto test X is different from the projection of test X onto test Y. See *linkage*.

proposed interpretation A summary, or a set of illustrations, of the intended meaning of test scores, based on the construct(s) or concept(s) the test is designed to measure.

protocol A record of events. A test protocol will usually consist of the test record and test scores.

psychodiagnosis Formalization or classification of functional mental health status based on psychological assessment. See *neuropsychodiagnosis*.

psychological assessment A comprehensive examination of psychological functioning that involves collecting, evaluating, and integrating test results and collateral information, and reporting information about an individual. Various methods may be used to acquire information during a psychological assessment: administering, scoring and interpreting tests and inventories; behavioral observation; client and third-party interviews; analysis of prior educational, occupational, medical, and psychological records.

psychological testing Any procedure that involves the use of tests or inventories to assess particular psychological characteristics of an individual.

random error An unsystematic error; a quantity (often observed indirectly) that appears to have no relationship to any other variable.

random sample See *sample*.

raw score The unadjusted score on a test, often determined by counting the number of correct answers, but more generally a sum or other combination of item scores. In item response theory, the estimate of test taker proficiency, usually symbolized $\hat{\theta}$, is analogous to a raw score although, unlike a raw score, its scaling is not arbitrary.

reference population The population of test takers represented by test norms. The sample on which the test norms are based must permit accurate estimation of the test score distribution for the reference population. The reference population may be defined in terms of examinee age, grade, or clinical status at time of testing, or other characteristics.

relative score interpretation The meaning of the test score for an individual, or the average score for a definable group, derived from the rank of the score or average within one or more reference distributions of scores. See *absolute score interpretation*.

reliability The degree to which test scores for a group of test takers are consistent over repeated applications of a measurement procedure and hence are inferred to be dependable, and repeatable for an individual test taker; the degree to which scores are free of errors of measurement for a given group. See *generalizability theory*.

reliability coefficient A unit-free indicator that reflects the degree to which scores are free of measurement error. The indicator resembles (or is) a product-moment correlation. In classical test theory, the term represents the ratio of true score variance to observed score variance for a particular examinee population. The conditions under which the coefficient is estimated may involve variation in test forms, measurement occasions, raters, scorers, or clinicians, and may entail multiple examinee products or performances. These and other variations in conditions give rise to qualifying adjectives, such as alternate-form reliability, internal consistency reliability, test-retest reliability, etc. See *generalizability theory*.

response bias A test taker's tendency to respond in a particular way or style to items on a test (i.e., acquiescence, social desirability, the tendency to choose 'true' on a true-false test) that yields systematic, construct-irrelevant error in test scores.

response process A component, usually hypothetical, of a cognitive account of some behavior, such as making an item response.

response protocol A record of the responses given by a test taker to a particular test.

restriction of range or variability Reduction in the observed score variance of an examinee sample, compared to the variance of the entire examinee population, as a consequence of constraints on the process of sampling examinees. See *adjusted validity/reliability coefficient*.

rubric See *scoring rubric*.

sample A selection of a specified number of entities called sampling units (test takers, items, etc.) from a larger specified set of possible entities, called the population. A random sample is a selection according to a random process, with the selection of each entity in no way dependent on the selection of other entities. A stratified random sample is a set of random samples, each of a specified size, from several different sets, which are viewed as strata of the population.

scale 1. The system of numbers, and their units, by which a value is reported on some dimension of measurement. Length can be reported in the English system of feet and inches or in the metric system of meters and centimeters. 2. In testing, *scale* sometimes refers to the set of items or subtests used in the measurement and is distinguished from a test in the type of characteristic being measured. One speaks of a test of verbal ability, but a scale of extroversion-introversion.

scale score See *derived score*.

scaling The process of creating a scale or a scale score. Scaling may enhance test score interpretation by placing scores from different tests or test forms onto a common scale or by producing scale scores designed to support criterion-referenced or norm-referenced score interpretations. See *scale*.

score Any specific number resulting from the assessment of an individual; a generic term applied for convenience to such diverse measures as test scores, estimates of latent variables, production counts, absence records, course grades, ratings, and so forth.

scoring formula The formula by which the raw score on a test is obtained. The simplest scoring formula is "raw score equals number correct." Other formulas differentially weight item responses. For example, in an attempt to correct for guessing or nonresponse, zero weights may be assigned to nonresponses and negative weights to incorrect responses.

scoring rubric The established criteria, including rules, principles, and illustrations, used in scoring responses to individual items and clusters of items. The term usually refers to the scoring procedures for assessment tasks that do not provide enumerated responses from which test takers make a choice. Scoring rubrics vary in the degree of judgment entailed, in the number of distinct score levels defined, in the latitude given scorers for assigning intermediate or fractional score values, and in other ways.

screening test A test that is used to make broad categorizations of examinees as a first step in selection decisions or diagnostic processes.

security (of a test) See *test security*.

selection A purpose for testing that results in the acceptance or rejection of applicants for a particular educational or employment opportunity.

sensitivity In classification of disorders, the proportion of cases in which a disorder is detected when it is in fact present.

Spearman-Brown formula A formula derived within classical test theory that projects the reliability of a shortened or lengthened test from the reliability of a test of specified length.

specificity In classification of disorders, the proportion of cases for which a diagnosis of disorder is rejected when rejection is warranted.

speededness A test characteristic, dictated by the test's time limits, that results in a test taker's score being dependent on the rate at which work is performed as well as the correctness of the responses. The term is not used to describe tests of speed. Speededness is often an undesirable characteristic.

split-halves reliability coefficient An internal consistency coefficient obtained by using half the items on the test to yield one score and the other half of the items to yield a second, independent score. The correlation between the scores on these two half-tests, adjusted via the Spearman-Brown formula, provides an estimate of the alternate-form reliability of the total test.

stability The extent to which scores on a test are essentially invariant over time. Stability is an aspect of reliability and is assessed by correlating the test scores of a group of individuals with scores on the same test, or an equated test, taken by the same group at a later time.

standard error of measurement The standard deviation of an individual's observed scores from repeated administrations of a test (or parallel forms of a test) under identical conditions. Because such data cannot generally be collected, the standard error of measurement is usually estimated from group data. See *error of measurement*.

standard score A type of derived score such that the distribution of these scores for a specified population has convenient, known values for the mean and standard deviation. The term is sometimes used to signify a mean of 0.0 and a standard deviation of 1.0. See *derived score*.

standardization 1. In test administration, maintaining a constant testing environment and conducting the test according to detailed rules and specifications, so that testing conditions are the same for all test takers. 2. In test development, establishing scoring norms based on the test performance of a representative sample of individuals with which the test is intended to be used. 3. In statistical analysis, transforming a variable so that its standard deviation is 1.0 for some specified population or sample. See *standard score*.

standards-based assessment Assessments intended to represent systematically described content and performance standards.

stratified coefficient alpha A modification of coefficient alpha that renders it appropriate for a multi-factor test by defining the total score as the composite of scores on single-factor part-tests.

stratified sample See *sample*.

systematic error A consistent score component (often observed indirectly), not related to the test performance. See *bias*.

technical manual A publication prepared by test authors and publishers to provide technical and psychometric information on a test.

test An evaluative device or procedure in which a sample of an examinee's behavior in a specified domain is obtained and subsequently evaluated and scored using a standardized process.

test developer The person(s) or agency responsible for the construction of a test and for the documentation regarding its technical quality for an intended purpose.

test development The process through which a test is planned, constructed, evaluated, and modified, including consideration of content, format, administration, scoring, item properties, scaling, and technical quality for its intended purpose.

test documents Publications such as test manuals, technical manuals, user's guides, specimen sets, and directions for test administrators and scorers that provide information for evaluating the appropriateness and technical adequacy of a test for its intended purpose.

test information function A mathematical function relating each level of an ability or latent trait, as defined under item response theory (IRT), to the reciprocal of the corresponding conditional measurement error variance.

test manual A publication prepared by test developers and publishers to provide information on test administration, scoring, and interpretation and to provide technical data on test characteristics. See *user's guide*.

test modification Changes made in the content, format, and/or administration procedure of a test in order to accommodate test takers who are unable to take the original test under standard test conditions.

test security Limiting access to the specific content of a test to those who need to know it for test development, test scoring, and test evaluation. In particular, test items on secure tests are not published; unauthorized copying is forbidden by any test taker or anyone otherwise associated with the test. A secure test is not for publication in any form, in any venue.

test specifications A detailed description for a test, often called a test blueprint, that specifies the number or proportion of items that assess each content and process/skill area; the format of items, responses, and scoring rubrics and procedures; and the desired psychometric properties of the items and test such as the distribution of item difficulty and discrimination indices.

test user The person(s) or agency responsible for the choice and administration of a test, for the interpretation of test scores produced in a given context, and for any decisions or actions that are based, in part, on test scores.

test-retest reliability A reliability coefficient obtained by administering the same test a second time to the same group after a time interval and correlating the two sets of scores.

timed tests A test administered to a test taker who is allotted a strictly prescribed amount of time to respond to the test.

top-down A method of selecting the best applicants according to some numerical scale of suitability. Often, "best" is taken to mean "highest scoring on some test."

translational equivalence The degree to which the translated version of a test is equivalent to the original test. Translational equivalence is typically examined in terms of the language used, the scores produced, and the constructs measured by the translated version and the original test. See *back translation*.

true score In classical test theory, the average of the scores that would be earned by an individual on an unlimited number of perfectly parallel forms of the same test. In item response theory, the error-free value of test taker proficiency, usually symbolized by θ.

unidimensional Having only one dimension, or only one latent variable.

user norms Descriptive statistics (including percentile ranks) for a sample of test takers that does not represent a well-defined reference population, for example, all persons tested during a certain period of time, or a set of self-selected test takers. Also called program norms. See *norms*.

user's guide A publication prepared by the test authors and publishers to provide information on a test's purpose, appropriate uses, proper administration, scoring procedures, normative data, interpretation of results, and case studies. See *test manual*.

validation The process through which the validity of the proposed interpretation of test scores is investigated.

validity The degree to which accumulated evidence and theory support specific interpretations of test scores entailed by proposed uses of a test.

validity argument An explicit scientific justification of the degree to which accumulated evidence and theory support the proposed interpretation(s) of test scores.

validity generalization Applying validity evidence obtained in one or more situations to other similar situations on the basis of simultaneous estimation, meta-analysis, or synthetic validation arguments.

variance components In testing, variances accruing from the separate constituent sources that are assumed to contribute to the overall variance of observed scores. Such variances, estimated by methods of the analysis of variance, often reflect situation, location, time, test form, rater, and related effects.

vocational assessment A specialized type of psychological assessment designed to generate hypotheses and inferences about interests, work needs and values, career development, vocational maturity, and indecision.

weighted scoring A method of scoring a test in which the number of points awarded for a correct (or diagnostically relevant) response is not the same for all items in the test. In some cases, the scoring formula awards more points for one response to an item than for another.

INDEX

Numbers in this index refer to specific standard(s).